Edinburgh Textbooks in Applied Linguistics
Series Editors: Alan Davies and Keith Mitchell

Pragmatic Stylistics

D0238764

Elizabeth Black

Edinburgh University Press

© Elizabeth Black, 2006

Edinburgh University Press Ltd
22 George Square, Edinburgh

Typeset in 10/12 Adobe Garamond
by Servis Filmsetting Ltd, Manchester, and
printed and bound in Great Britain by
MPG Books Ltd, Bodmin, Cornwall

A CIP record for this book is available from the British Library

ISBN 0 7486 2040 0 (hardback)
ISBN 0 7486 2041 9 (paperback)

The right of Elizabeth Black
to be identified as author of this work
has been asserted in accordance with
the Copyright, Designs and Patents Act 1988.

Undergraduate Lending Library

Contents

For my Mother, and in memory of my Father and daughter Julia, 'My priuy perle wythouten spotte'.

Series Editors' Preface

This series of single-author volumes published by Edinburgh University Press takes a contemporary view of applied linguistics. The intention is to make provision for the wide range of interests in contemporary applied linguistics which are provided for at the Master's level.

The expansion of Master's postgraduate courses in recent years has had two effects:

1. What began almost half a century ago as a wholly cross-disciplinary subject has found a measure of coherence so that now most training courses in Applied Linguistics have similar core content.
2. At the same time the range of specialisms has grown, as in any developing discipline. Training courses (and professional needs) vary in the extent to which these specialisms are included and taught.

Some volumes in the series will address the first development noted above, while the others will explore the second. It is hoped that the series as a whole will provide students beginning postgraduate courses in Applied Linguistics, as well as language teachers and other professionals wishing to become acquainted with the subject, with a sufficient introduction for them to develop their own thinking in applied linguistics and to build further into specialist areas of their own choosing.

The view taken of applied linguistics in the Edinburgh Textbooks in Applied Linguistics Series is that of a theorising approach to practical experience in the language professions, notably, but not exclusively, those concerned with language learning and teaching. It is concerned with the problems, the processes, the mechanisms and the purposes of language in use.

Like any other applied discipline, applied linguistics draws on theories from related disciplines with which it explores the professional experience of its practitioners and which in turn are themselves illuminated by that experience. This two-way relationship between theory and practice is what we mean by a theorising discipline.

The volumes in the series are all premised on this view of Applied Linguistics as a theorising discipline which is developing its own coherence. At the same time, in order to present as complete a contemporary view of applied linguistics as possible other approaches will occasionally be expressed.

Each volume presents its author's own view of the state of the art in his or her topic. Volumes will be similar in length and in format, and, as is usual in a textbook series, each will contain exercise material for use in class or in private study.

Alan Davies
W. Keith Mitchell

Acknowledgements

I owe much stimulus to successive generations of students on the M.Sc. in Applied Linguistics at the University of Edinburgh. I am also very indebted to former Ph.D. students, particularly to Carol Chan, Alexandra Georgakopoulou, Anne Pankhurst, Sonia S'hiri and Peter Tan whose interests were close to mine. I am grateful for the friendship, stimulus, entertainment and advice from former colleagues, particularly Tony Howatt, at the former Department of Applied Linguistics, and Hugh Trappes-Lomax of the Institute of Applied Language Studies. Finally to my husband, who has been exceptionally patient and tolerant. He spent many hours resolving problems that Microsoft might have spared me. For that, and for nearly forty years of tolerance, I am deeply grateful. Alan Davies and Keith Mitchell have proved very patient and helpful editors.

Grateful acknowledgement is made to the following sources for permission to reproduce material previously published elsewhere. Every effort has been made to trace the copyright holders, but if any have been inadvertently overlooked, the publisher will be pleased to make the necessary arrangements at the first opportunity.

Alice Thomas Ellis, *The 27th Kingdom*. Reprinted by permission of PFD on behalf of Gerald Duckworth & Co. Ltd.

Alice Thomas Ellis, *The Other Side of the Fire*. Reprinted by permission of PFD on behalf of Gerald Duckworth & Co. Ltd.

From 'The Snows of Kilimanjaro'. Reprinted with permission of Scribner, an imprint of Simon and Schuster Adult Publishing Group, from *The Short Stories of Ernest Hemingway*. © 1936 by Ernest Hemingway. Copyright, renewed 1964 by Mary Hemingway.

D. H. Lawrence, 'Tickets, Please' from *England, My England, and Other Stories*. Reproduced by permission of Pollinger Ltd. and the Estate of Frieda Lawrence Ravagli.

The Society of Authors as Literary Representative of the Estate of Virginia Woolf.

I am unable to quote from James Joyce's texts, since permission was refused by his heirs. The books are available in libraries. I regret the inconvenience caused to readers, should any wish to follow up the comments.

Acronyms

CP: the co-operative principle with four associated maxims: of quantity, quality, manner and relation

DD: direct discourse

FDD: free direct discourse

FDS: free direct speech

FDT: free direct thought

FID: free indirect discourse

FIT: free indirect thought

FIS: free indirect speech

FTA: face threatening act. Part of Politeness theory: an FTA can threaten positive face (desire to maintain a positive self-image) or negative face (desire not to be imposed upon)

ID: indirect discourse

IN: implied narrator. A bundle of features (knowledge, attitudes etc.) necessary to account for the text

IR: implied reader. One who has the necessary knowledge and background to understand a text fully

N: narrator. The voice that tells the story

NRSA: narrator's report of speech act

NRTA: narrator's report of thought act

Glossary

Code switching: shifting from one dialect or language to another.

Deictic expressions: pointing words that link the situation and text.

Echoic discourse: any discourse where two voices are heard. It includes irony and FIT. See Chapters 7 and 8.

Heteroglossia: the combination of registers, jargons, sociolects, dialects in a natural language.

Hybrid discourse: the co-presence of two consciousnesses within a single bit of discourse (for example in FID).

Implicature: (conversational implicature). What is implied, but not stated: a hearer accesses an implicature to rescue the CP – when, taken literally, a statement does not satisfy it. Implicatures may be used for reasons of politeness, or to increase interest.

Intertext: the echo or quotation of other texts.

Edinburgh Textbooks in Applied Linguistics

Titles in the series include:

Introduction

This book tries to show that Applied Linguistics can make a contribution to the study of literature. When I was an undergraduate, I was impressed – and very puzzled – by colleagues who declared that something was 'symbolic'. This was generally approved by the lecturer, but no one said why or how. When I began to teach, I encountered the same problem. My students were avid in the recognition of symbols. Sometimes I saw why, at other times I was baffled. This book is an attempt to de-baffle me, and, I hope, others. I believe that there is a linguistic explanation for many tropes in literature, and I hope to show how they work. The ways in which we interpret ordinary language use are relevant to the ways in which we interpret literary discourse – which is only the language of the time, written by people who are more adept at manipulating its nuances than most of us. But I shall try to show that we follow roughly the same procedures whether we are listening to a friend, reading a newspaper, or reading a literary work.

I begin with an account of traditional approaches to literary discourse. This is because pragmatics is the study of language in context, and the ways in which novelists create character and situation are relevant to our interpretation of the discourse. I then move on to introduce the theories of Austin and Grice, who offer basic groundwork in pragmatics. Then I consider the kinds of 'signposting' that help us through our reading. The theories considered here are pragmatic in the sense that they contribute to the contextualisation of the text, and offer hints as to its interpretation – the equivalent of intonation in spoken language. More technically, I move on to consider the complexities of prose fiction in the variety of 'voices' offered the reader, and, in the following chapter, the ways in which direct and indirect discourse are manipulated. The argument then becomes more technical, as I consider the role of politeness theory and relevance theory, and then consider how these theories show us something about how we interpret the books we read. In particular, I show how these theories can explain how we interpret metaphor and symbolism in a coherent manner. It is not an arbitrary decision, but one grounded in an (implicit) understanding of how language works. I have attempted to avoid excessive use of technical terms throughout, which may offend the purists, but I offer no apology.

Chapter 1

Pragmatics and Stylistics

1.1 INTRODUCTION

The first stylisticians seem to have felt that the language of a text perfectly reflected the textual world (see Fasold 1990; Joseph, Love and Taylor 2001). In this they were – perhaps unconsciously – following the ideas of Whorf. The weak interpretation of the Whorfian hypothesis holds that people's world view is at least partially conditioned by their language. A linguistic study would therefore reveal its meaning. Nowadays it is more fashionable (and probably more accurate) to think that meaning is the result of interpretive processes. We do not assume that all readers will come to share the same view of all aspects of a text's meaning (see Weber 1996: 3–5), though a general consensus is of course likely, and a grossly deviant interpretation may signal problems with the production or reception of the text. We will therefore understand a text differently according to what we bring to it: we cannot assume that it has a single, invariant meaning for all readers. Since Pragmatics is the study of language in use (taking into account elements which are not covered by grammar and semantics), it is understandable that stylistics has become increasingly interested in using the insights it can offer. We are in a world of (relatively) unstable meanings; the role of the reader is that of an interpreter, not a mere passive recipient.

I propose to consider here some of the basic elements which are crucial to the interpretation of written, and in particular, literary discourse. Some of the topics will be developed more fully later. I shall consider whether it is possible to identify such a thing as literary discourse; the nature of context; the interpretation of deictic expressions (especially the verb and pronouns); and what these tell us about the relationship implied between text and reader.

1.2 LITERARY AND NON-LITERARY DISCOURSE

It has become conventional wisdom in recent years to say that there is no principled way in which to distinguish between literary and non-literary discourse. The same linguistic resources are used in the spoken and written language; figures of speech such as metaphor and simile are found in speech and all kinds of writing (see Short 1986: 154). One of my aims here will be to suggest ways in which the same devices may be more effective in literary than in non-literary discourse. I will argue, for example, that the impact of some metaphorical structures is greater in literary texts, because they form part of a 'package' and make a greater contribution to meaning than the random use of (often trite) metaphors and similes in everyday conversation.

It is to be expected that literary discourse will differ from ordinary conversation and some written discourse since any published work is subject to a process of careful composition and much revision. Even in fictional dialogue the slips of the tongue, repetitions, elisions and opaque reference which characterise the spoken language are seldom represented, save occasionally for humorous effect.

Written discourse is addressed to an absent audience: even a shopping list is intended for a future 'I' who does not know what I do now about the gaps in the larder. Private diaries may be meant only for the author, but typically they will be read at some later time, so the author may well be surprised by some attitudes or comments, to say nothing of having forgotten incidents which once seemed important. That is, in almost any written text an element of 'decentreing' enters in: even if we are addressing ourselves, it is a future or other self, who does not necessarily know all that we do; hence the need for shopping lists.

1.3 CONTEXT

Context is usually understood to mean the immediately preceding discourse and the situation of the participants (see Brown and Yule 1983: 35–67). In a written text the beginning provides the necessary orientation into the discourse, since nothing precedes it. But it should be noted that the title, appearance, author, even publisher of a book or magazine provide the reader with many hints as to the kind of text they can expect, and so contextualise it to some extent. Werth (1999) develops an elaborate and very precise view of context. The context in which discourse takes place is identified as the discourse world, while the topic is the text world. It is the text that drives the evocation of knowledge and establishes common ground which is arrived at by negotiation between the participants. To this is added the background knowledge of the participants, enriching and giving meaning to the ongoing discourse. In short, he argues that context is dynamic, the mutual creation of the discourse participants. (This applies equally to written or spoken discourse.) In this view, the search for coherence is text driven. While the prototypical situation of discourse is face-to-face interaction, there is no reason to suppose that written texts operate any differently. This view stresses the incremental nature of discourse: added information clarifies what has gone before, and/or may alter our perception of it.

Another view of context (considered below in Chapter 7) is developed by Sperber and Wilson (1986/1995). They argue that context is the responsibility of the hearer, who accesses whatever information is necessary in order to process an utterance, on the assumption that it has been made as relevant as possible by the speaker. Without discounting the importance of the points discussed above, they stress that encyclopaedic knowledge plays an important role. Thus different people may interpret the same utterance differently according to the information they possess, what they deem relevant, and their knowledge of social conventions. Consider for example:

> Mrs Dalloway said she would buy the flowers herself.
> For Lucy had her work cut out for her. The doors would be taken off their hinges; Rumpelmayer's men were coming. And then, thought Clarissa Dalloway, what a morning – fresh as if issued to children on a beach. (Virginia Woolf, *Mrs Dalloway*, 1925/1964: 5)

We may infer from these initial sentences of *Mrs Dalloway* a number of things. The social relationship between Lucy and Mrs Dalloway is hinted at by the fact that one is referred to by first name only, the other is more fully introduced with title and two names. Mrs Dalloway makes an apparently generous offer in the first sentence – to reduce Lucy's workload – but it sounds more fun to buy flowers than be involved with the removal of doors, and the arrival of Rumpelmayer's men. We do not know who they are, but the purchase of flowers suggests a party rather than removal men or painters. It is in this way that the reader feels her way into a text. The social relationship between these women would have been immediately clear to the first readers of the novel: it might be opaque to a modern reader. Early readers of the novel might also assess the social situation of the family by observing that when Mrs Dalloway returns home, it is Lucy, and not a butler, who opens the door for her. The development of our understanding of discourse is incremental.

1.4 DEICTIC EXPRESSIONS

There are a number of significant differences between most written and spoken discourse. This applies particularly to deictic expressions. Deictics are 'pointing' words. They include tensed verbs (temporal deixis), personal pronouns, demonstratives (*these, this, that*), and time and place expressions such as *now, then, here, yesterday, today*, and so forth. These words relate our linguistic expression to the current situation. They are bridges between language and the world (Lyons 1977: 637ff.; Hurford and Heasley 1983: 62–75; Huddleston and Pullum 2002: 1,451ff.). They take their basic meaning from the so-called canonical situation of discourse: face-to-face interaction. (This is clearly the basis of human interaction: one notices, even on the telephone, the need to provide a context for some utterances.) In written texts, particularly in fictional discourse (where the 'world' is created by the text), they have a role that is somewhat different to that found in ordinary language use, so some attention will be paid to them here. They play a significant part in establishing the spatio-temporal perspective of a narrative, and may suggest whether the perspective of narrator or character is invoked. I will now consider in some detail how deictic expressions work in written texts.

1.4.1 Pronouns

In one crucial respect fictional discourse differs from other types of discourse. As Widdowson (1975: 50–3) shows, the referents of the pronominal system differ from that of spoken language. The 'I' of the lyric poet cannot be identified with the author of the text, any more than the reader (save in exceptional circumstances) identifies with the 'you' in a love poem. The same point applies to the whole pronominal system in a text. We cannot identify the sender of the message directly with the author, just as the reader is the ultimate addressee, but not the one addressed directly in the text. Thus, the first person has elements of the third person, and the second person has elements of the third, since it refers to an addressee who is not the receiver of the message. That is particularly clear in the case of lyric poems, where the 'speaker' may be an inanimate object, dead, an animal, or whatever the poet chooses.

1.4.2 Articles

The definite article is normally used to refer to unique entities (*the sun*), or items already known from previous discourse. Therefore when it occurs at the beginning of a text, the reader is informed of what is to be taken as part of the 'given' of the fictional discourse: this may imply the perspective from which events are viewed: *At first Joe thought the job O.K. He was loading hay on the trucks, along with Albert, the corporal* (D. H. Lawrence, 'Monkey Nuts', 1922/1995: 64). The definite articles, and the verb *thought* urge this reading.

An alternative explanation for the occurrence of the definite article at the beginning of a narrative derives from script theory (that is, pre-existing knowledge structures which enable us to process discourse speedily). Tannen (1993), in discussing Schank and Abelson's concept of a script, cites the minimal narrative: *John went into the restaurant. He ordered a hamburger and a coke. He asked the waitress for the check and left* (Tannen 1993: 18). The use of the definite articles, it is suggested, is an argument for the existence of a script, which has 'implicitly introduced them', by virtue of our knowledge of restaurants and the habits of customers. (One might note similarly that no mention is made of John paying for his meal: the reader assumes he has done so; otherwise the story would be far more interesting than it is.) The definite article referring to the waitress here clearly implies 'the one who served John' rather than any passing waitress. The definite article referring to the restaurant is a typical way of introducing entities in a fiction: it simply tells us that this restaurant is to be taken as part of the 'given' elements in this world.

The role of deictics in establishing the spatio-temporal perspective of a narrative is perhaps most obvious at the beginning of a text. In particular, odd combinations of proximal (close) and distal (distant) deictics occur. One case is the first sentence of Ernest Hemingway's 'The Short Happy Life of Francis Macomber': *It was now lunch time, and they were all sitting under the double green fly of the dining tent, pretending that nothing had happened* (1947/1964: 413). In ordinary discourse, the past tense of the verb is normally accompanied by a distal deictic, so we would expect the past tense to be followed by *then* rather than *now*. The use of the proximal deictic seems to shift the perspective to that of the characters in the fiction. Together with *pretending*, it suggests that something unpleasant had happened not long before (see Simpson 1993: 14). A comparable example is: *Evvie arrived again at supper time on*

Saturday. Tonight she wore baggy cotton trousers with a drawstring at the waist and a fairisle pullover . . . (Alice Thomas Ellis, *The Other Side of the Fire*,1983/1985: 30). The *tonight* suggests that the perspective is of a character in the fiction, since the past tense would normally be followed by *that night*. The verb *arrive* also helps to establish that the perspective is that of a member of the host household.

One of the effects of the use of such proximal deictics is to draw the reader into the text, creating a sense of involvement at the beginning of the narrative. A rather curious use of *ago* occurs at the beginning of D. H. Lawrence's *Sons and Lovers* (1913/1948). The first paragraph describes a situation, which is said to have occurred since the reign of Charles II: *Then, some sixty years ago, a sudden change took place.* Here, in the absence of other evidence, the temporal reference appears to be that of the time of writing.

1.4.3 Tense

Tense is normally reckoned to be part of the deictic system, since it locates actions or events in relation to the moment of speaking. However, the situation in fictional discourse differs from the canonical situation. The normal narrative tense in fiction is the simple past: it is best interpreted not as a temporal or deictic marker, but as a generic marker. That this is so is readily seen by the fact that we are not disturbed by the normal combination of past-tense narrative with the present tense in dialogue. (In dialogue, of course, tense has its normal deictic values, as it is mimetic of real world discourse.) It is also appropriate because fictions are often told by a narrator who relates events as though they are past, with genuine or assumed hindsight, whether or not the author has decided how the story will end. That is why even novels set in the future may be narrated in the past tense: it is used for the narration of any imagined world, past, present or future.

Of course, tense functions deictically within narratives, which essentially means that the perfect tenses have a deictic function within the fictional discourse, whereas other tenses do not normally have this function. In *The Prime of Miss Jean Brodie* (1961/1965: 54), Muriel Spark writes: *The sewing sisters had not as yet been induced to judge Miss Brodie* . . . Note the complexity of the temporal system here: the perfect tense works in relation to the normal base line of the narrative, while *as yet* is the narrator's hint that the situation will change in the (fictional) future. The reader is juggling with information which will, in the light of other elements in the fiction, have to be organised in a temporal sequence in order to work out the development of the plot. In this respect, as in some others, the language of literary discourse differs interestingly from standard language. Thus the pragmatic interpretation of a perfect tense differs from the interpretation of the simple past.

1.4.4 Present tense

Stanzel (1984: 22–44) draws attention to the widespread use of the present tense in texts such as synopses, chapter headings and author's notes. He considers that this signals that the narrative is 'unmediated': that is, the author may not have decided what kind of narratorial voice to use. In any case, such instances are not part of narrative proper, and in that sense are also related to some of the uses of the present tense when the narrative past is temporarily abandoned, which will be considered here. The issue is interesting precisely because tense is so commonly used to signal changes in the focalisation or perspective, or even its total absence, as in the text types considered by Stanzel. Huddleston and Pullum (2002: 129) consider that this use is simply that the perspective in such texts is that of a text that can be read at any time; they note that it is commonly used in stage directions – as such, it is a timeless use of the tense.

1.4.4.1 Present tense for past event

The present tense is occasionally used to suggest simultaneity of narration and event: *So now I am at Avignion . . . in three minutes you will see me crossing the bridge upon a mule . . .* (Sterne 1765/1980: VII, 41). It is quite clear that this is retrospective narration (there is a wilful confusion between the temporal situations of the character, writing time and reading time).

Occasionally whole novels, or parts of them, are written in the present tense, as a substitute for the narrative past. These uses are not particularly interesting, since the novelty soon wears off, and the interpretive process is seldom affected by the base tense of the narrative. Some chapters of Dickens' *Our Mutual Friend* are in the present tense; in the case of those dealing with the Veneerings, it may be that the present suggests that they are as superficial as their name suggests, and lack a 'past'. Spark's *The Driver's Seat* (1970/1974) is in the present tense, and therefore the future is used for prolepses (anticipations): *She will be found tomorrow morning dead from multiple stab-wounds . . .* (25); *On the evening of the following day he will tell the police . . .* (27). Such passages prove that the narrative is in fact retrospective; here the present tense does not mean that the narrative is simultaneous with the events. This use of the present tense is essentially the 'historical' present, and so differs radically from the instantaneous present, which describes an activity as it takes place.

1.4.4.2 Present in vernacular narrative

The present tense is frequent in oral narratives, apparently for the sake of added emphasis; it certainly seems designed to increase interest and involvement by the audience (see Brown and Levinson 1987: 205; Georgakopoulou 1993; Georgakopoulou and Goutsos 1997). As such, it draws attention to a significant point in the narrative. The use of the present in vernacular narratives (discussed in Leech 1971; Georgakopoulou and Goutsos 1997) is echoed by Dickens in *Our Mutual Friend: It being so, here is Saturday evening come, and here is Mr Venus come, and ringing at the Bower-gate* (1864/1971: 350). Georgakopoulou and Goutsos also draw attention to the use of the present tense to segment narrative.

1.4.4.3 Instantaneous present

Another use of the present tense is the instantaneous present, where the action is simultaneous with narration. It is common in broadcast sports commentaries, and in demonstrations, when the action is described as it takes place. This use of the present tense is, unsurprisingly, rare in fiction, but it is occasionally found. In *Our Mutual Friend* a young man describes what he sees from a window:

> 'Two belated wanderers in the mazes of the law,' said Eugene . . . 'stray into the court. They examine the door-posts of number one, seeking the name they want. Not finding it at number one, they come to number two. On the hat of wanderer number two, the shorter one, I drop this pellet. Hitting him on the hat, I smoke serenely, and become absorbed in the contemplation of the sky.' (1864/1971: 340)

The first part of the paragraph is odd, since we would normally use the present progressive to describe an on-going activity. This example is not, of course, in the narratorial voice: Eugene is reporting the view from the window to his companion, but is doing so in a narratorial style; the base form for narrative is the simple tense (see Dahl 1985: 112). It is interesting that at the end of the passage Eugene does describe an act just as he carries it out. As Leech (1971: 3) points out, it is more common to use the present continuous when describing an action as it is performed. Leech considers that this use of the present tense is rather theatrical.

Spark's *Not to Disturb* (1971/1974) is a novel where the instantaneous present is used: the narration is synchronous with the events described, and thus has an organic motivation since it is written in 'real time'. The 'three unities' of Greek drama are observed: the action takes place overnight, the characters are all gathered in one house; (it is perhaps a precondition of a fiction of this type that the time should be sharply limited). The action consists of the suicide of the owner, after he has murdered his wife and secretary, events which have been planned, or at the very least foreseen, by the servants, who are the main characters in the fiction. When the time for the action arrives, the servants treat it as though it had already taken place:

> 'He was a very fine man in his way. The whole of Geneva got a great surprise.'
> 'Will get a great surprise,' Eleanor says.
> 'Let us not split hairs,' says Lister, 'between the past, present and future tenses.'
> . . .
> 'The poor late Baron,' says Heloise.
> 'Precisely,' says Lister. 'He'll be turning up soon. In the Buick, I should imagine.'
> (Spark 1971/1974: 6)

There is a play here on the analogy between the omniscience of the narrator and God's foreknowledge. The narrative proceeds in the present tense, with occasional occurrences of the perfect in summarising passages: *The doctor has scrutinised the bodies, the police have taken their statements, they have examined and photographed the room* (1971/1974: 89). The present perfect is used here to mark the current relevance of the event, and return to the base line of the narrative. Leech calls this use the 'resultative past' (1971: 34).

There is, however, one interesting use of the 'historical' present, when a clergyman is summoned to the house. He explains his presence: '*I was in bed and the phone rings. Sister Barton is asking for me. It's urgent, she says, he's screaming. So here I am. Now I don't hear a sound. Everyone's gone to sleep*' (1971/1974: 49). This may be accounted for in the ways considered above; it is also the case that the speaker is not highly educated, so a vernacular style of narrative may be held to be particularly appropriate. The speaker probably intends to convey irritation at being disturbed. It does not break the present tense of the narrative, which is established as the norm, and so does not draw special attention to itself, though the past tense might be expected in such a situation. There is, in fact, a single instance of the past tense in the fiction, when the quasi-omniscient butler is told the real identity of the madman in the attic: '*That,' said Lister, 'I did not know*' (1971/1974: 38). This must be a very rare instance of the commonest reporting verb in fiction used in a contextually deviant way; it draws attention to itself, being foregrounded against the norms established by the text. The knowledge that Lister acquires here is highly significant, and brings about a change in the servants' 'plot'. (It appears that the madman in the attic is not a remote relation, but the heir; the clergyman is promptly compelled to marry a pregnant housemaid to the lunatic, thus ensuring even greater financial rewards than the servants had expected to receive.) The novel ends with the future tense: *By noon they will be covered in the profound sleep of those who have kept faithful vigil all night . . .* (1971/1974: 96).

The present tense is effective in this fiction because of the synchronicity between event and narration; the fiction also demonstrates the manipulative qualities of the narrator (embodied in this case in the servants, who have not only foreseen or plotted the events, but intend to make their fortunes by selling the story to the press.) Their manipulation is analogous to the author plotting the fiction before beginning to write. Lister, the butler, is fully aware of the grammatical and indeed narratological implications of tense. When discussing his memoirs, he slips into the past tense:

'There might be an unexpected turn of events,' says Eleanor.
'There was sure to be something unexpected,' says Lister. 'But what's done is about to be done and the future has come to pass. My memoirs up to the funeral are as a matter of fact more or less complete.' (1971/1974: 9)

Lister, counting a bribe he has just received, remarks:

'Small change,' he says 'compared with what is to come, or has already come, according as one's philosophy is temporal or eternal. To all intents and purposes they're already dead although as a matter of banal fact, the night's business has still to accomplish itself. (1971/1974: 12)

Lister later remarks that his employers *have placed themselves . . . within the realm of predestination* (1971/1974: 37). An omniscient narrator foresees the future while narrating; the characters are predestined to carry out the plot, just as the unfortunate

Baron is in this novel. Lister's comment is thus concerned with the nature of narrative.

A seamless web is created by the congruence of plot, narrative technique and the comments thereby implied on the nature of fiction. There is a marked contrast between this novel, where the instantaneous present tense is organic and closely linked to the plot and Spark's constant interest in the relationship between narrators and God, and the trivial use of the instantaneous present in Dickens, cited above.

1.4.4.4 Present tense within past tense narrative

Within narratives in the past tense, the present is used for a number of purposes. It functions contrastively in most fictions in which it occurs. It is often used at the beginning of narratives to set the scene, or indicate that the narrative proper has not yet begun. It seems usually to be the case that a shift into the present tense marks a departure from the narrative proper. Such departures are of various types, which I will consider now.

The present tense is used in certain fictions where characters' thoughts are represented in free direct discourse (for which see Chapter 5). This is a distinctive use, quite different from a narrator using the present tense for a narrative which is clearly retrospective (as happens in *The Driver's Seat*). The latter are in what used to be termed the historical present, whereas the thoughts or words of a character focaliser will most naturally be reported in the present tense when there is no (visible) narratorial presence. This happens in, for example, William Faulkner's *As I Lay Dying*, a novel in which the reader has to piece together the narrative from the perceptions of the characters involved, without any comment from the narrator other than the ascription of the various chapters to the characters:

> The signboard comes in sight. It is looking out at the road now, because it can wait. New Hope. 3 mi. it will say. New Hope. 3 mi. New Hope. 3 mi. And then the road will begin, curving away into the trees, empty with waiting, saying New Hope three miles. (1930/1963: 93)

1.4.4.5 Iterative present

The iterative present is used, as the name implies, for actions which occur regularly, of the type *John walks to work*. It is very common in spoken language, but less common in literary discourse. It is used for actions which are perceived to extend from the past into the future (Leech 1971): '*Wanda looks out of the window*,' I told Martin York. '*She sees spies standing at the corner of the road. She sees spies in the grocer shop, following her.*' (Spark, *A Far Cry from Kensington*, 1988/1989: 39). Here the narrator is reporting the mental suffering of a refugee who believes herself to be persecuted; the iterative present marks the habitual nature of her activity. It is clearly distinct from other uses of the present tense discussed above.

1.4.5 Suspension of narrative

When a narrator temporarily abandons his narratorial role to generalise, comment, or otherwise depart from his storytelling role, the tense often marks this departure, by a shift from the past to the simple present. The narrator may engage in generalisations or gnomic utterances (of the type *a rolling stone gathers no moss*), draw conclusions which are only tangentially relevant to the purpose at hand, or invite the reader to consider various alternatives. With generalisations, we are invited to perceive the general applicability of a comment. The move into the present tense suspends the narrative, however briefly. The effect of the present tense in these instances is to alter the scope of authority claimed by the narrator, and it creates an interpersonal bond with the reader. The fact that the present tense is more immediate perhaps also has the effect of drawing the reader's attention both to what is being said, and also to the fact that its relationship with the narrative is problematic: it thus invites thought and attention. Often such passages are more or less entertaining, or address the reader in an intimate way, suggesting shared knowledge and attitudes: *I offer this advice without fee: it is included in the price of this book* (Spark, *A Far Cry from Kensington*, 1988/1989: 11). We find such generalisations in the present tense, with the following clause returning to the narrative base line. Judgements may be offered on plot development or a character:

> Such thoughts are known as *hubris* and are, on the whole, unwise.
> At half past twelve she wondered briefly whether she should drop in on one of her London friends for lunch. (Ellis, *The Other Side of the Fire*, 1983/1985: 28)

Occasionally one wonders whether a generalisation is attributable to character or narrator. It may of course be both – this seems to be the case in a passage in *Pride and Prejudice*: *What praise is more valuable than the praise of an intelligent servant?* (Jane Austen 1813/1972: 272). The norms of Elizabeth and the narrator are very close, so it makes little difference to the overall interpretation.

Tenseless clauses may have a comparable effect of making generalisations when the semantic content is appropriate:

> It had caused a major earthquake in the nineteenth century, and a repetition of this disaster was confidently predicted by seismologists and local millenarian sets: a rare and impressive instance of agreement between science and superstition. (David Lodge, *Changing Places*, 1975/1979: 55)

Occasionally, narratorial generalisations which one might expect to occur in the present tense are in the narrative past: *She did not know then that the price of allowing false opinions was the gradual loss of one's capacity for forming true ones* (Spark 'Bang Bang You're Dead', 1987: 67). The motivation here may be to avoid breaking the narrative line, but it suggests that the character subsequently acquires this knowledge (*know then* contrasts with a later position of knowledge.) Another, uncommon way of involving the reader is to ask a question: *'Or is it just that the past seems to contain more local colour than the present?'* (Julian Barnes, *Flaubert's Parrot*, 1984/1985: 15).

1.4.6 Other uses of the present tense

The present tense is sometimes used to set the scene at the beginning of a narrative, where it indicates that the narrative proper has not yet begun. It is also used for descriptions that are felt to be of an enduring character. D. H. Lawrence does this sometimes at the beginning of his fictions: in 'Tickets, Please' for example, the story is prefaced by a general account of the countryside in which the events take place, and the types of people involved in the fiction: *There is in the Midlands a single-line tramway system* . . . (1922/1995: 34). The text continues for some paragraphs in a descriptive mode. When the narrative proper begins, the tense shifts to the past.

The present tense is also used of situations that are thought to hold generally (and so are essentially descriptive), with the past tense marking a return to the narrative line. Again, Lawrence offers an interesting example in 'Tickets, Please': *During these performances pitch darkness falls from time to time, when the machine goes wrong. Then there is a wild whooping, and a loud smacking of simulated kisses. In these moments John Thomas drew Annie towards him* (38). If the present tense does indeed have an empathetic function, it may suggest a motivation for its use in such instances.

Such shifts of tense within a text are interesting because they often mark a change in the scope of authority claimed by the narrator (see Fowler 1981: 90). They are therefore significant for the pragmatic meanings encoded in the text, since the interpretation of any utterance depends upon the situation and the implied relations between addresser and addressee. The effect is thus to separate comments made in the 'authorial' voice from the narrative proper. The precise effect of the change in tense will vary according to the context and perhaps the norms established in the text, but its primary function is to mark some change in the narrative mode. It is this use of the present tense, marking a departure from – or better, a comment on – the narrative that we have when the narrator addresses the reader: *It is not to be supposed that Miss Brodie was unique at this point of her prime* . . . (Spark, *The Prime of Miss Jean Brodie*, 1961/1965: 42).

The present tense is also used by narrators who comment explicitly on the development of their narrative. It is characteristic of Fielding: *Reader, I think it proper, before we proceed any farther together, to acquaint thee, that I intend to digress* . . . (1749/1973: I, 2, 28) and occurs in Spark, when she draws attention to apparently arbitrary shifts in the narrative: *It is time now to speak of the long walk through the old parts of Edinburgh where Miss Brodie took her set* . . . (*The Prime of Miss Jean Brodie*, 1961/1965: 27). In sum, the present tense functions contrastively in most fictions where it occurs. It is often used at the beginning of narratives to set the scene, which suggests that the narrative proper has not yet begun. In other instances, it is always worthy of extra attention.

1.4.7 Imperative

The imperative in the narrator's voice occasionally breaks the fictional discourse. It is probably more common in verse than prose, but the effects are similar. As happens with the gnomic present (and perhaps with other uses of the present), the reader is drawn into the discourse situation, and this creates empathetic involvement (see Fowler 1981). *Tristram Shandy* offers numerous examples, since the narrator is engaged regularly in a discourse with the (constantly shifting) figure of the reader, who sometimes even intrudes upon the writer (when, for example, 'madam' is accused of sitting on his cap (VII, 26). Thus the reader is invited to:

> Imagine to yourself a little, squat, uncourtly figure of a Doctor *Slop*, of about four feet and a half perpendicular height, with a breadth of back and a sesquipedality of belly which might have done honour to a Serjeant in the Horse-Guards. (II, 9)

These examples are from a first-person narrative, but it can equally occur in third-person texts:

> Imagine, if you will, that each of these two professors of English Literature (both, as it happens, aged forty) is connected to his native land, place of employment and domestic hearth by an infinitely elastic umbilical cord of emotions, attitudes and values . . . (Lodge, *Changing Places*, 1975/1978: 8)

The effect is similar to a rhetorical question, in that the imperative demands a reaction, which in this case is perfectly feasible, since readers are reminded of their duty to read collaboratively in order to actualise the meaning of the text. In most instances, the fictional situation clearly makes such a response impossible, or at best unlikely. Thus when Tristram Shandy cannot adequately describe Widow Wadman, the reader is invited to:

> – call for pen and ink – here's paper ready to your hand. – Sit down, Sir, paint her to your own mind –as like your mistress as you can – as unlike your wife as your conscience will let you – 'tis all one to me – please but your own fancy in it. (VI, 38)

1.4.8 Pronominal references to the narrator

In one way or another, tense changes such as those considered here draw attention to the narratorial voice by problematising it, or changing the relationship implied between text and reader. There are occasions when third-person narrators refer to themselves in the first person. This can have various effects. Ellis (1982) begins *The 27th Kingdom* with: *The story I shall tell begins like this.* The first person is resumed only at the end of the novel: *As for me, the story-teller, I was in the pub by the river at the time* . . . It is a framing device, reminiscent of folk tales, suggesting the voice of an oral storyteller, and the echo continues when the narrative proper begins: *Once upon a time in the Year of Our Lord 1954* . . . There is no confusion of roles here, since these passages are outside the narrative proper. It is almost as though the author were addressing us directly before giving way to the narratorial voice; it is perhaps a rather jokey way of drawing attention to the fact that author and narrator are clearly distinct entities.

Other occurrences of apparent authorial intrusion into a text are more unsettling. The 'gnomic present' is occasionally found with the first personal pronoun, thus apparently breaking out of the omniscient narratorial role:

> But there was also about him an indescribable air . . . the air common to men who live on the vices, the follies or the baser fears of mankind; the air of moral nihilism common to keepers of gambling hells and disorderly houses; to private detectives and enquiry agents to drink sellers, and, I should say, to the sellers of invigorating electric belts and to the inventors of patent medicines. But of that last I am not sure, not having carried my investigations so far into the depths. For all I know, the expression of these last may be perfectly diabolic. I shouldn't be surprised. (Joseph Conrad, *The Secret Agent*, 1907/1963: 21)

This is (I think) the only time the narrator uses the first-person pronoun in the novel. The effect is therefore disturbing. Consequently, the reader may quibble with the list of immoral men as it develops; by the end it is simply bizarre, and, for me at least, the intended effect is lost. The confusion arises because roles and voices are confused. An omniscient narrator destroys his authority the moment he says *I*. As the term suggests, no ordinary human has the capacities of such a narrator: it is a voice, a textual stance, not a human being. Gnomic generalisations should be relevant to their context, and in harmony with the norms of the fiction. They are typically presented as quasi-proverbial utterances, without the citation of authority: when the authority becomes an 'I' as in Conrad, the result is to undermine the authority claimed. A similar explanation accounts for the problem posed by this passage: *Sleep is still most perfect, in spite of hygienists, when it is shared with a beloved* (Lawrence, *Sons and Lovers*, 1913/1965: 87). The dig at hygienists undercuts the effect of the generalisation because it reminds us forcefully that two opinions are possible.

The identity of the 'I' addressing the reader is seldom problematic. However, a number of interesting cases occur, where the conventions appear to be broken. When Fielding introduces Sophia, the heroine of *Tom Jones*, he begins rather ironically (the chapter heading *A short Hint of what we can do in the Sublime* . . . suggests as much). He begins by comparing Sophia to various beauties of the day. The passage concludes:

> She was most like the Picture of Lady *Ranelagh;* and I have heard more still to the famous Duchess of *Mazarine;* but most of all, she resembled one whose Image never can depart from my Breast, and whom if thou dost remember, thou hast then, my Friend, an adequate Idea of Sophia. (1749/1973: IV, ch. 2)

The problem here is that the 'I' ceases to be that of the narrator, and becomes authorial. In this respect it is similar to the Conrad passage cited above. The effect is similar to that, and to the passage from *Sons and Lovers*. The problem in all of these cases is that the distinctions between the author and the narratorial voice are blurred; in each case the problem arises because the scope of authority claimed is acceptable for the narrator. When the human author intrudes, the implicit pact with the reader is destroyed.

1.4.9 Second-person pronouns

The second-person pronoun can occasionally be used in a rather odd manner. At the beginning of Spark's *A Far Cry from Kensington* (1988/1989) the first-person narrator uses 'you' with the sense of 'one': it is a common use of the pronoun in English, which, in most varieties, lacks an impersonal pronoun. But later in the passage it seems that the 'you' addressed is in fact the interlocutor, presumably the reader, since there is no other addressee in the text:

> You can lie awake at night and think; the quality of insomnia depends entirely on what you decide to think of. Can you decide to think – Yes, you can. You can put your mind to anything most of the time. You can sit peacefully in front of a blank television set, just watching nothing; and sooner or later you can make your own programme much better than the mass product. It's fun, you should try it. You can put anyone you like on the screen, alone or in company, saying and doing what you want them to do, with yourself in the middle if you prefer it that way. (1988/1989: 5)

If one attempts to replace 'you' by 'one' in this passage, the moment when the referent changes becomes clear. It is difficult to interpret *It's fun, you should try it* as anything other than an invitation to the reader. In this respect its effect is comparable to the use of the imperative. Consider the effects of this rewritten version:

> *One* can lie awake at night and think; the quality of insomnia depends entirely on what *one* decides to think of. Can *one* decide to think – Yes, *one* can. *One* can put *one's* mind to anything most of the time. *One* can sit peacefully in front of a blank television set, just watching nothing; and sooner or later *one* can make *one's* own programme much better than the mass product. It's fun, *you* should try it. *One* can put anyone *one* likes on the screen, alone or in company, saying and doing what *one* wants them to do, with *oneself* in the middle if *one* prefers it that way.

There is a regular instability in the use of *we, he,* and *you* without any apparent motivation, change of meaning, or distance in a passage of introspection by the focaliser in Hemingway's 'The Snows of Kilimanjaro:

> *We* must all be cut out for what *we* do, he thought. Wherever *you* make *your* living is where *your* talent lies. *He* had sold vitality, in one form or another, all *his* life and when *your* affections are not too involved *you* give much better value for the money. *He* had found that out, but *he* would never write that, now, either. No, *he* would not write that, though it was well worth writing. (1939/1964: 450)

It is difficult to see this as anything other than carelessness.

1.5 CONCLUSION

There is no evidence that literary discourse differs from non-literary texts as text: as discourse it is clearly different. Literary discourse uses any devices available in the language. The text is self-contained: the context is created by the discourse. All elements necessary for its interpretation must be built in. It is addressed to an absent audience; the message is conveyed indirectly through the words of characters, which may be transmitted through the voice of a narrator. The result is an embedded discourse, where the meaning of a token can change according to the level it is placed on. These matters will be considered in Chapter 4.

Referentially, fictional discourse does not refer to the real world, but to an imaginary construct. While ordinary language may be described as 'doing things with words', literary discourse does not usually have, or expect to have, a direct impact upon the world. This clearly affects the reader's attitude to narrative, which will be considered below.

One area where there is a linguistic difference between literary and other kinds of discourse is deixis. Deictics are used in ways that differ from ordinary usage, in tense and other forms. The fact that 'I' is not identical with the sender or 'you' with the ultimate addressee results in a multilayered discourse which demands interpretation on various levels. Furthermore, the communication is uni-directional, unlike the canonical situation. The role of the reader becomes duplicitous also. Our attitude to events is detached; we assume the text is the result of conscious planning, and search for meanings. On one level we read with a measure of credulity: we play the game, even as we see through it. At the same time, we refrain from the kind of response that might be appropriate in life. We do not sue love poets for breach of promise; we read of murders in detective fiction without considering the gore that attends murder in real life. We allow (relatively) free play to inferences generated by the text in a way that might be unwarranted in real life. The fact that we can re-read a text until we are satisfied with our interpretation means that written language can be much denser than the spoken language: it is recoverable, and often repays special attention. Thus literary discourse is in part created by the kind of attention a reader is prepared to bring to it. Thorne (1988) argues that the kind of reading we give a literary text differs qualitatively from that we give other texts: our attention is rewarded by extra meanings. We bring that extra attention to the text because we recognise its deviant status, and are prepared to make an effort in the expectation of a reward.

Having reviewed here some of the eminent features of literary discourse, in the next chapter I will look at various theories that suggest how we assess all verbal interactions.

Chapter 2

Pragmatic Theories

2.1 INTRODUCTION

The theories to be considered here were developed primarily in relation to spoken interactions, but it will be argued that they are not irrelevant to the interpretation of written texts. I do not propose to give a full account of speech act theory here: as I hope to show, it is of limited usefulness for the explication of literary discourse. Pratt (1977) was among the first to show the usefulness of pragmatic theories to the study of literary texts. A clear, concise account of matters not considered here (such as the performative verb hypothesis) may be found in Thomas (1995).

2.2 SPEECH ACT THEORY

The term speech act does not refer simply to the act of speaking, but to the whole communicative situation, including the context of the utterance (that is, the situation in which the discourse occurs, the participants and any preceding verbal or physical interaction) and paralinguistic features which may contribute to the meaning of the interaction. We are, in short, concerned with contextualised speech (see Leech 1983: x; Yule 1996: 3–8). That is, the concern is not so much whether or not an utterance is grammatically correct, but whether or not the speaker achieves her communicative purpose; hence, Austin's title *How to Do Things with Words*. For instance, to say *Cold, isn't it* out of doors on a winter's day may be no more than a phatic utterance; if the speaker is addressing her hostess indoors, it may be interpreted as a hint to turn up the central heating; if the interlocutors are looking at a house with a view to purchase, it may be interpreted metaphorically and so be tantamount to rejecting the possibility of buying it.

Whenever we produce an utterance we are engaged in three acts. A **locutionary** act is the production of a well-formed utterance in whatever language one is speaking. The **illocutionary** act is the meaning one wishes to communicate: the illocutionary force we attach to a locutionary act is the meaning we intend to convey. The **perlocutionary** act is the effect of our words. If I say, *please open the window* and you do so, I have achieved my perlocutionary aim. Without entering into fruitless speculation about the intentions of authors, it seems that, in general terms, to look for the perlocutionary aim of most literary works is pointless. Arguably, most works of fiction do not have a perlocutionary aim in any obvious sense (though one might argue that Dickens, for example, wished to change social conditions through his writing) (see Cook 1994: 45). Within the fictional discourse, characters certainly have perlocutionary aims. The aim of Browning's Duke in 'My Last Duchess' is presumably to impress the envoy whom he is addressing, and to persuade him that the proposed marriage would be an excellent arrangement, provided that the bride behaves better than the last Duchess. If the ambassador reacts in the way many readers do, the Duke's aim will fail miserably.

In order for a speech act to be well formed, certain circumstances must obtain. These are known as felicity or appropriacy conditions (for a summary, see Searle 1969: 66). For example, for a question to be felicitous, not only must the social circumstances be appropriate (you do not interrupt formal proceedings to ask the time) but the speaker must want to know the answer, and must also think that the hearer both knows the answer and is prepared to supply it. It follows then that neither exam questions nor rhetorical questions are true questions.

It is quite possible for a well-formed locutionary act to fail:

> 'I discovered her with a young man in a tweed coat and flannel knickerbockers. They were kissing one another in the summerhouse.'
> Lord Emsworth clicked his tongue.
> 'Ought to have been out in the sunshine,' he said, disapprovingly. (P. G. Wodehouse, *Lord Emsworth and Others*, 1937/1966: 15)

Quite clearly, Lord Emsworth, by accident or intent, fails to pick up his companion's intention in speaking. The illocutionary force (the effect she is aiming at) of her utterance is concerned with the kiss, not the location. She is far more worried about inappropriate suitors than about wasting rare English sunshine. The misfiring of illocutionary acts is common. Such failures can be the result of simple misunderstanding, as well as of a wilful decision to be obtuse. Narrators sometimes make clear that this has happened:

> 'Love's young dream,' says Leslie 'ain't what it used to be. It comes of all this living together before you get married. Takes all the romance out of it.'
> This is a pointed comment, aimed at Trevor, who however pretends to misunderstand. 'Right,' he says. 'That's what I tell Michelle: marriage is fatal to romance.' (Lodge, *Paradise News*, 1991/1992: 7)

Or:

> 'Can I see them?' asked Miriam.
> 'I don't know,' said Eloise again, apparently taking the question at face value. (Ellis, *Fairy Tale*, 1996/1997: 99)

(This example neatly illustrates the loss to the language of the distinction between *can* and *may*.)

2.2.1 Direct speech acts

These occur when there is a direct correlation between the grammatical form of an utterance and its illocutionary force (*Shut the door*, for example). Commonly however, the mapping is not straightforward:

> 'Stop it. Harry, why do you have to turn into a devil now?'
> 'I don't like to leave anything,' the man said. 'I don't like to leave things behind.'
> (Hemingway, 'The Snows of Kilimanjaro', 1939/1964: 448)

Here we have an imperative, an interrogative and a declarative sentence, used appropriately though the illocutionary force of the question is a complaint rather than a request for information, which is how Harry interprets it. In such a case, where there is no direct mapping between form and function, we have what are known as indirect speech acts.

2.2.2 Indirect speech acts

When we use one speech act rather than another, and leave our hearer to work out the meaning we intend, we are dealing with indirect speech acts. Often they are used for reasons of politeness. In English, for instance, we normally avoid the imperative except in specific circumstances (of great intimacy; in the military; in addressing small children; or in situations of imminent danger). So, *Can you turn the radio down?* addressed to an adolescent is almost certainly a polite way of avoiding the imperative. Without that context, we cannot be certain: if addressed to a paraplegic, it may be a question about physical capacity, and thus a direct speech act. When a Glaswegian says *Was you looking at me Jimmy?*, he is not asking a question, but issuing an invitation to fight. In short, questions have many different functions according to context; it is up to our pragmatic experience to interpret them appropriately. This is not usually a difficult problem, since most of these are fixed collocations which occur in predictable situations, and therefore the interpretative burden on the hearer is not significant. It is part of our experience as members of a speech community to interpret them appropriately. Levinson (1983) and Grundy (1995) think that we can do without the concept of indirect speech acts. Levinson (1983: 274) suggests that it may be a mistake (and is certainly un-pragmatic) to attempt to map syntax onto speech acts; it may be preferable to look at the function of each speech act in context, and accept that they can serve a wide range of purposes. Grundy argues that language is made up of segments that are meaningless in isolation: morphemes and phonemes only convey meaning when they combine into words, which in turn combine into sentences (so that *tap* can be a noun or a verb, according to the context in which it appears) (Grundy 1995: 101–5). These are possible solutions to the problem posed by indirect speech acts; they simplify analysis and are thoroughly pragmatic in their attention to context rather than syntactic form. In the case of the Hemingway extract cited above, the question is clearly a complaint, not a request for information (which is available in any case to the speaker, who knows quite well that the man is dying, and has a right to be upset). It offers a solution to such oddities as the fact that English avoids the imperative in most circumstances, whereas other languages do not. It is simply a matter of politeness in English, which is encoded differently in other languages.

2.3 CLASSIFICATION OF SPEECH ACTS

Various types of speech acts have been identified (see, for example, Yule 1996), and they are described below.

2.3.1 Representative speech acts

Representative speech acts are statements and descriptions. The speaker offers her view of the world as she understands it. Much fiction, like much ordinary language use, consists largely of representative speech acts; in particular, much of the narrator's activity consists of representative speech acts. An interesting problem may arise when, in a first-person narrative, the representative speech acts of the narrator suggest a world view at odds with our own. The governess narrator in Henry James' *The Turn of the Screw* believes in ghosts (possibly influenced by her reading of gothic novels like *The Mystery of Udolpho*, which she admits to); she interprets events in a way which we might not. In considering types of narrator, we will see that a first-person narrator cannot say things that show inner knowledge of a character's mind, any more than in real life we can say *You are tired* whereas *You look tired* is perfectly acceptable (see Chapter 4). This is because of the felicity conditions attaching to representative speech acts. We are expected to believe that what we say is true, and to have evidence for it. (Note that this theory does not seem to take account of the possibility that we may lie.) Some narrators break this kind of rule regularly: one of them is Conrad's Marlow, in *Heart of Darkness*, who says: *But his soul was mad. Being alone in the wilderness, it had looked within itself, and, by heavens! I tell you, it had gone mad. I had – for my sins, I suppose – to go through the ordeal of looking into it myself* (1902/1983: 108). Such instances, when a narrator is perhaps being less than fully honest, are identifiable if we look at the kinds of speech acts involved, and consider whether or not they are used appropriately. It is at its most interesting and relevant when the act performed is in some way malformed: this is the case in the extract above, when Marlow comments on the state of Kurtz's soul. This passage shows that Marlow and Kurtz have at least *hubris* in common.

2.3.2 Expressive speech acts

Expressive speech acts are those that reveal the speaker's attitude, such as congratulating, condoling, or expressing pleasure. They have a strongly interpersonal function. One may therefore expect to find more of them in the discourse of characters within fiction than in the narratorial voice, though they are found here too. An example occurs in the introductory section of Ellis' *The Other Side of the Fire*: *she fell in love with her husband's son. Bloody hell!* (1983/1985: 7). It is a puzzling and disquieting remark; it seems difficult to attribute the exclamation to any but the narrator's voice, since no other has yet been heard. The reason for the uneasiness aroused by this remark may be explained by an analysis of interjections as deictic items. If they are deictic, they must be rooted in the situation of utterance, and be attributable to someone whose reactions are encoded. A remark of this kind is normally interpretable by a bystander with reference to something in the context, in the same way as deictic items like *here, there* and the tense of verbs are interpreted (see Wilkins 1995). So here we are presumably invited to adopt a particular view of this illicit love.

A more straightforward example occurs near the end of *Pride and Prejudice*, when the narrator remarks:

> I wish I could say, for the sake of her family, that the accomplishment of her earnest desire in the establishment of so many of her children, produced so happy an effect as to make her a sensible, amiable, well-informed woman for the rest of her life; though perhaps it was lucky for her husband, who might not have relished domestic felicity in so unusual a form, that she was still occasionally nervous and invariably silly. (Austen 1813/1972: 393)

The eponymous narrator of *Moll Flanders*, when describing one of her exploits as a thief, comments:

> I say, I confess the inhumanity of this action moved me very much, and made me relent exceedingly, and tears stood in my eyes upon that subject; but with all my sense of its being cruel and inhuman, I could never find in my heart to make any restitution. (Defoe 1722/1978: 202)

There is, in first-person narratives, sometimes an interesting correlation between expressive speech acts and representative speech acts which, as in the example above, are not necessarily well formed. This is a notable feature of Browning's 'My Last Duchess', and arguably one source of the reader's sense that the Duke is a thoroughly manipulative and slippery man. This feature, and its implications, is considered more fully in the context of first-person narrators (see Chapter 4).

2.3.3 Directives

Directives are essentially commands: again, these are more likely to be found within character to character discourse. Directives addressed to the reader occur rarely in the narrator's voice, for the obvious reason that readers exist outside the communicative framework of the fiction. Sterne regularly addresses his (fictional) readers, who become quasi-characters in themselves. In this particular instance, the real reader shares 'Madam's' puzzlement, and might almost be inclined to follow the instruction:

> How could you, Madam, be so inattentive in reading the last chapter. I told you in it, *that my mother was not a papist* . . . I do insist upon it, that you immediately

> turn back, that is, as soon as you get to the next full stop, and read the whole
> chapter over again. (*Tristram Shandy*, 1760/1980, I: 20)

Not that re-reading the chapter will illuminate the matter, unless one's mind is as
contorted as the narrator's. A comparable example is:

> You are about to begin reading Italo Calvino's new novel, *If on a winter's night a
> traveller*. Relax. Concentrate. Dispel every other thought. Let the world around
> you fade. Best to close the door; the TV is always on in the next room. (Calvino
> 1982: 9)

Like Sterne, Calvino is interested in probing the conventions of literary discourse.

Directives may function in a manner analogous to rhetorical questions that is, as
devices that promote engagement with the text. For example, Lawrence writes: *See
him stand on a wet gloomy morning . . .* ('Tickets, Please', 1922/1995: 36). All these
examples may remind us that the novel's origins lie (however remotely) in oral narratives, with a storyteller entertaining a real audience. In *Tom Jones* Fielding addresses
the real reader regularly: he was deeply conscious of being an innovator in the writing
of fiction, and he wanted the ground rules clearly understood by his audience. This
happens, for instance, in some of the prefaces to the books in *Tom Jones*, when the
reader is instructed in his task: *First, then, we warn thee not too hastily to condemn any
of the Incidents in this our History, as impertinent and foreign to our main design . . .*
(1749/1973: 398) Here it is Fielding as author, not narrator, who is offering instruction. He has stepped out of his narratorial role temporarily, to comment on the work
(see Chapter 1). Thus the relationship with the reader is wholly different.

2.3.4 Commissives

Commissives are acts which commit the speaker to some future course of action.
They include promises (and their converse, threats: the difference depends on how
the hearer will be affected by the proposed act); they are common in the discourse of
characters in fiction, but rarer in the narrator's discourse, though arguably the beginning of some novels functions as a commissive: *The story I shall tell begins like this*
(Ellis, *The 27th Kingdom*, 1982: 7). *Once upon a time* might also be regarded as a
commissive: including the implied promise of a particular type of story. That is a
matter of our knowledge of genre, and the expectations aroused by this particular
opening.

2.3.5 Declarations

Declarations are a unique form of speech act, in that their successful performance
depends upon the status of the speaker, and the precise circumstances surrounding
the event. They are institutionalised in a society. Declarations include sacking a
worker, performing a marriage, and sentencing a criminal. Given that a declaration
is the one speech act that has an effect in the real world, in bringing about the state

to which it refers, it can hardly occur within literary discourse except as a pseudo-speech act, as when characters marry, or are sent to prison. Of course, there is a view that all speech acts in literature are pseudo-speech acts; this is ultimately a rather fruitless debate, which is not, I think, relevant to how readers interpret a text, knowing as we do that the whole is designed to entertain, and mirrors, however distortedly, the real world (see Petrey 1990: 67).

2.3.6 Speech acts and interpretation

This section may seem to readers to have something of the butterfly-collecting spirit about it: there are plenty of examples, but little in the way of concrete or useful ways of using speech act theory in interpreting literary texts (except perhaps when they are malformed, particularly in first-person narratives, as exemplified in some of Marlow's discourse, and that of Browning's Duke). Speech act theory in itself does not seem to me to offer many insights into how literary language works, or how it achieves its effects. Fish offers an interesting interpretation of *Coriolanus* using the theory, and a good account of Searle's thoughts on fictional discourse, but at the end of a lengthy discussion he concludes: *Speech-act theory is an account of the conditions of intelligibility, of what it means to mean in a community, of the procedures which must be instituted before one can even be said to be understood* (1980: 245). Petrey (1990), on the other hand, offers a defence of the contribution of speech act theory to the study of literary texts.

2.4 THE CO-OPERATIVE PRINCIPLE

The philosopher H. P. Grice developed a co-operative principle (1967/1987) which, he considers, underlies successful verbal communication. That is, we assume, in normal circumstances, that these are the ground rules that we observe when speaking and interpreting utterances.

The **co-operative principle** states: *Make your conversational contribution such as is required, at the stage at which it occurs, by the accepted purpose or direction of the talk exchange in which you are engaged.* To this he appends four **maxims**, which clarify how the co-operative principle works:

Maxim of quantity
1. Make your contribution as informative as is required (for the current purposes of the exchange).
2. Do not make your contribution more informative than is required.

Maxim of quality
Try to make your contribution one that is true.
1. Do not say what you believe to be false.
2. Do not say that for which you lack adequate evidence.

Maxim of relation
Be relevant.

Maxim of manner

Be perspicuous.
1. Avoid obscurity of expression.
2. Avoid ambiguity.
3. Be brief.
4. Be orderly.

The co-operative principle is intuitively attractive, and it seems likely that we (unconsciously) use it, or some very similar approach, in our interpretation of discourse. Of course, different societies may interpret the maxims differently: there is bound to be cross-cultural variation, but it is difficult to imagine a society in which some such fundamental assumptions are not made about the *bona fides* of interlocutors, however much surface realisations may vary.

On the other hand, it is not clear to what extent a 'conversational' principle can be generalised: the Gricean maxims are not equally applicable to every situation. Phatic utterances are not designed to fulfil any of the maxims. They oil the wheels of social discourse by acknowledging the existence of other people, and suggesting (possibly inaccurately) the speaker's continued interest in them. Furthermore, many verbal interactions are not conversations, or at least, there are sub-types, such as gossip or storytelling. To gossip interestingly, speakers are likely to engage in exaggeration, depart in various ways from the strict truth, and generally try to make their comments interesting, at the expense of various maxims. Some interactions, such as quarrels, are inherently unco-operative. (Maybe that is how we recognise what is going on.) We all lie, from time to time, for good or bad reasons. We all say irrelevant things, but are irritated when others do so. Thus Grice presents an idealised account of the average verbal interaction. And there are other types of linguistic activity, which may involve the CP to varying degrees: committee meetings, lectures, interviews are tightly structured linguistic events, where decisions about the application of the maxims are dependent on the decisions of the chairman or lecturer. While the rules for each of these events vary, some at least of the maxims should be observed. The maxim of manner is very much a matter of convention in such situations, but the maxims of quantity, quality and relation are supposed to be observed by co-operative speakers. In sum, unless we trust our interlocutors – except when we have reason for not doing so – and assume that they are obeying the Co-operative Principle in some form, there might seem to be little point in talking in the first place.

The maxims are not always observed, and the failure to do so can take a number of forms.

1. **Opting out**: making clear that one is aware of the maxim, but is prevented for some reason from observing it. Politicians and reporters observing an embargo on the publication of news are in this situation.
2. **Violating a maxim**: often with the intention to mislead, this is often a quiet act, also known as lying.
3. **A clash** arises when one cannot be fully co-operative. For instance, to fulfil one maxim (say, of quantity) might require one to break another (of quality), in a

situation where one is not certain of the accuracy of some information, and hence uncertain whether to say something which may be helpful, but where one's evidence is inadequate. One may therefore hedge one's contribution. Phrases such as *I understand that,* or *it seems to me* may indicate this.

4. **Flouting**: this is the most interesting way of breaking a maxim. One makes clear to the hearer that one is aware of the co-operative principle and the maxims, so that the audience is led to consider why the principle or a maxim was broken. The assumption, in other words, is not that communication has broken down, but that the speaker has chosen an indirect way of achieving it. It may be that something in the situation prevents giving a direct answer to a question; considerations of politeness may inhibit the speaker. This is one of the most crucial aspects of Grice's theory for the interpretation of literary texts. We assume that flouts generate implicatures, and it is up to the reader to pick up appropriate ones. Thus the maxim of manner is flouted when we use a metaphor or irony, but we assume that it has communicative effects. The same maxim is involved when a non-chronological order is selected for telling a story. If I begin a conventional whodunnit with the murderer approaching his victim, I will spoil the story, and doubtless lose all my readers, unless, of course, it turns out that what amounts to a flout within the genre of detective fiction turns out to be a psychological study of the motivation of murderers, where the loss of the mystery element may be insignificant. In considering the effects of the implicatures that may be generated by flouting a maxim, we should always remember that the whole act of reading a novel is a slow process, which takes place over time (in that way, it is comparable to music, and perhaps contrasts with the initial impact of looking at a painting). It is easy to lose sight of the fact that during the reading process, implicatures will accumulate, and that we balance one against another in order to arrive at an interpretation. In that respect, a book like this, which inevitably deals with short extracts, traduces the reading process. It can only be hoped that readers will consult their memories, and their own knowledge of texts, to supply examples and so enrich the reading process.

2.5 CONVERSATIONAL IMPLICATURE

Conversational implicatures arise from a combination of language and situation: the same utterance on different occasions might not generate an implicature, or might suggest a different one. They are rooted in the situation in which they occur, and must be interpreted taking the context into account. If we assume that our interlocutor is obeying the co-operative principle when one of the maxims appears not to be fulfilled, we will attempt to infer the meaning intended. Exploiting a maxim may happen because allowing the hearer to work out the point of a remark may be a polite way of avoiding what are known as face threatening acts (FTA). For instance, if you ask me to lend you five pounds, I may find it difficult to refuse politely. If you simply say that you will have to walk home because you have no money, the implicature might be that I should lend you some, but neither of us suffers damage to our self-esteem if I fail to do so. This kind of implicature is commonplace in everyday language, and plentiful in literary texts:

> Meanwhile Miss Brodie was being questioned by the girls behind on the question of the Brownies and the Girl Guides, for quite a lot of the other girls in the Junior School were Brownies.
> 'For those who like that sort of thing,' said Miss Brodie in her best Edinburgh voice, 'that is the sort of thing they like.'
> So Brownies and Guides were ruled out. (Spark, *The Prime of Miss Jean Brodie*, 1961/1965: 31)

Here the narrator spells out the implicature that the girls derive from their teacher's comments: they are keen to keep her good opinion. A reader (like Sandy, one of the children) may derive other implicatures. Sandy acutely perceives that the Brownies might be seen as rivals to Miss Brodie, offering the children an alternative focus of interest and activity. Readers may also recognise the control Miss Brodie exercises over her pupils, or they may perhaps look back nostalgically to the days when teachers commanded respect.

Leech (1983) points out that the maxims and the implicatures they generate explain in a principled way why we may exploit the maxims rather than obeying the co-operative principle: interpreting an implicature is partly the responsibility of the hearer, as well as being encouraged by the encoder of the message. It may be the most economical way of saying something, or it may simply add to the interest of an utterance. My grandfather used to introduce my mother as *my daughter by my first wife*. In fact, he had only one wife. The implicature, however, is that he must have had more than one, since he was being so specific. The maxim of quantity is clearly flouted here, and perhaps also that of relation. The only motivation appears to be to arouse curiosity about his private life.

Rhetorical questions often generate implicatures, and tend to involve the maxim of manner:

> 'Let's get back to this loathsome plot to ruin my life's whole happiness. Why can't you be a sport, Uncle Clarence, and stand up for me? Can't you understand what this means to me? Weren't you ever in love?'
> 'Certainly I was in love. Dozens of times. I'll tell you a very funny story – '
> 'I don't want to hear funny stories.'
> 'No. No. Quite. Exactly.'
>
> (Wodehouse, *Lord Emsworth and Others*, 1937/1966: 19)

Here Uncle Clarence, by answering a series of rhetorical questions, effectively aborts the force of his niece's complaints. Clearly she has no wish to hear about his past love life; her only concern is with his present conduct.

2.6 THE CO-OPERATIVE PRINCIPLE AND LITERARY DISCOURSE

One would expect that the Gricean maxims should have some relevance for the processing of literary discourse, on the innermost level of character-to-character interactions. It is perhaps more interesting to consider whether it is not also applicable to our processing of the whole text, in the interaction between narrator and reader, and the relationship between narrator and characters. If Grice is right in his hypotheses, then it seems most likely that we use the co-operative principle in interpreting any discourse. Furthermore, arriving at meaning via the maxims involves effort, and so increases engagement with the text.

The issue is whether using Grice in the interpretation of literary discourse can usefully guide our reading. Just as in ordinary conversation, we may judge that a work is too long, obscure, or whatever. What Grice does is to suggest the ways in which, via the implicatures, we may be guided toward interpretation – though we may, of course, conclude that our initial judgement was correct and that, *Finnegan's Wake*, for example, is indeed unco-operative throughout. Grice's maxims, in relation to literary work, suggest interpretative procedures – procedures which we are familiar with from our daily conversational interactions. As Brown and Yule (1983: 13) point out, the spoken language is used primarily for interpersonal communication, while the written is predominantly transactional. Fictional discourse bridges these two functions: one might suggest a higher degree of transactional elements in much of the narratorial commentary, while conversations between characters are (to varying degrees) mimetic of the spoken language. On the character-to-character level, the maxim of quality operates in a way analogous to real-life interactions. Characters will lie, or exaggerate, or conceal. The only difference is that, sometimes at least, the reader may know more than the characters, and so be in a better position to arrive at possible implicatures not available to them. More interesting are those cases where the narrator plays fast and loose with the maxims. There are some fictions where the narrator may be regarded as unreliable – the Governess in James' *The Turn of the Screw*, for example. Marlow in Conrad's *Heart of Darkness* is perhaps another example, though in this case it is his interpretations that a reader may question, rather than the events he describes. General violation of the maxims is a feature of unreliable narrators.

Clashes between the demands of various maxims occur in the interaction of characters, but perhaps more interestingly in the narrator's discourse. One might argue, for instance, that a writer of detective stories is faced with clashes throughout the writing, because she knows 'who dunnit' and conceals, for as long as possible, the murderer's identity from the reader. More broadly, this applies to any of us telling a story, and any narrator trying to engage the interest of the reader. Spark, in *The Prime of Miss Jean Brodie*, plays with this: she reveals the broad outlines of the plot early in the fiction, but teasingly does not directly answer major questions readers may have.

It should be noted that the first three maxims refer to what is said, while the maxim of manner refers to how it is said, and so is under the most direct control of the speaker or writer. It might also seem that this maxim is hardly relevant to literary dis-course, which sometimes seems to abound in ambiguities, may be obscure, prolix or unduly compressed, and is certainly not necessarily orderly. Novelists regularly re-order the way in which a story is told: it is common for narratives to interweave the present with the past, most often in the interests of the maxims of manner and rela-tion; it is thus a most useful way of guiding readers, who are invited to consider the implicatures of such departures from the conversational maxims. The maxim of quantity is difficult: what is the appropriate amount of information required in a fiction? We have to take it on trust that the narrator has judged appropriately, and given us all that is required. But there are interesting exceptions to this generalisa-tion, in fictions such as James' 'Paste' or *The Turn of the Screw* (1898/1969), where the amount of information offered is insufficient to allow secure interpretation: there are permanent gaps which are never filled. These matters are considered more fully below. Another kind of example is found in Agatha Christie's *The Murder of Roger Ackroyd:* the first-person narrator is also the murderer. His narrative is, on the whole, true, but he withholds crucial evidence, so violating the maxim of quantity. Some readers feel that the concealment this necessitates makes the whole fiction rather a cheat: it might be held to break a convention of the genre, which normally requires that the reader should be in possession of sufficient information to anticipate the detective's conclusions.

2.6.1 Character-level interaction and implicatures

We shall consider a dialogue from the end of Hemingway's 'The Short Happy Life of Francis Macomber' (1939/1964). The story tells of a disastrous safari: Macomber runs away from a lion; his wife sleeps with Wilson, the white hunter; finally Macomber regains his courage and is confronting a wounded buffalo when his wife *shot at the buffalo . . . as it seemed about to gore Macomber and had hit her husband about two inches up and a little to one side of the base of his skull* (1939/1964: 440). The narrator is thus committed to the proposition that the shooting of Macomber was an accident. (Of course, that does not mean that the characters are aware of the true facts of the case.) There is a distinction between 'shooting at' (and missing), and 'shooting' (and hitting). This is an example of a conventional implicature, which depends upon our knowledge of the grammar of a language (see Levinson 1983). As Mrs Macomber weeps, Wilson says:

'That was a pretty thing to do,' he said in a toneless voice. 'He *would* have left you too.'
'Stop it,' she said.
. . .
'There's a hell of a lot to be done,' he said . . . 'Why didn't you poison him? That's what they do in England.'
'Stop it. Stop it. Stop it,' the woman cried.
. . .

'Oh, please stop it', she said. 'Please, please stop it.'

'That's better,' Wilson said. 'Please is much better. Now I'll stop.'

(1939/1964: 441)

Wilson violates the maxim of quality since he did not see what happened; nor is he in a position to predict the future. The maxim of manner is involved too: this is a most inappropriate way to address a widow. The implicature is that she murdered him; this is not true, as the narrator points out. Further, he has no evidence of this, so the quality maxim is violated. It is also grossly inappropriate to demand politeness, in the manner of a nanny, at such a juncture. The maxim of manner is thus violated throughout. Note that Wilson has no problems with any clash, but is happy to say 'that for which he lacks adequate evidence'. (This, of course, ignores the possibility that psychologically Mrs Macomber is a murderer, in the sense that, in the long term, she may be quite pleased at what happened.) Thus the implicatures generated here are partly available only to the reader: the communication of implicatures is not only between characters, but between narrator and reader.

2.6.2 Higher-level interaction: narrator-reader implicatures

2.6.2.1 Exemplification

I shall now consider the contribution that each of the maxims can make to the interpretation of fiction. The narrative of Joyce's 'A Painful Case' (1914/1988) concerns Mr Duffy, a middle-aged bank clerk, who becomes friendly with Mrs Sinico. They meet at concerts, and for conversation. The relationship is broken off when she takes his hand and presses it to her cheek. Four years later, she is run over by a train and Duffy feels first revulsion, then (very briefly) remorse, before regaining his composure. Captain Sinico plays no part in the story: he is at sea most of the time; the narrator tells us he hoped Mr Duffy might marry his daughter – a revealing comment, given that Duffy is closer to the mother's age than the daughter's.

2.6.2.2 Quantity

This maxim requires that we offer the appropriate amount of information. On one level, it is clearly irrelevant to literary discourse, since the situation, information and so on are all fictional. There cannot therefore be a particular quantity of information that is required or useful. However, the maxim of quantity may explain why a reader seeks meaning in apparently trivial or irrelevant details. We are likely to attend to such details precisely because of the implied guarantee of relevance made by any published work. While we may pay little heed to the clothing or appearance of an acquaintance, in a literary text we may see it as an index of character and/or social position. At the beginning of 'A Painful Case' we are offered a description of the room inhabited by the protagonist, which he furnished himself. The passage is full of negatives. The colours are predominantly black and white, with a black and scarlet rug. Initially more interesting are the books, arranged by size, and ranging from a copy of the *Maynooth Catechism* sewn into a notebook (which suggests a relic of his school-days) to Wordsworth's complete works. The selection of books seems to trace his intellectual development (later in the story we are told of books he buys after break-ing off his affair with Mrs Sinico), but, since the narrative deals with a failed love affair, which does not take place in this room, the reader may justly wonder whether the maxim of relation has not also been violated. When the narrator describes Mr Duffy, negatives are also prominent. Colour is mentioned in the description of his physical appearance: his face is the colour of Dublin's streets. This may suggest that the narrator intends that the preceding description of the room should encourage the reader to interpret the character via his surroundings. That is, metonymic discourse of this type may be interpreted through the maxims of the co-operative principle.

We may also find that the same incident is told more than once. The motivation can be of many types, but sometimes it may be that an omniscient narrator is showing agreement with an interpretation offered by a character within the fiction. This will increase the credibility of the character, and may affect our overall interpre-tation. In contrast, a character's assessment of a situation may differ from that of the narrator, as in the extract from 'The Short Happy Life of Francis Macomber' above, where the narrator and character have different interpretations of events.

2.6.2.3 Quality

This maxim has to do with the truth or falsity of an utterance. Characters within fic-tions will lie, or exaggerate, or conceal, and, as we have seen, narrators do too. More interestingly, discrepancies between the views of narrator and character may emerge. In 'A Painful Case' the neglectful husband tells the inquest into his wife's death that the marriage had been happy until she had taken to drink a couple of years before. The narrator has already offered another view: the captain is so uninterested in his wife that it never occurs to him that she might be attractive to someone else. It is up to the reader to reconcile these views, bearing in mind that an omniscient narrator's views normally take precedence over those of a character.

2.6.2.4 Manner

This maxim refers not to what is said, but to how it is expressed. It is therefore most firmly under the control of the speaker or writer. On the highest level of textual organisation, any departure from chronological order involves this maxim (and that of relation). Any figure of speech breaks the maxim of manner, since a metaphor, for instance, is not literally true; ironies are often expressed in terms either of exaggera-tion or a contrafactual statement. Metaphors and other figures of speech are consid-ered in Chapter 8. Instances of re-phrasing suggest different views of an event, and also involve this maxim. In George Mackay Brown's 'The Two Fiddlers', Gavin, one of the protagonists, tells his companion, Storm, of a mutual attraction between himself and a guest at a wedding. The narrator comments that *Storm was popular with the island girls and Gavin had no success with them at all* (1974: 14).

2.6.2.5 *Relation*

On the face of it, one assumes that, given the editorial process undergone by any published work, everything within a fiction will be relevant. This maxim explains why it
is that we seek for relevance in trivial details – such as the arrangement of books on
Duffy's shelves – which perhaps would not strike us as significant in real life. This
maxim is crucial for the interpretation of figures of speech, where one is invited to
consider the relevance they may have to the narrative. One might further consider
that the account of Duffy's meals can be considered here. This (very) short story
begins with a description of the suburb and house where he lives. From his windows
he could look into a derelict distillery. This begins the series of negatives with which
the narrative is peppered. Duffy's lunch consists of beer and dry biscuits: this sounds
like a parodic communion. We are told that his friendship with Mrs Sinico nour-
ished him. Taking the emphasis on food and nourishment together, one may conclude that the initial reference to the distillery is highly relevant: it begins a chain of
metaphors, metonymies and similes which together illuminate Mr Duffy's miserable
existence. Just as Duffy has rejected the consolation the Church could offer, so he
refuses also Mrs Sinico's companionship, and condemns himself to a solipsistic existence. Even the apparently trivial (and so violating the maxim of relation) reference
to the distillery can be interpreted as encouraging a particular reading of the text. It
is not suggested that this reading is only available through consideration of the
maxims: that is plainly not the case.

Grice's maxims offer one way of approaching a text, and suggest elements in it
which can be considered in their light, with useful results. Perhaps the main contribution that an awareness of the maxims can make is that they inform our reading:
any kind of deviation from a maxim may be significant. It is here (as perhaps also in
life) that the maxims guide interpretation.

2.7 THE CO-OPERATIVE PRINCIPLE AND THE
INTERPRETATION OF LITERATURE

In a wide-ranging review of the applicability of pragmatic theories to literary discourse, Cook (1994) argues that the co-operative principle is inapplicable to literary
discourse. In a discussion of its limitations, he suggests that it applies primarily to
relations between acquaintances, not intimates or those in disparate power relationships. He notes that the maxims are regularly broken in quarrels, when we are repetitive, irrelevant and probably do not pay much attention to the truth. One response
to that is that it is precisely because the maxims are infringed that we are aware of
the nature of the interaction: we judge it against a norm of co-operative behaviour.
But the more profound point is that, when we are reading a literary text, we are essentially *voyeurs*. As such, we observe with interest, and are perhaps prepared to adopt
whatever attitudes may be necessary for the 'willing suspension of disbelief'. *Voyeurs*
are interested in the minutiae of others' lives; they live vicariously. They may therefore be expected to judge the language they encounter using the same means they

would were it to occur in real life, with the crucial difference that a *voyeur* can enjoy a quarrel, or a love affair, without having to endure the consequences.

Cook further considers that the wide range of works regarded as literary, which range from the fairly factual to the fantastic, means that the question of the truthfulness (the quality maxim) of an utterance is irrelevant or unhelpful. He similarly considers the quantity maxim to be irrelevant, since a literary work has no practical or social function. Therefore the work must be too long, but some works are praised for concision. One can respond to this on two levels. First, the application of the cooperative principle and maxims may work differently on different levels of the discourse. In dialogue, which is analogous to real-life conversation, one should be able to apply the maxims as usual. In the discourse of the narrator, the matter is more complex, though the real-life analogy exists too: we tell each other stories, often for a range of interpersonal reasons. This can clearly be an imposition upon the audience, for which it may or may not feel adequately rewarded. Secondly, he ignores the implied contract we all enter into when we read a fictional work: we may suspend some of our disbelief, but nevertheless we are likely to process the text in much the same way as other types of discourse, though we play the credulous reader.

In place of these theories, Cook suggests that we read literature in order to change our mental representations of the world. But arguably this is covered by the maxim of relation, and is certainly fundamental to Sperber and Wilson's Relevance theory. (Pilkington 2000 considers the issue of literariness, and why we read literature, in the light of relevance theory. His contribution is considered below, in that context.) It is ultimately difficult to see why we should attend to any discourse unless it affects us in some way. Cook proposes that a crucial function of literary discourse is the refreshing of schemata (essentially, our pre-existing knowledge structures, whether of our 'world view' or encyclopaedic knowledge, of language or text structure). A difficulty with this view is that we continue to read novelists like Jane Austen. Cook suggests that her fictions did originally function to overturn schemata: a reader, whose views had been formed by *Tom Jones* as to the behaviour of the middle classes in the country, would find *Emma* offered a very different view (1994: 194). He admits that this does not account for the fact that we continue to read, and even re-read fictions which we know well. Sometimes, of course, it is we who have changed, and so we return to the text with new experiences and perceptions, which may change our view of the text, as he also admits. Cook's argument is in many respects attractive, but, while noting that affecting cognitive change must be the intended effect of any discourse in some sense (as relevance theoreticians hold), it does not seem to solve the problem of defining 'literariness' or explaining why and how people read literature in the first place. Of course, as Cook points out (1994: 44), we cannot know what Homer intended when he composed the *Iliad*. We can be absolutely certain that our understanding will differ radically from that of its original audience. Much scholarly effort may allow us to recover something of its world view, cultural assumptions and so on, but when we first approach the poem, it will almost certainly have a novelty effect which could not be assumed for the original audience. Heroic poems, like folk and fairy tales, are part of the common stock of their community. An audience may judge one performance against another, but the story itself will be familiar and unlikely to change the cognitive environment of the audience. The same point applies to the reading of Jane Austen: we may read for information about a past society, and so create – or refresh – our schemata of what it was like. But that is to read for sociohistorical reasons, which is a valid approach, but irrelevant to the literary qualities of the texts. If Cook were correct in his suggestions, one might expect that experimental poetry, fiction (and music!) would attract major audiences. But, as he notes, the evidence shows that this is not the case (1994: 192). It takes time for such works to be assimilated, which almost suggests that we prefer that the critics endure cognitive change, and then tell us what to think. He is probably right to suggest that schema refreshment is one of the effects of literature (and certain other types of discourse) (1994: 195), but the theory does not answer the question of what literariness really is, or why we value literary discourse. It does suggest ways in which text is processed, and so may account for some of the effects it has on the reader.

Cook does not seem to me to have found the answer to what 'literariness' is. Certainly, speech act theory and the co-operative principle were not designed to answer this problem, nor are they able to do so. What they do is offer an explanation of how texts may be processed, some of the attitudes readers bring to the processing of text, and why we arrive at certain interpretations. Thorne proposes what I believe to be the *raison d'être* of literary discourse (though he is discussing only poetry).

> We read poems (or should) in a way which is quite different from the way in which we read other texts, because in the case of other texts it is the imposition of one, and only one, meaning that is important. Learning to read a poem . . . is a matter of learning to hear what normally we must be deaf to: the inexhaustible ambiguity of utterances. (1988: 290)

It would be difficult to sustain an argument that most novelists (or poets) are exceptional thinkers: what they can do is manipulate language in interesting ways, and thus teach us something of the potential of language.

Cook also argues that the politeness principle (Brown and Levinson 1987; Yule 1996), which basically refers to our wish to get our own way and maintain a satisfactory public self-image or 'face', is violated in literary discourse because it always imposes on the reader's face (owing to the intimate topics it discusses). However, this ignores the fact that we can choose to read or not read a particular work – as Wodehouse points out, if readers are not interested, *they throw him aside and go out to picture palaces* (*A Damsel in Distress*, 1919/1961: 5).

The interpersonal element is prominent in some novels, when the relationship between narrator and reader is very important: Fielding in *Tom Jones* spends much time addressing the reader (Booth (1961) calls the relationship between narrator and reader a sub-plot). Fielding begins by saying that an author should consider himself to be like a man who *keeps a public ordinary, at which all Persons are welcome for their money* (I, 1), and not like a gentleman who invites his friends to dinner. Therefore, the author must be attentive to the taste of his guests. In the final volume, he takes leave of the reader, comparing the experience of reading the novel to travelling on a stage-coach: the destination, and so the moment of parting, has arrived. One might argue that Fielding is, at least at times, very conscious of the 'face' wants of his readers, and attentive to them. (The apparent attentiveness may owe something to his anxiety to instruct readers in the art of reading fiction.) In contrast, one might consider the thoroughly antipathetic voice of the narrator in Spark's *The Driver's Seat*, which is unsettling in its understandable refusal to enter into the mind of a character who is apparently bent upon getting herself murdered. The text is full of *as ifs* and similar formulations. The narrator rarely exercises omniscience: when it occurs, it remains unsettling: *she will come forward and repeat all she remembers and all she does not remember, and all the details she imagines to be true and those that are true . . .* (1970/1974: 23). It is difficult to establish a strong interpersonal relation with such a narrator, and this is presumably the point.

2.8 INTEREST PRINCIPLE

Leech (1983) proposes that there is also an interest principle, analogous to the co-operative principle, which would explain many features of everyday discourse as well as aspects of literary language. The existence of understatement or litotes, hyperbole, even irony (which he prefers to consider an aspect of politeness) and metaphor may be accounted for under this heading. More obviously, the interest principle seems to be at work in some textual features that seem designed purely to amuse:

> 'In fact,' he went on, laying the whole deck of cards on the table and talking turkey without reserve, 'he loves you like a ton of bricks and his dearest wish is that you will consent to sign your future correspondence Monica Allsop.' (Wodehouse, *Galahad at Blandings*, 1965/1966: 75)

The ludicrous juxtaposition of a string of (judiciously amended) fixed collocations; the redundant formulation *talking turkey* and speaking *without reserve*); the misapplied simile (does 'he' also love bricks?), finishing with the bathetically commonplace reference to changing a name upon marriage can only be designed to amuse the jaded reader by the elevation of common linguistic infelicities almost to an art form.

Other aspects of Leech's interest and politeness principles will be considered in the context of irony. It suffices to note here that litotes is common in Old English poetry; in the modern language it survives primarily for self-deprecation (*not bad if I do say so myself*) and, as Leech suggests, as a counterweight to the very common use of hyperbole (*you are out of your mind*). As he points out, these formulations apparently violate the maxim of manner: they do so primarily to attract our attention and amuse. While the proliferation of principles and maxims seems undesirable, Leech has drawn attention via this principle to what is, I think, one of the major motivations for reading literature: we do so to enjoy ourselves. The ludic principle might well be the prime motivation for reading fiction, even if one might think it takes a warped mind to say that reading some works is a pleasure in the usual sense. As Leech concedes, the interest principle draws attention to things that can, by and large, be handled via the maxim of manner, so long as we are prepared to admit that a major motivation in a lot of language use is not transactional, but designed to entertain.

2.9 THE CO-OPERATIVE PRINCIPLE AND SYMBOLISM

While Cook argues that the Gricean maxims apply only to a very limited range of conversational situations, and are unhelpful for the interpretation of literary discourse, Eco (1984) explores the possibility of applying them to explain the interpretation of symbols. This is considered in Chapter 9.

2.10 CONCLUSION

I hope I have shown that, on a range of different levels, texts can be studied in the light of the co-operative principle with some benefit. The use of speech act theory is, on the whole, less valuable as a tool. But it is worth stressing that these tools allow us to explain how it is that we have arrived at a particular interpretation. They are not infallible guides which point to meaning. Marlow's discourse may make us uneasy: looking at the way he uses the wrong speech act tells us why we mistrust him. Similarly, we can explain why we come to certain views via the implicatures we access. This may lend a measure of respectability to our reading. This is a general point about how language works: if it were always used in a fully transparent manner, the world would be much less interesting, though some linguists might be happier. In the next chapter, I will review some of the ways in which writers try to guide readers through texts.

Chapter 3

Signposts

3.1 INTRODUCTION

This chapter considers the way narratives are structured, and methods of analysis. The structure and organisation of a narrative offers vital clues to interpretation. The theories of Labov (on textual organisation) and Genette (on temporal organisation) are considered in detail, in the context of a pragmatic assumption that all the devices considered here function in some way as macro-implicatures which help us to interpret a text. Most of the topics considered here form part of the 'deep structure' of narratives: they are prior to the surface structures such as syntax and lexis. The theories described here might, metaphorically, be regarded as a grid which we impose on a text to interpret and make sense of it, or as map references which enable us to find where we are – and where we want to be. I will start with the most general, large-scale categories, and then move to smaller devices. I begin with a consideration of genre, which is perhaps the most obvious indication of what we are reading, and how we should approach it.

3.2 SCHEMATA

This section considers the kinds of knowledge we bring to reading. We bring certain expectations to any text, based upon our previous experience of texts and the world. Discourse analysts work with concepts such as schemata and scripts (see Brown and Yule 1983: 241–50). These terms, though coming from different traditions (see Tannen 1993: 16; Segal 1995; Semino 1995: 119–92; Werth 1999: 103–13), refer to pre-existing knowledge structures which enable us to process discourse quickly. While they are, up to a point, subject to individual variation, they work by assuming that, in a particular cultural community, some things will be automatically understood by most members. Thus, a reference to a restaurant will, other things being equal, allow reference to waiters, tables, napkins, menus and so on as part of the 'given' elements in the situation, whereas mentioning a transport café will more likely suggest a menu on a blackboard, while a tea urn might replace the wine waiter. Such 'given' elements in a situation are often signalled by use of the definite article to refer to items which, technically, are 'new' in the discourse situation, so theoretically requiring the indefinite article (see above, Chapter 1). Thus schemata allow for a relatively quick and allusive style, in both spoken and written language. The assumption that schemata exist rests in part upon the speed with which we are able to process language, and the inexplicit styles we commonly use. We need not be explicit if we can rely on our interlocutors' knowledge to supply appropriate contextual elements to complete our discourse. Indeed, to over-specify might be considered impolite, suggesting that we consider our interlocutor to be inferior, ignorant or a member of a different speech community. The interpretation we give any verbal message is affected by the schemata we use in interpreting it. Semino (1997) develops Cook's theory of literary discourse, considered in the previous chapter, and shows its uses as an analytic tool. Stockwell (2002: 80) develops Cook's insights in the light of cognitive theories, and suggests that schemata for literature may exist, which might include appropriate language and style. These are certainly vital to interpretation.

3.3 GENRE

Genre is comparable to schema: it draws on our previous knowledge and experience, and offers a framework for interpretation. Genre is part of our knowledge structure, and functions in a way similar to schemata. Both underlie our initial approaches to a text. Genre is a kind of pre-setting device, which predisposes the reader to approach a text in a particular ways, it tells us whether what follows is likely to be a joke, business discussion, chat, novel or poem.

The expectations we bring to a text are also affected by its appearance including what Genette (1982) calls paratextual features. This encompasses the physical appearance of the text including the binding, the cover, the identity of author and publisher, the date of publication and other factors. We are aware, for instance, that informative text is often set out in columns: as in newspapers, dictionaries and encyclopaedias. We would be surprised to find a novel set out in this way, just as the convention has developed that poetry is set out in such a way that the line breaks indicate the rhythm. All of these things guide our initial approach to a text. In that sense, they are physical clues to the genre to which it belongs (or is aping). It is essential to a full understanding of a text to know what generic conventions the author is invoking, and the system of expectations that a competent reader brings to its interpretation. The games Sterne plays in *Tristram Shandy* (1760–7/1980), though coming very early in the development of the novel, have allowed some to question its genre. Certainly its appearance, with footnotes, marbled, blank and black pages, asterisks, and text in Latin and English presented like a crib on opposite pages, with the Latin curse carefully annotated for single or multiple victims (III, 11), regularly surprises the reader.

3.4 THE COMPETENT READER

Culler (1975) develops the notion of the competent reader. Competence is developed through experience of texts; one might regard it as the awareness of genres and the kinds of schemata we expect to find in a particular type of discourse. An English speaker learns early that *Once upon a time* usually signals the beginning of a fairy tale, and expects it to end *and they lived happily ever after* or some variation of the formula. So, when we come to Joyce's *A Portrait of the Artist as a Young Man* (1916) which begins with the traditional opening of a fairy tale, and comments on what a fine time it was, expectations are aroused which affect at least our initial approach to the text. The ironies it generates reverberate through the reading. In the world of fairy tales (as in most others), there are questions that should not be asked. George Mackay Brown, in 'The Two Fiddlers', retells a folk tale of a fiddler who disappears for twenty-five years. The narrator's voice is the omniscient one of the conventional fairy tale. The genre is cued from the first words, so the reader is prepared to expect fairies and supernatural events, though the tale is nicely balanced – the death of a young woman is presented as mysterious, though to the modern reader it is clearly the result of tuberculosis. In a final section a different narratorial voice is heard, subverting the values and norms of the first narrator:

> There the tale stops abruptly. The old story-tellers did not seem to be interested in what happened afterwards to Storm . . . The story-tellers left many fascinating questions unanswered. Did Storm marry and grow old and die, like everybody else in the island? . . . or had the magical food and drink put timelessness on him, so that he was a young man for ever – a lyrical statue among perpetual witherings? If so, that might have been the greatest burden of all to bear. ('The Two Fiddlers', 1974: 23)

To read this text successfully, we need to recognise the traditional fairy-tale elements in it, and so be able to recognise the games Brown is playing.

Genre also functions as a kind of intertextual device; it might perhaps be described as a matrix within which we seek to interpret a text in the first instance. Clearly, in the case of Joyce's *Portrait*, the final interpretation will be very different, and far more complex than an innocent reader's naïve response to the first sentences. It may be illuminating to recall that there are texts which cause massive interpretative difficulties precisely because we are not sure what they are. An example is the fourteenth-century poem *Pearl* which has been interpreted variously as a highly personal statement of grief for a dead child, a dream poem, and a theological study. It is clear that we will interpret it very differently according to the genre to which we assign it. In sum, genre can be seen as a kind of schema: it affects our initial interpretation of a text; it influences what we look for, as well as what we expect to find. Perhaps most crucially, it influences what we are inclined to take for granted as part of the 'given' of a situation. An extreme example of the influence of schemata to induce or influence interpretation might be Fish's attempt to discredit stylistics by inviting his students to interpret a list of names on his blackboard and allowing his class to assume that they represented a poetic text, but this shows only that readers are predisposed to find meaning in anything that is presented as a text, perhaps especially in a classroom (1980: 323).

The beginning of a novel often serves to indicate the genre:

The story I shall tell begins like this.

Once upon a time in the year of Our Lord 1954 . . . (Ellis, *The 27th Kingdom*, 1982: 7)

But others are more problematic:

I wish either my father or my mother, or indeed both of them, as they were in duty both equally bound to it, had minded what they were about when they begot me; had they duly considered how much depended upon what they were then doing . . . (Sterne, *Tristram Shandy*, 1760–7/1980: I, 1)

This beginning is not inappropriate for an autobiography, which the title (*Life and Opinions of Tristram Shandy* . . .) might lead us to expect.

3.5 LABOV'S NARRATIVE THEORY

Labov's (1972) theory of naturally occurring narratives was developed to handle oral narratives told by young Black Americans. It is, however, also useful for the analysis of written narratives. Pratt (1977) was the first to consider its relevance to literary texts. Toolan (2001) summarises the arguments of those who do not consider it relevant to literary texts. Labov defines a narrative as consisting minimally of two temporally ordered clauses, such that reversing the order of the clauses would change the story. Thus *Jane got married and had a baby* is not the same story as *Jane had a baby and got married*. This seems unproblematic: most would probably agree that a sequence of tensed declarative clauses lies at the heart of narrative. (I will show below that this need not be the case.) A more elaborate narrative will consist of:

1. Abstract
2. Orientation
3. Complicating action
4. Evaluation
5. Result or resolution
6. Coda.

The **abstract** is characteristically a summary of the story: in literary works the title sometimes serves this purpose ('The Short Happy Life of Francis Macomber', for example). Quite often, in modern narrative, there is no abstract, though the beginning of Ellis' *The Other Side of the Fire*, cited above, is clearly an abstract.

The **orientation** gives the 'who, what, when, where' information introducing the narrative. Nineteenth-century fiction often begins with a fairly lengthy orientation section. Lawrence's 'Tickets, Please' (discussed in Chapter 1), like *Sons and Lovers*, begins with an account of the Midlands and general scene-setting for the following narrative. In 'Tickets, Please' the orientation is marked by being in the present tense (and so marked off from the narrative proper), and it is lengthy in relation to the narrative, possibly because it sets the scene psychologically as well as literally. (It should be noted that the proportion of a narrative is in itself an evaluative device, since it clearly suggests the focus intended by the narrator.) The core of a narrative is the **complicating action**. It is here that one expects to find narrative clauses. The **result** signals the end of the story proper: it is the natural outcome of the preceding action. The **coda** is a final rounding-off: it is the tidying-up of the lives of characters which was prevalent in classical fiction though less common today. The fairy-tale ending *and they lived happily ever after* is perhaps the prototypical coda.

Evaluation is the most interesting and complex category. It can be found anywhere in the text, and Labov suggests it explains why the story is felt to be tellable. Evaluative devices are often clustered at significant moments in a narrative. While we might not expect to find precisely the same devices used in written as in oral narratives, Labov's scheme offers a useful framework for analysing such texts. Literary discourse is, after all, grounded in ordinary language, so we should expect to find the same devices in both.

Labov considers evaluative devices in two categories: external and internal. These are discussed below.

3.5.1 External evaluative devices

These are where the narrator interrupts the narrative to stress the significance of the events described: *I was terrified.* Such a comment clearly has a strong interpersonal function, which applies also to written texts. In literary fictions, external evaluation is most likely in first-person narratives such as Conrad's Marlow stories. At the beginning of *Heart of Darkness* Marlow comments obliquely on the story he is about to tell: *And this also . . . has been one of the dark places of the earth* (1902/1983: 28). Later he comments on the narrative to his companions:

> 'You can't understand. How could you? – with solid pavement under your feet, surrounded by kind neighbours ready to cheer you or fall on you, stepping delicately between the butcher and the policeman, in the holy terror of scandal and gallows and lunatic asylums – how can you imagine what particular region of the first ages a man's untrammelled feet may take him into by the way of solitude – utter solitude without a policeman – by the way of silence – utter silence, where no warning voice of a kind neighbour can be heard whispering of public opinion?'
> (Conrad, *Heart of Darkness*, 1902/1983: 85)

Such comments are rare in fictions with an omniscient narrator, though the *Bloody hell!* in *The Other Side of the Fire* may be an example, since it is not attributed to a character and so is, one assumes, a narratorial comment. It may possibly be interpreted analeptically: the reader may decide later that the comment is attributable to a character in the fiction. Though it is not characteristic of Mrs Bohannon's idiolect, she does use the term at least once. Generalisations and gnomic utterances by the narrator might also be regarded as external comments, such as: *history suggests actions performed for lofty motives are more likely to be dangerous than those performed for selfish ones* (Salley Vickers, *Instances of the Number 3*, 2001/2002: 42–3). Comments of this type always have the effect of suspending the narrative, albeit briefly. Note also that the present tense contrasts with the normal past tense of narrative clauses.

In oral narratives, the teller sometimes attributes evaluative comments to another person, who is not necessarily a character in the story (Labov 1972: 373); or the event is evaluated by the action of characters. One of Marlow's audience in *Heart of Darkness* comments:

> The others might have been asleep, but I was awake. I listened, I listened on the watch for the sentence, for the word that would give me the clue to the faint uneasiness inspired by this narrative that seemed to shape itself without human lips in the heavy night air of the river. (1902/1983: 58)

Comparable effects in fictions with an omniscient narrator may result from changes in focalisation, which may contribute to the network of evaluative devices. And dialogue, of course, offers various perspectives on the action.

3.5.2 Internal evaluative devices

Toolan (1998: 139) suggests that internal evaluative devices are generally more subtle than external evaluation. That is certainly true of oral narratives. Amongst internal devices, comparators are elements such as negatives, future tenses and modal verbs that temporarily suspend the narrative syntax to move away from the story line, and consider unrealised possibilities. They can occur in dialogue, in passages of indirect discourse, or in the narrator's voice. For example in *The Other Side of the Fire*, the protagonist reflects on the time that she wasted bringing up her children:

> And for what? They would never live with her again for long. They would go off to public schools, then university, then into careers. She would see them briefly in the holidays when they weren't on school trips. Oh. What a goddamn waste of time, thought this Claudia. (Ellis 1983/1985: 137)

Such self-questioning, and moving between past, present and future are all characteristically evaluative devices. As this example suggests, they are often associated with depiction of a character's thought, and are therefore more likely to be found in written, rather than oral stories. Narrators also offer such comments or guidance: *So far the girls had found no evidence to the contrary, nor were they ever to do so* (Spark, *The Prime of Miss Jean Brodie*, 1961/1965: 93). Here the narrator looks forward to the end of the narrative (incidentally stressing her own privileged position). Changes of this sort in the time line, offering hints of the future, always have an evaluative function. They disrupt the story line, interrupting the flow of narrative (marked here by a change in tense). The effect is similar to cases of narrative instance, when a first-person narrator draws attention to his storytelling role, so reminding the audience of all the possibilities of forgetting, rehandling the material and generally cooking the books characteristic of telling a story. These devices often function as a kind of macro-punctuation of the narrative; they can be emphatic markers; and often signal the emotional state of the narrator. The effects of such references are considered more fully in the context of first-person narratives (see Chapter 4).

Other devices with an evaluative function are metaphor and a change of narrator such as occurs in Brown's 'The Two Fiddlers' or Spark's 'Miss Pinkerton's Apocalypse'. In both these texts, the norms and attitudes of the first narrator are subverted by a different voice appearing towards the end of the story. This effect is not unlike what happens when there is a move from the narratorial voice to internal focalisation through a character. Labov identifies such effects in the oral texts he studied. Rhetorical devices, such as variation of syntactical patterning (considered below), can also clearly have an evaluative function, when the norms of a text are temporarily disrupted. I will argue that intertextuality and considerations of genre are also linked to the notion of evaluation.

Labov's category of evaluative devices in narrative is interesting and seemingly heterogeneous. They are, however, linked by one feature: they are predominantly interpersonal in their effect. In some cases this is because they address the reader directly, but more often it is because they invite speculation, or indicate that the reader might wish to pursue a particular line of thought. These include irony, metaphor and other tropes which involve the reader's interpretive effort. More obviously, 'considering unrealised possibilities' helps the reader to understand the depths of the protagonist's solipsism. This happens, for example, in Joyce's 'A Painful Case' when the protagonist asks himself whether he could have lived with his friend Mrs Sinico – but he does so only after her death (the idea never came to him while she was alive!). Questions, whether rhetorical or not, have the same effect. As Fowler (1981) points out, any question has the effect of drawing the reader into the discourse.

Most people would agree with Labov when he states that a narrative consists minimally of a temporally ordered sequence of clauses in the past tense: tensed declarative clauses, or TCDs. However, we seem to have a propensity for seeing narrative in all sorts of texts. Consider Wendy Cope's 'Reading Scheme' (1986):

Here is Peter. Here is Jane. They like fun.
Jane has a big doll. Peter has a ball.
Look, Jane, look! Look at the dog! See him run!

Here is Mummy. She has baked a bun.
Here is the milkman. He has come to call.
Here is Peter. Here is Jane. They like fun.

Go, Peter! Go, Jane! Come, milkman, come!
The milkman likes Mummy. She likes them all.
Look, Jane, look! Look at the dog! See him run!

Here are the curtains. They shut out the sun.
Let us peep! On tiptoe, Jane! You are small!
Here is Peter. Here is Jane. They like fun.

I hear a car, Jane. The milkman looks glum.
Here is Daddy in his car. Daddy is tall.
Look, Jane, look! Look at the dog! See him run!

Daddy looks very cross. Has he a gun?
Up milkman! Up milkman! Over the wall!
Here is Peter. Here is Jane. They like fun.
Look, Jane, look! Look at the dog! See him run!

As the title suggests, the poem (a villanelle) is parodic of children's early readers. The parallels between the two text types – both rely heavily on patterned repetition – are exploited by the poet. Early readers are heavily illustrated. This probably explains the rather peculiar discourse situation. It is unclear who is speaking much of the time: which bits are to be attributed to the 'narrator' and which to participants in the story.

One must, I think, postulate two different audiences for this text, with very different perceptions. To a child, it is not a narrative: it lacks causality, and appears to be essentially descriptive of the accompanying pictures, which support the early reader.

An adult reader, making use of schemata, intertextual references and plays on words, does perceive a narrative here: a trite tale of suburban dalliance. This reading is supported by the odd 'she has baked a bun' (one surely bakes many: so the reader thinks of the slang expression 'having a bun in the oven', meaning pregnant). The 'innocent' remark that Mummy likes them all supports this, as does Daddy's sudden arrival, possibly with a gun. The last line, characteristic of a good villanelle, has a different meaning: now the dog may be running away in fear.

What is clear is that, despite the absence of tensed declarative clauses, this text does seem to be a narrative: implicitly, at least, it tells a story. The knowing adult perceives an adulterous woman found out by her husband; the child reader (if there were one) would be no more than normally bored or interested in the antics of Peter, Jane, the dog and the milkman. The narrative must, of course, be pieced together from the information supplied: it is a matter of deriving implications from the text. But it is as much a narrative as Browning's pair of poems 'Meeting at Night' and 'Parting at Morning'; like them, this poem has is a gap in the middle: the reader has to infer the actions implied by the texts.

3.6 TEMPORAL ORDERING

Since, as Labov points out, the norm for narrative is a temporally ordered sequence of clauses (Cope's 'Reading Scheme' is so interpreted), deviations from this order will almost certainly contribute significantly to the network of evaluative devices. To consider the temporal organisation of a narrative, it is first necessary to reconstruct the *fabula*: the chronologically ordered sequence of events that underlie the text. It is quite rare for a story to be told in strictly chronological order (A-B-C). Some re-orderings are virtually required by a genre: detective stories, for instance, conventionally begin with the discovery of a corpse, and gradually reveal the sequence of events leading to murder (often, C-B-A). In effect, the readers' wits are pitted against the detective's in attempting to find the solution first; that is, to discover the *fabula* underlying the fiction. The text we read, with all its anachronies (that is, departures from chronological order) is the *sužet*. Genette (1980, 1988) identifies three aspects of the temporal organisation of narrative:

Order: Answers the questions: What happened first, next, last?
Duration: How long?
Frequency: How often?

3.6.1 Order

The category of **order** is perhaps the most obvious. Departures from chronological order are not merely designed to maintain interest in detective stories. In *The Prime of Miss Jean Brodie* (1961/1965) Spark employs both large and small-scale departures from the chronological order. Whittaker (1982: 131) reckons there are fourteen analepses and fourteen prolepses. The reader is put in possession of the future lives of a group of schoolgirls early in the narrative: by page 35 we know the broad outlines of the plot, so one of the usual motives for reading is gone. But central questions remain unanswered, and much of the motivation remains obscure; even the narrator feigns ignorance at times: *It was impossible to know how much Miss Brodie planned by deliberation or how much she worked by instinct alone* (Spark 1961/1965: 78–9).

This is slightly disingenuous, since an omniscient narrator precisely does know these things. But it is this teasing quality of the narrative that maintains interest, and directs attention to Spark's concerns in the fiction; readers are left speculating about the motivation of the characters throughout. Such elaborate departures from chronological order are often due to the exigencies of a particular story. Vickers' *Instances of the Number 3* (2001/2002) begins with a man's death. The narrative is concerned with the developing relationship between his widow and mistress and, through a long series of cunningly woven analepses, the lives of the three protagonists are revealed.

The question arises, why tamper with chronological ordering (so violating the co-operative principle, in particular the maxim of manner), making life more difficult for the reader? The answer must be related to what Leech (1983) labels the interest principle. Re-ordered chronology teases the reader, involving us more closely in the text. In the case of Vickers' novel, it is intriguing to learn that the mistress does not attend her lover's funeral because, the last time she visited the graveyard, they had indulged in particularly inspired love-making. So too, in Spark's novel, she directs attention where she wants it by a revelation of the basic story very early on. By depriving us of one of the motivations for reading, we attend to perhaps more interesting matters. Thus such dislocations function as a kind of evaluative device with the narrator implicitly suggesting where our interest should lie. In effect, they are the equivalent of a massive punctuation, or intonation in oral narrative.

3.6.2 Duration

This is the most difficult and elusive of these categories, because it attempts to relate the time taken for the putative events to occur in the 'real world', that is in 'story time', to the time taken to narrate them. But since it is impossible to measure the time taken to narrate something, Genette proposes that the amount of space devoted to events in a narrative be used as a rough guide. Thus the temporal is measured spatially. Sterne recognises the problem, and refers to it repeatedly in *Tristram Shandy* (1760–7/1980) (which begins with the eponymous hero's conception): at I, 14 he remarks *I have been at it these six weeks, making all the speed I possibly could,–and am not yet born . . .*

The only place where one can assume a rough equivalence between reading time and lapsed time in the real world is in dialogue. But even the speed at which dialogue is read varies from reader to reader, just as the pace of talk varies from speaker to speaker, and according to the topic or circumstances. However, if it is taken as the base line and labelled **scene**, then **summary** will be those passages where the narrator compresses the narrative, when discourse time is shorter than story time, for example: *So he went to Harvard and was extremely miserable for several months* (Lodge, *Changing Places*, 1975/1978: 19). **Ellipsis** occurs when time passes (and events occur) with no space/words devoted to it in the text (this is what happens in Cope's 'Reading Scheme' and Joyce's 'A Painful Case', and Browning's 'Meeting at Night' and 'Parting at Morning', discussed above.) Ellipsis is common: most fictions skip the less interesting parts of their character's lives. It is also significant because central mysteries remain in many texts: in Joyce's 'A Painful Case', for example, we are left uncertain whether Mrs Sinico committed suicide or died accidentally. Only she could have told us. James' short story 'Paste' depends upon ellipsis for its effect, also a permanent gap. Again, Leech's interest principle may explain the motivation for ellipsis. Not only is it a source of uncertainty (so allowing readers to speculate) but, as Fielding points out, a novel is not a history or newspaper, so, when nothing interesting happens, he will skip whole years (*Tom Jones*, 1749/1973: II, 1).

Stretch is the other extreme: the events take longer to narrate than their occurrence would. The prototypical example here is Bierce's 'An Occurrence at Owl Creek Bridge' (1946/1988). The reader follows the thoughts of a man awaiting execution, who imagines he escapes, and apparently spends days on the journey home – all in the few minutes before he is hanged. Another example, also concerning the moment before death, is found in *The Secret Agent*.

He was lying on his back and staring upwards. He saw partly on the ceiling and partly on the wall the moving shadow of an arm with a clenched hand holding a carving knife. It flickered up and down. Its movements were leisurely. They were leisurely enough for Mr Verloc to recognize the limb and the weapon.

They were leisurely enough for him to take in the full meaning of the portent, and to taste the flavour of death rising in his gorge. His wife had gone raving mad – murdering mad. They were leisurely enough for the first paralysing effect of this discovery to pass away before a resolute determination to come out victorious from the ghastly struggle with that armed lunatic. They were leisurely enough for Mr Verloc to elaborate a plan of defence, involving a dash behind the table, and the felling of the woman to the ground with a heavy wooden chair. But they were not leisurely enough to allow Mr Verloc time to move either hand or foot. The knife was already planted in his breast. (Conrad 1907/1963: 212)

The narrator here reports Verloc's perceptions though words like *that armed lunatic, his wife* and they suggest a brief shift to Verloc's perspective. On the whole, however, the passage is distanced and objective. The absence of modality is notable, and contributes to the alienating effect. The repetition of near-identical phrasing emphasises the effect of a slowed-down narrative. From the third sentence, *Its movements were leisurely,* almost all the following sentences repeat *leisurely.* The phrase *leisurely enough* is repeated until the formula is ended with *not leisurely enough* and the murder. Syntactic repetition underlines the effect of the slowed-down narrative: the action is much faster than reading time. The speed of thought, shown in the development of Verloc's plan, also emphasises the disparity between reading time and elapsed time that is characteristic of narrative stretch.

In Bierce's story, the overall effect crucially depends upon the use of stretch; in *The Secret Agent* the effect is more local: the technique is used to show the slowing-down of perceptions at moments of anguish or extreme danger.

Finally there is **pause**, where the story time is suspended, but the discourse continues. This occurs in descriptive passages. Genette considers that only descriptive passages in the narrator's voice can be regarded as examples of pause. If they are focalised through a character, then they contribute in some way to our knowledge of the character, and how he sees the world, and thus are not strictly pause, since they forward the narrative, or at least develop the reader's understanding of the character. In one sense this is clearly the case. Nevertheless, however focalised, any description retards the narrative, and so creates a (possibly minute) measure of suspense. Therefore the perspective adopted here considers that all of these options contribute to the evaluation of narrative, since they so clearly influence the rhythm of our reading and reception of the text. Some of these choices are superficial (such as the syntactical variation discussed below) while others (such as narratorial changes and temporal manipulation) reflect a series of choices made by an author at a relatively 'deep' level in the creation of the text.

It would be endlessly tedious were synchrony between real time and reading time to be observed. Who would read a description of a ball that took as long to read as to attend the ball itself? But the proportion of space within a fiction dedicated to an incident is almost always telling.

3.6.3 Frequency

The category of **frequency** is less problematic, and perhaps interpretively less interesting. It concerns the number of times an incident occurs in the *fabula* and the number of times it is related in the *sužet*/text.

The possibilities are:

1. To tell once what happened once, or *n* times what happened *n* times (singulative).

2. To tell once what happened *n* times (iterative).
3. To tell *n* times what happened once (repetitive).

Lodge, in *How Far Can You Go?* (1980/1981: 150), makes the point amusingly: that telling once what happens *n* times is reserved for the narration of marital love scenes, while telling *n* times what happened *n* times is usually kept for extra-marital affairs. Singulative narratives are almost the norm, and need not be exemplified here. The formula of telling *n* times what happens *n* times often gains its effect through small changes in an otherwise invariant and so predictable pattern. The 'Parable of the Talents' is an example: each of the servants is rewarded for having doubled his master's money, save for the last, who has not invested it, but returns the original sum, and is cast into darkness for his sloth (Matthew 25: 14–30). Repetitive narratives are not easy to find, since they are, if absolutely invariant, a recipe for boredom. *Tristram Shandy* (1760–7/1980: VIII, 19) has an example: Trim attempts to tell the story of 'The King of Bohemia and his Seven Castles' but for various reasons is never able to get beyond the first few words. The immediate context thus varies slightly. If one allows, as Genette does (1980: 115), that different narrators are permissible in this type of narrative, then Faulkner's *As I Lay Dying* might be classed as an example. However, it is not an altogether happy choice, since the individual characters' contributions are in the form of their thoughts, memories and fragments of dialogue, sometimes with reference to the immediate situation; the reader slowly pieces together the *fabula* implied by the text. Ellis' trilogy of *The Clothes in the Wardrobe* (1987/1989), *The Skeleton in the Cupboard* (1988/1989) and *The Fly in the Ointment* (1989/1990) is a more apposite case. Here the 'same' story is told by a young woman, her fiancé's mother, and an old friend. Of course, many details, and indeed incidents, are different in the three novels, and one of the interests in reading them is noting the effect that a different interpretation of the same incident may have.

Iterative narratives are also commonplace: they are characteristically marked by items such as *always, would* or *often*. For example:

> Always my father would locate the planet or the constellation first, then touch my shoulder and say: 'Look now.' And I would see, suspended in silence as if he had conjured it, the cosmic dust of a nebula unimaginably far, or a planet turning in silence like a gold coin . . . he would say startling things: that beyond our own galaxy lay an estimated hundred thousand million more, some measuring hundreds of thousands of light years across . . . (Colin Thubron, *Distance*, 1996/1998: 39)

or:

> The car would swerve off in any old direction and Jack would start cursing and she would shout back. Our journeys usually found us bogged in the sand at Southport . . . (Hilary Mantel, *Learning to Talk*, 2003: 53)

All the devices discussed here can be explained by Grice's co-operative principle because they have the effect of generating implicatures in the overall speech act of the text. They are therefore elements which we are expected to exploit when arriving at our interpretation. It will be noted that many of them involve the maxim of manner, which, as has been pointed out, relates not to what is said, but how it is expressed. That is, they are significant because they focus the reader's attention on particular aspects of the narrative.

3.7 EVALUATION AND TEMPORAL ORGANISATION

As I have suggested, the temporal organisation of narrative is very likely to function as a major evaluative device; on a more local level too, there are often interesting correlations between Labov's evaluative devices and the temporal organisation of narrative. It seems obvious that the major textual dispositions considered by Genette contribute enormously to the overall impact of a work. The proportions of a text – the number of words, the degree of attention allocated to various parts of the narrative – are suggestive of the narrator's interests, and will obviously affect the reader's approach to a narrative. Thus decisions to treat an incident as scene, or to summarise it, are suggestive of the attention it deserves, though other points are also to be considered: summary may allow more in the way of ironic intervention by a narrator.

The proportions of Lawrence's 'Tickets, Please' are illuminating in this respect. The short story tells of a philandering ticket inspector on a tram system. He arouses the ire of his victims, the female conductors, who beat him up ferociously. The story has analogues with the Dionysian stories of the dismembering of Pentheus, and the attack on Orpheus (also motivated by sexual jealousy). The proportions of the text are intriguing. The narrative proper is prefaced by a descriptive passage in the present tense, amounting to almost one quarter of the text. The description begins with the countryside and the tram's route:

> There is in the Midlands a single-line tramway system which boldly leaves the county town and plunges off into the black, industrial countryside, up hill and down dale, through the long, ugly villages of workmen's houses, over canals and railways, past churches perched high and nobly over the smoke and shadows, through stark, grimy, cold little market-places, tilting away in a rush past cinemas and shops, down to the hollow where the collieries are, then up again, past a little rural church, under the ash trees, on in a rush to the terminus, the last little ugly place of industry, the cold little town that shivers on the edge of the wild gloomy country beyond. There the green and creamy-coloured tram car seems to pause and purr with curious satisfaction. But in a few minutes – the clock on the turret of the Co-operative Wholesale Society's Shops gives the time – away it starts once more on the adventure. Again there are the reckless swoops downhill, bouncing the loops: again the chill wait in the hill-top market place: again the breathless slithering round the precipitous drop under the church: again the patient halts at the loops, waiting for the outcoming car: so on and on, for two long hours, till at last the city looms beyond the fat gas works, the narrow factories draw near, we are in the sordid streets of the great town, once more we sidle to a standstill at our terminus, abashed by the great crimson and cream-coloured city cars, but still

perky, jaunty, somewhat daredevil, green as a jaunty sprig of parsley out of a black colliery garden. (1922/1995: 34)

The paragraph is remarkable in a number of ways. It is very rhythmical: this effect derives primarily from the syntactical structure, with two very long sentences sandwiching two short ones between them (these correspond to the moments when the tram is stopped). The syntax of the first sentence is linear, with little embedding except in post-nominal position (for example, *down to the hollow where the collieries are*), though the string of sixteen prepositional adjuncts found here must be exceptional. Semantically, perhaps the most obvious feature is the personification of the tramway system: it moves *boldly*; it *plunges*; it is *perky, jaunty, somewhat daredevil*; it *purrs with curious satisfaction* (where animacy, though not humanity) is attributed to it. This contributes to a sense of excitement in the passage, though the description of the scenery is bleak: it is almost devoid of colour (the one tree mentioned is the ash); instead, colour comes from the trams, which are green or cream or crimson. Yet the scene is created by man: the results of his activity are everywhere, from the churches to the *black, industrial countryside*, the dreary houses and villages and the tramway itself. The city itself is also unattractive with *sordid* streets and *narrow* factories – where people work – contrasting with the *fat* gas works. The paragraph works well as an orientation into the story where, despite the war and poverty, the people are ebullient. The rhythm of the passage is mimetic not only of the tram's journey *up hill and down dale* but, as the lexis of the fourth sentence hints, of sexual activity (for example, *breathless slithering*).

These introductory paragraphs are not only orientating, but predominantly evaluative in Labov's terms: they prepare the reader for the sexual encounters and violence to follow. In that respect they are, albeit allusively, an abstract of the narrative. When a description seems exceptionally long or otherwise at odds with the context in which it appears, the reader assumes that it will be relevant in some way to the narrative that follows. We hold them in mind until their relevance is apparent, when they can be integrated into the on-going interpretation of the text. The initial paragraph of 'Tickets, Please' is a prototypical example of pause.

3.8 INTERTEXTUALITY

Intertextuality is a term subject to many different definitions (see Wales 1989). The narrowest is to say that it denotes the echo or invocation of another text (in that sense Bakhtin is right when he argues that we cannot speak without echoing earlier uses of the language (1981: 276)). Intertextuality is part of the network of evaluative devices found in literary discourse, which works in complex ways to deepen the meaning of the text. I have chosen one text from Joyce's *Dubliners* to suggest the ways in which these intertextual elements contribute to the interpretation of the text. The term can be stretched to include the choice of genre, which implies knowledge of a particular communicative code that is shared by the participants in the situation: in this case, author and readers.

In 'A Painful Case' Joyce exploits the rather trite convention of the triangular love story (there are references to Tristan and Isolde via the place name Chapelizod (supposedly 'Isolde's chapel') where the protagonist lives. But Duffy is hardly a Tristan; the lady's husband is uninterested in her (as Mr Duffy also proves to be). The reference to Chapelizod very economically establishes a whole set of implied contrasts between the story and the 'unrealised possibilities' that Labov identifies as evaluative devices. The generic expectations we bring to triangular love stories (the 'love nest' schema of the popular press) probably include a good deal of passion, with two men interested in the woman, rather than the woman being abandoned by both. The almost total absence of dialogue in the story runs counter to the expectations that many readers bring to such texts. It is therefore ironic that the only direct discourse in the whole text with the canonical form of question and reply occurs in the report of the inquest into the death of the 'heroine'. This death, whether by suicide or accident, stirs Duffy to only brief remorse. The reader's appreciation of the story is enhanced if it is played off against the story of Tristan, one of the classical stories of deep passion in European literature.

A narrower definition of intertextuality as the echo or quotation of another literary text includes the miserable reflections of Gavin, the unsuccessful lover in George Mackay Brown's 'The Two Fiddlers', when he reflects '*There is no end of labour . . . All is vanity and vexation of spirit*' (Brown 1974: 21), quoting Ecclesiastes. A difficulty with the use of intertextuality, which is here understood as built into a text by the author, is that a reader may fail to recognise it (the same point can be made about irony, of course). This constitutes a face threatening act and may thus be construed as impolite. It may also be thought to be a violation of the maxim of manner: like many textual strategies, it runs the risk of being misunderstood, or simply missed. In the case of the intertextual references in 'A Painful Case', the references to Tristram and Isolde enrich the text by reminding the reader of the possibility of romantic love, and they implicitly contrast it with the impoverished emotional life of the protagonists of this story. On the other hand, the echo of Ecclesiastes in 'The Two Fiddlers' reminds us of the cultural milieu of the story, where even a poor crofter is very familiar with the Bible, to the extent that he quotes it as a comment on his life. Missing the quotation would not, perhaps, radically affect interpretation, though it impoverishes our reading. Recognising them, on the other hand, promotes a warm feeling of inclusion: we are part of the implied readership of the story, and able to appreciate its effects. The creation of solidarity is important as part of the interpersonal rhetoric of the text. A further point about intertextual quotations from other literary works needs to be made here, though it is developed further in the context of Bakhtin's contributions to the analysis of fictional language. Any such quotation creates a mingling of voices in the text. Locally, the effect is to remind the reader of other people, other worlds, other ways of looking at life. It is particularly apposite when considering a solipsistic character like Duffy.

3.9 SYNTAX

The foregrounding of one textual element can also be regarded as an evaluative device within the Labovian framework. While in oral narratives syntactical variation is unlikely to be noticed, even if it occurs in a deviant way, the same does not apply to written texts. Consider the following:

> They spoke about the events of the evening, the bonny face of the bride, the parsimony of the bride's father, the unworthiness of the bridegroom to possess such comeliness, the good ale contributed by this farm, the sour ale from that croft, the clumsiness of the dancers, the marvellous cheese and oatcakes. (Brown, 'The Two Fiddlers', 1974: 13)

The rhythmical prose here results from the variation in the nominal groups: *the events of the evening* (post-nominal modification only); *the bonny face of the bride* (pre-nominal adjective, noun, post-nominal modifier); *the parsimony of the bride's father* (no pre-nominal modification, but a repetition of the previous post-nominal modifier); *the unworthiness of the bridegroom to possess such comeliness* (no pre-nominal modification, but a more complex post-nominal modifier, with an infinitival clause); then a return to the earlier pattern with pre-nominal modification and a post-nominal modifier: *the good ale contributed by this farm, the sour ale from that croft* (with simpler post-nominal modification). The passage is rounded off with a noun with post-nominal modification: *the clumsiness of the dancers*; parallel to the first phrase is *the marvellous cheese and oatcakes*, with pre-noun modification for *cheese*, and nothing for oatcakes. The variation lends interest to an essentially trite narrative: this is the kind of thing conventionally said after weddings, particularly when the speakers were (possibly) rivals to the groom for the bride.

3.10 CONCLUSION

This chapter has been concerned with aspects of text which guide the reader in interpretation, hence the reference to signposts. Labov defines evaluation in terms of the relations between teller and audience. These devices reassure the audience that the story is worth listening to. In literary texts, the guarantee of interest is in a sense there already: the publisher, editor and author's name all assure the reader of some sort of quality control. So the devices considered here are not necessarily designed primarily to reassure us, but rather to show us how to read the text and suggest the general cultural context in which it is placed. The strategies considered here involve the reader directly in the text; they are pragmatic, in that they are contextually situated, and invite direct and active reader participation.

The various devices considered in this chapter are relevant to interpretation, and clearly contribute to readers' developing understanding of the text. Pragmatically speaking and in a Gricean framework, all can be said to generate implicatures which contribute to the developing interpretation of the text. That is, for instance, if we tell a story in the canonical way – A-B-C – then no particular implicature is generated.

If, however, we alter the order in which we narrate, thus creating suspense, puzzlement or throwing emphasis on one feature of the narrative rather than another, we are generating implicatures. As is always the case, it is up to the reader to work out what they may be. Similarly, changes in focalisation or in the predicted pattern of a narrative (breaking or distorting generic conventions) will have a similar effect. That is why all these function as evaluative devices in Labov's terms.

Genre may seem an unexpected dimension of narrative to consider in this section. However, it is argued that without knowing the genre being invoked, the reader is not in a position to understand fully what the author is attempting. One notes some self-conscious novels, such as Lodge's *Changing Places* where the narrator comments on his sudden move into a partly epistolary style – hardly used for centuries. Similarly, Ellis' title *Fairy Tale* prepares the reader for what follows. That is why I consider genre relevant in this context: it is not in the spirit of butterfly collecting that it is relevant (where taxonomy is all-important), but in the ways in which it guides the reader. Intertextuality works in much the same way, inviting the reader to identify a source, and wonder why it is echoed here. In short, all these are signposts which direct the reading process, and suggest the degree of importance to be assigned to various parts of the text. In the next chapter I shall consider the various kinds of narrators we find, exploiting these devices.

Chapter 4

Narrative Voices

4.1 INTRODUCTION

Narrative is a basic human activity. We all tell stories – to ourselves, to others. First-person narratives are commonplace, from pub conversations to parents telling children about their past. The so-called omniscient narrator of third-person narratives traces its ancestry to the oldest forms we are familiar with: folk tales are universal; their narrators are constrained by the tradition within which they work, and by the knowledge that their audience is probably as familiar with the story as they are themselves. So the basic types of narration which are considered here are, very nearly, as old as the human race itself.

4.2 NARRATIVE VOICES IN FICTIONAL DISCOURSE

We noted above (in Chapter 1) Widdowson's demonstration that the voice within fictional discourse must be distinguished from that of the author, just as the recipient of a message within the discourse is not identical with the reader. Booth (1961) argues that a novelist creates an 'implied author'. This is thought necessary to explain that the same author may seem to espouse different views in various novels, or may indeed create a narrator whose views are at odds with those of the author. Genette (1988) argues strongly against the concept of the implied author, on the grounds that such a construct is not only unnecessary, but impossible to sustain. He accepts that the 'implied author' exists to the extent that it represents everything the reader can infer about the author from the text. The reason for mentioning the implied author here is that the concept can serve to clarify matters for naïve readers. In a similar way, it can be helpful to assume a balancing construct of the implied reader – that is, a reader who has the necessary linguistic and cultural knowledge to understand and appreciate the text. The need for such a construct is shown when one considers the difficulties in interpreting texts produced in another culture or age. One may be baffled because of uncertainty about the function of the text; certain references may be unclear; it may be apparent that implicatures are intended to be drawn, but it is uncertain what they are. It is also necessary to suspend one's personal attitudes when reading some works, in order to react empathetically with the text. One's distaste for

Nabokov's Humbert Humbert may be acute in real life, but it need not prevent us reading *Lolita*. As real readers, we may be more or less close to the implied reader. The greater the distance, the more difficult reading becomes. As the term suggests, these constructs are merely *implied* by the text: they have no 'real' existence: they are a bundle of norms used in the creation and interpretation of the fiction. This already creates a complex response on the part of the reader: on one level, we react to the text as we might to similar events in real life, feeling sympathy or revulsion as appropriate. On another, we refrain from such reactions, knowing that we are reading fictional discourse: the blood on the library floor where the baronet lies is, we know, not our problem. We read detective fiction for entertainment: there can be few ghouls who would enjoy the same events in real life.

Leech and Short (1981) offer a widely accepted view of the structure of fictional discourse. The writer and the reader lie outside the direct communicative flow established in a text. Within the text, the narrator, who may be first or third person, tells the story. The narrative may include dialogue between characters: only at this level is the discourse of a fiction directly mimetic of ordinary language use. We have thus an embedded discourse, in which a real author addresses us via the implied author (who, in third-person narratives, may be identical to the narrator), within whose discourse we have characters' dialogue: outside this frame are the real readers. Rimmon-Kenan (1983) argues that we also require a narratee: the recipient of the narrative. She also considers that there is a narrator for every text, regardless of whether there is a narratorial voice in the text. Its existence is postulated to account for the selection of letters in an epistolary novel, chapter headings, divisions and so on.

Some writers build narratees into their texts. Conrad regularly has Marlow addressing a group of companions, who comment (very slightly) on the story. Marlow's direct addresses to his immediate audience sometimes occur when he is emotionally involved in the narrative. Sterne, in *Tristram Shandy* (1760/1980), invokes a number of readers: 'Madam' is a far from ideal reader. She is regularly berated: *I told you my father was not a papist* . . . (I: 20). On at least one occasion the reader is invited into the study, and papers are moved from a chair to accommodate him. It cannot be argued that these intra-diegetic (that is, internal to the narrative) addressees are approximations of the implied reader: on the contrary, they are often very limited in their appreciation of the narrative. They may thus help to educate the real reader and help her to approximate to the norms of the implied reader.

4.3 NARRATOR

The choice of narratorial voice affects many subsequent decisions about the development of the story, and the choice of techniques. The 'same' story, told with different kinds of narrators, can have very different effects. Ellis' trilogy, considered below, is an example of this technique. The 'same' story is told from the perspective of the three main participants (*The Clothes in the Wardrobe, The Skeleton in the Cupboard, The Fly in the Ointment*). This places a considerable onus on the reader, as re-reading is virtually essential, partly to perceive ironies when the same event is presented from different perspectives, and when the intentions of a narrator/participant are revealed, but also because one narrator may be privy to things the others are either unaware of or conceal in their stories.

4.3.1 Types of Narrators

Narrators can be broadly divided into two types: first-person or 'I' narrators, who may or may not participate in the story they present. Those who are participants (homodiegetic narrators, in Genette's terms), such as Conrad's Marlow, are somewhat different from those who are essentially observers of the activities of others (thus heterodiegetic narrators) such as Nick in Fitzgerald's *The Great Gatsby*. The second type is the third-person narrator.

4.4 SIMPSON'S TYPOLOGY OF NARRATORS

Simpson (1993) develops a typology of narrators based on the modality of the discourse. Modality is particularly important because of its strongly interpersonal function. It is often enlightening to consider it in the context of the Gricean maxims. Narrators who are participants in the story (homodiegetic) are Type A; third-person narrators are Type B. **Positive** Type narrators (whether first or third person) are those who use evaluative adjectives and *verba sentiendi* (words denoting feeling, thoughts or perceptions) appropriately. The modal systems encoding the narrator's desires (the boulomaic system) and obligation and duty (the deontic system) occur, while the epistemic system (which has to do with knowledge) is less prominent. Narrators whose discourse exhibits **negative** shading exploit the epistemic modal systems, with attention paid to perceptions; terms of estrangement are also prominent. Narratives with **neutral** shading are those whose discourse is lacking in modality: it is characterised by assertions, and the absence of evaluative terms. It is, in short, essentially a reportorial style.

4.4.1 First-Person Narrators

Many early novels are first-person narratives. Scholes and Kellogg (1966) consider that the motivation for this choice was verisimilitude: 'I was there, I saw it'. However improbable some of the activities of a character like Moll Flanders may appear, there is no doubt some truth in this argument. More recently, such fictions have exploited this feature of first-person narratives, while at the same time making the reading more problematic for the reader. James' *The Turn of the Screw* may, on one level, trade on the credulity of the reader, but sufficient clues are provided in the text to make reading it an unsettling experience (cf. Brooke-Rose 1981). Cook (1994) offers a clear analysis of the multilayered discourse that constitutes this fiction, creating instability at every level: it is a report of a report of a report . . . It is impossible to know who is ultimately responsible for the text we read.

Epistemic modality is one of the prime ways in which the observance (or nonobservance) of the Gricean maxims is likely to be apparent in a first-person narrative. This is especially true of the maxim of quality, with its requirement that one have adequate evidence for a statement. One who asserts matters that must be outside her knowledge is immediately suspect. Thus the governess in *The Turn of the Screw*, describing her reception by the housekeeper, says: *Oh, she was glad I was there!* (James 1898/1969: 20). This is the kind of observation that a first-person narrator cannot properly make: no one can make such categorical assertions about another's state of mind. This is, of course, one of the major limitations of first-person narratives: the narrator should not make assertions about the motives, thoughts or intentions of the other characters in the fiction, though speculation is possible. In this respect, first-person narratives are closer to the real world and its norms than third-person narratives, with their potential for omniscience. A difficulty in interpreting such blatant ignoring of the maxims of quality and manner (and perhaps of others, too) is that the reader may be uncertain as to whether the speaker is flouting the maxims, and so attempting to convey an implicature, or wishing to deceive, or whether this is an idiolectal matter, that is, she is infringing the maxims – the speaker habitually expresses herself this way. Certainly the governess appears to have a Manichean cast of mind, as is hinted at by the first sentence of her narrative: *I remember the whole beginning as a succession of flights and drops, a little see-saw of the right throbs and the wrong* (14) On meeting her first charge she compares her to *one of Raphael's holy infants* (16). Then, when she believes the child has been with the ghost of her previous governess, she describes her as *hideously hard; she had turned common and almost ugly* (100) In these, and countless other cases, implicatures are generated on two levels. On the one hand, the reader may conclude that the governess is inexperienced and innocent (as is indeed the case). Her abuse of the maxims of quality and manner may do no more than reflect this. But, given the embedded nature of literary discourse, the implied author may be suggesting, via these flouts, that she is mentally unbalanced. It seems impossible to determine whether she is violating the maxims, flouting them or infringing them: that is, she is incapable of expressing herself in another way (cf. Thomas 1995: 74). In terms of speech act theory, the governess' comments are representative speech acts, though readers may consider them to be ill-formed (cf. Mey 1993: 164 who points out that representative speech acts convey a subjective state of mind). The governess' discourse is characterised by absolute certainty of her interpretation of events. That is, she may genuinely believe what she says, just as flat-earthers are honest in their assertion that the earth is flat. We disagree, but do not attack them for lying, rather for ignorance. This is a genuine difficulty with novels of this type: readers must decide whether the narrator is honest, but holds opinions we may not, or whether she is dishonest and manipulative.

Ellis (1987/1989) in *The Clothes in the Wardrobe*, one volume of the trilogy that tells the 'same' story three times, from the perspective of different participants, has a first-person narrator who is essentially of Simpson's A Positive type. However, she is also given to offering many comments and details which are inappropriate for a first-person narrator. Indeed, at times her discourse sounds as though it were that of a third-person narrator. *To her, religion was morality and appearance, and she kept it in the same compartment of her mind as her dinner napkins.* (Ellis 1987/1989: 50). The style makes the text very reader-friendly, in much the same way as a narrative with an omniscient narrator, but at the expense of the credibility of the narratorial voice. Such obvious failures to attend to the maxim of quality invite censure. Some speakers doubtless express themselves in such a loose way to make their discourse more entertaining, but it scarcely makes them more reliable.

On the other hand, Marlow in *Heart of Darkness* is usually careful in this respect. Indeed, Marlow appears to be an example of Simpson's Type A with negative shading. His discourse is full of terms of estrangement (Uspensky 1973). Many of his comments are hedged by *perhaps, possibly, appear, seem* and similar terms qualifying his observations. The narrative is full of epistemic modality (words denoting the knowledge and perceptions) of the narrator. Marlow constantly stresses his own uncertainty; the Congo is obscured by fog; the activities of most of the Europeans appear to be pointless when not positively malicious. A profusion of metaphors enhances the problematic nature of Marlow's (and hence the readers') experience. Dying men are referred to as *bundles of acute angles* (1902/1983: 45); a boiler *wallows* in the grass. The boundaries between animate and inanimate are blurred or disappear. These devices together mirror the uncertainty of the narrator, and create it in the reader. The effects created by the modal choices in the text are further enhanced by other elements in the fiction. It is, metaphorically speaking, a case where the deep grammar and surface realisations in the text are in harmony. There are rare exceptions to this pattern: Marlow's criticism of an exploring expedition finishes: *To tear treasure out of the bowels of the land was their desire, with no more moral purpose at the back of it than there is in burglars breaking into a safe* (61). He also says of Kurtz: *his soul was mad . . . being alone in the wilderness it had looked within itself, and, by heavens! I tell you it had gone mad* (108). Here, as in the James and Ellis examples cited above, the failure to observe the maxim of quality should create uneasiness in the reader. In his comments on Kurtz, Marlow is perhaps revealing how disturbing he finds the man: flouting the maxim of quality can be attributed to his emotional involvement.

First-person narrators may have many and varied motivations, certainly including telling a good story – obeying the interest principle (Leech 1983). Many such narratives are free-floating: there seems to be no particular motivation for the narrative, or an audience. This is the case with the Ellis trilogy. Conrad's Marlow, on the other hand, addresses a group of his friends.

4.4.2 Narrative Instance

A particular feature of first-person narratives is identified by Brooke-Rose (1981), that is, reference to the time of writing, in her study of *The Turn of the Screw*. She calls this *narrative instance*. It can take a simple form of the type 'I remember', or any item (including adverbials or sentence markers) that marks a distinction between the time of writing and the time when the events narrated purport to have taken place: *After two years I remember the rest of that day . . .* (Fitzgerald, *The Great Gatsby*, 1926/1962: 170). Narrative instance has two effects in addition to marking a temporal gap. It implies that the narrator is aware of his or her role, and may suggest awareness of an audience. The very act of reminding readers of the distinction between the times of the action and narration should invite particularly critical attention to the text. The reader is made aware that the narrator has had time to reconsider, to distort, to forget; it allows for the artistic re-handling of events, and so demands critical reading. The use of terms such as *I remember* also has the pragmatic effect of involving the reader: perhaps the use of the first person automatically suggests the answering *you*. Such terms seem to involve an interlocutor. This does not apply of course to all cases: adverbial shifters do not have this kind of effect.

If there is a substantial temporal gap between the time of the events and the time of narration, it is likely that, even if the narrator and protagonist is the same person, the perspective on events will have changed: the narrator may be looking back critically on an earlier self. Of course, some first-person narratives are told by someone who is still more or less involved in the events depicted. If the time of writing is very close to the time narrated, narrative instance may be absent, or unremarkable. An example is Spark's short story 'You Should Have Seen the Mess' (1958/1987). What this all means is that the reader of a first-person narrative may have a more complex interpretive task than in reading a traditional third-person narrative, where the narrator is a trusted guide and interpreter.

Some narrators are highly self-conscious and analytical: in this (Type A negative) passage, full of markers of epistemic uncertainty, the narrator is very dubious about a crucial moment in his past. His uncertainty extends even to the participants in the conversation.

> I am fairly sure I have remembered its essence accurately enough, turning it over in my mind again, I find myself less certain about some of the details. For one thing, I am no longer sure she actually put to the inspector the actual words: 'How is your conscience able to rest while you owe your existence to such ungodly wealth?' . . .
>
> In fact it is even possible I have remembered incorrectly the context in which she uttered those words; that it was not to the health inspector she put this question, but to my father, on another morning altogether, during that argument in the dining room. (Kazuo Ishiguro, *When We Were Orphans*, 2000/2001: 71)

When the narrator refers to his role, it automatically brings in a number of temporal dimensions: minimally, the time of writing and the time referred to in the fiction, though it can be more complex. In *The Turn of the Screw* the governess narrator reports on sounds she thought she heard on her first night in the house:

> But these fancies were not marked enough not to be thrown off, and it is only in the light, or the gloom, I should rather say, of other and subsequent matters that they now come back to me. (1898/1969: 16)

Here she refers to writing time, the time of her arrival, and hints at other events which lie in the (narrative) future: the reader may infer that her story will be told with some eye to the effect it produces. From the beginning she hints at the problems that lie ahead. (Such hints are characteristic of this fiction, and contribute to the uncertainties and suspense in the text.)

Cases of narrative instance are sometimes used as a way of securing added emphasis, in that they may occur at particularly significant moments of the narrative, and thus have an evaluative function. This kind of effect is exploited very fully by Marlow, in Conrad's *Heart of Darkness* (1902/1983). Since the fiction purports to be an oral narrative, told to a group of cronies, it is quite natural for Marlow to refer to his role of narrator as well as participant in his story. He often addresses them directly, and is clearly concerned about their reactions to his words. One consequence is that he presents himself as a reflective man, who invites a similarly thoughtful reaction from his audience. He sometimes refers to the difficulty of explaining his experiences in the Congo, as here when he tries to explain his thoughts about Kurtz before they met:

> I did not see the man in the name any more than you do. Do you see him? Do you see the story? Do you see anything? It seems to me I am trying to tell you a dream – making a vain attempt, because no relation of a dream can convey the dream-sensation . . .' (1902/1983: 57)

Awareness of audience can, I think, also be counted as a form of narrative instance, since it implicitly encodes the difference between story time and time of narration. Demonstrations of the narrator's awareness of their role can take many forms. In cases such as *Heart of Darkness* and *The Turn of the Screw* a naturalistic explanation for the narrative is provided in an outer frame. The governess in *The Turn of the Screw* leaves a manuscript account, which is read to a group of the recipient's friends after her death. Sometimes narrators address the reader directly, or make comments that show they are concerned that the story should be well told. Nick Carraway, the narrator of *The Great Gatsby*, writes: *Reading over what I have written so far . . .* (Fitzgerald: 1926/1962: 62). It is not clear that Nick has in mind any audience but himself; however, in other cases it is clear that an audience is envisioned.

Not all first-person fictions have such naturalistic explanations for their origins. The narrator of Ellis' *The Skeleton in the Cupboard* (1988/1989), a very old woman, is clearly aware that she is narrating, as shown by comments such as: *I hasten to repeat* (28); *I've already said* (29); *I should have made clear* (89). What is opaque is to whom the narrative is addressed, what the motivation for it may be, though the remark *one more cause of shame to add to a life-time's roll of those things which I ought to have done* (110) may suggest that it is confessional. There is a difference between motivated first-person fictions, such as *Heart of Darkness* and *The Turn of the Screw*, which offer explanations of their origins and so contextualise the narrative to some extent, and those where no apparent motivation, or audience, is supplied.

Some first-person narrators seem unaware of an audience, or of the fact that they are narrating at all; in that case one might not expect to find the kinds of effects considered here. One of the peculiarities of such texts is that they may appear to be unmotivated and hence left hanging: readers are not quite sure why they should exist, why we should be addressed. An example is Spark's 'You Should Have Seen the Mess'

(1987). Though it begins with a clear reference to the time of writing (*I am now more than glad*), there is no apparent motivation for telling the story: it reads like a school essay (indeed, the narrator says she was very good at English at school). One of the most bizarre examples of an apparently free-floating novel is the beginning of *The Clothes in the Wardrobe* (Ellis 1987/1989): '*I remembered her all my life.*' It seems to imply that the narrator is dead (she is, at least, dead to the world, as she has become a nun).

Demonstrations of the narrator's awareness of their role can take many forms. In cases such as *Heart of Darkness* and *The Turn of the Screw*, a naturalistic explanation for the act of narration is provided in an outer frame to the narrative. Conrad's Marlow tells his stories to a group of cronies; the governess in *The Turn of the Screw* leaves a manuscript account. Such introductions contextualise the narrative to some extent.

The absence of any comments on the narratorial role may be interesting in themselves. There is, I suppose, no reason why first-person narrators should refer explicitly to the act of narration, and so show consciousness of their activities. The unawareness of an audience (which need not only depend on references to the narrator's role: there are other possibilities, such as comments addressed to the reader or audience) may leave such fictions somehow 'free-floating': that is, the motivation for their existence is unclear to the reader. This seems to be the case with Spark's *A Far Cry from Kensington*, though the fiction is full of advice from the narrator to readers: *It is my advice to any woman getting married to start, not as you mean to go on, but worse, tougher, than you mean to go on* (1988/1989: 117). The phrase *it is my advice* occurs repeatedly; often the advice is very quirky. There are other ways of showing awareness of an audience: the narrator of Ellis' *The Fly in the Ointment* apparently addresses the reader (there is no other interlocutor built into the text) directly:

> promiscuous men are bad lovers. I don't want to go into details, but it's true. If you think about it you'll find you agree with me. That is, of course, if you have had the poor sense to experiment with a promiscuous man. Yes, I know, I did, but I had reasons of my own . . . But as I was saying . . . (1989/1990: 75)

and

> I didn't really repent of confiding in Mrs Monro – even if I should have done, and if you think I should, I don't agree with you. (88)

At moments like this the reader feels drawn into the text as an interlocutor, an effect not unlike that posed by rhetorical questions and similar devices. One of the effects of the narrator making explicit the role is often to set up a fairly strong interpersonal relation with the reader. In this case the interlocutor is clearly female – this may suggest that the fiction is addressed to a female confidante (though other than a scattering of 'you', referring to the reader, there is nothing to indicate this in the text). It would seem unreasonable to hypothesise that the implied reader is female. At the very least, it shows that the narrative is not a *narrative that seemed to shape itself without human lips* . . . (Conrad, *Heart of Darkness*, 1902/1983) but has a suasive intention. The reader is meant to be involved.

The zestful but naïve narrative of Defoe's *Moll Flanders* is an instructive contrast to the artful and highly wrought texts considered here. Ostensibly (and only that), the purpose of the narrative is to warn readers against the lifestyle she followed, and to warn of the dangers surrounding us. She often uses words like *reflect*, usually in the context of considering her financial situation or her multiple marriages. But she seems wholly unaware of the likely reactions of her readers, or of her role as narrator. Such references to the narratorial role are major evaluative devices, and lend rhythm and proportion, as well as conveying an attitude to the texts in question.

4.5 THIRD-PERSON NARRATORS

Third-person narratives are Simpson's Type B. This type of narrator is a disembodied voice, characterised by ubiquity (that is, in principle it can inform the reader of events anywhere) and the ability (not always exploited) to enter into the minds of characters in the fiction. (The impersonal 'it' is used to refer to the narratorial voice to stress its impersonality: it is not always possible to say that it possesses male or female characteristics.) The flexibility of this type of narratorial voice permits a fusion of the voices of characters and narrator which presents some of the most interesting and complex features of fictional discourse. It is one of the principal sources of heteroglossia, the mingling of different voices in fiction (this is considered more fully in Chapter 7). The 'ground rules' for the interpretation of the so-called omniscient narrator (Simpson's Type B positive) require that we believe that, within the realms of the fictional discourse, what they present is 'true'. Thus we must rely on their judgements, which are partly encoded through the deontic system. We do this because they conform most explicitly to the co-operative principle: we trust them to provide sufficient information, of adequate quality, which will ultimately prove relevant to the narrative. The maxim of manner is also significant here, particularly through the ironic comments that often characterise this type of narrative. Such narrators may be given to generalisations (gnomic utterances) and be judgemental (using deontic and boulomaic modality). With this type of narrator, implied author and narrator are usually indistinguishable. This is, certainly in the traditional novel, the commonest type of narrator, found from folk tales to modern novels. It is a polite narrative style, in its attentiveness to the face wants of the reader. Below is an example of B positive narrative from *Pride and Prejudice*:

> Mr Bennet was so odd a mixture of quick parts, sarcastic humour, reserve, and caprice that the experience of three and twenty years had been insufficient to make his wife understand his character. (Austen 1813/1972: 53)

Since the narrator can report the thoughts of characters, this type of narration is in some respects the richest and most complex, with the potential for irony arising from the interplay of the perceptions of characters and narrator. With the use of various forms of reported speech and thought, it sometimes becomes problematic whether to attribute elements of text to narrator or character. This applies particularly to passages where focalisation is temporarily rooted in the character (Simpson's Type B(R)).

For example, Ellis describes a psychiatrist listening to his patient who *unreeled yet again a succession of memories, dreams and unseemly desires* (*The Inn at the Edge of the World*, 1990/1991: 21). It is unclear whether the judgemental *unreeled* and *unseemly* are attributable to narrator or character. Similarly,

> 'Wouldn't mind if me stepdad dropped dead.'
> Mr Golightly, who was no sentimentalist either, was still looking at the deceiving surface of the mire. 'Yes,' he agreed. 'Death improves some people.'
> The tragedy was these were so rarely the ones who were chosen. (Salley Vickers, *Mr Golightly's Holiday*, 2003: 161)

The final sentence can be interpreted as reporting Mr Golightly's thought, or be attributed to the narrator.

Simpson's Type B(N) neutral is an impersonal style of narration, largely devoid of modality, or the analysis of the thoughts and feelings of characters. The absence of evaluative devices is marked. This might seem to be the voice of a most reliable narrator, given the absence of any 'personality' in the narrating voice, the lack of evaluation or other signs of involvement. This is, however, not necessarily the case. Consider the beginning of one of the *vignettes* from Hemingway's 'In Our Time': *They shot the six cabinet ministers at half past six in the morning against the wall of a hospital* (1947/1964: 300). The reader is cast off-balance by the use of the definite article – we wonder which six cabinet ministers? This is followed by the indefinite article for 'a hospital'. This is essentially unco-operative.

Type B negative narratives are unsettling, because the narrator seems uncertain about how to interpret events. The use of terms of estrangement (*as if*) is common:

> She gathers up the handles of her bags, picks up her book and looks at him and through him as if he were already a distant memory and leaves without a good-bye, indeed as if she had said good-bye to him long ago.
> (Spark, *The Driver's Seat*, 1970/1974: 89)

Narratives of this type distance the reader, do not promote emotional involvement with the characters, and engender a sense of bafflement.

4.6 CONCLUSION

This chapter has sought to introduce the narratorial stances commonly found in fiction. In the next chapter we will consider some of the complexities which can arise, particularly in the depiction of words and thoughts of characters, embedded in the narrator's discourse.

Chapter 5

Direct and Indirect Discourse

5.1 INTRODUCTION

I will consider here the role of direct and indirect discourse in fiction, focusing on the ways in which they are used, the interpretive problems they present, and the contribution they make to give fictional discourse the complex layers of meaning and implicatures which they can generate. They are an important means of characterisation.

5.2 IDIOLECT

The moment we open our mouths we situate ourselves sociolinguistically: our lexis, pronunciation and the syntactic choices we make allow our interlocutor(s) to make inferences about our education, our geographical and social origins. Our choice among the options available to us in the language will also be influenced by the activity we are engaged in. Every speaker has unique features of language use: these are termed idiolect. (It should be noted here that few fictions provide sufficient evidence of a character's lect to enable an identification of idiolectal features which would satisfy a sociolinguist. Rather, what happens is that features of language are used contrastively with the language of the narrator, and so function to suggest idiolectal features of the character.) All of this means that the speech of fictional characters can make a most useful contribution to their characterisation: they can indicate what they are doing, suggest their relations with other characters, and mark their educational and social status. Some writers (Austen is the obvious example) manipulate the language of their characters in such a way that the closer the character's language to that of the narrator, the closer their agreement on significant moral and ideological matters. Those who do not see eye to eye with the narrator deviate from her linguistic norms. Dialect or idiolectal forms are sometimes used for the purpose of sketchy characterisation, or at least identification of the geographical and/or social class of a character. In an explanatory note Twain describes the various dialects he uses in *The Adventures of Huckleberry Finn*, and their sociolinguistic purpose. Huck is the narrator, Jim a runaway slave he is helping. If they reach Cairo, Jim is free:

'We's safe, Huck, we's safe! Jump up and crack yo' heels, dat's de good ole Cairo at las', I jis knows it!'
I says:
'I'll take the canoe and go see, Jim. It mightn't be, you know.' (Mark Twain 1884/1985: 282)

Hints of a dialect may be sufficient: *'T'ink ob your liver, man,' the cook had implored him. 'Think of your responsibilities,' the priest had exhorted him* (Ellis, *The 27th Kingdom*, 1982: 49). The suggestion of a generalised West Indian dialect, with a sociolectal indication of the language of the educated priest, is sufficient in the context: neither cook nor the priest play any further part in the fiction, so local colour is all that is required here.

Sometimes the reader can be surprised. In one of Irvine Welsh's short stories, the protagonist, who speaks the Edinburgh dialect Welsh has made familiar, is addressed by a man in a pub:

– You. Boab Coyle. Nae hoose, nae joab, nae burd, nae mates, polis record, sair face, aw ain the space ay a few ooirs. Nice one . . .
– How the fuck dae you ken? . . . – It's ma fuckin business tae ken. A'hm God. (Boab disbelieves this, so God goes on) – Robert Anthony Coyle, born on Friday the 23rd of July, 1968, to Robert McNamara Coyle and Doreen Sharp . . . You have a sickle-shaped birthmark on your inner thigh . . . (Welsh, 'The Granton Star Cause', in *The Acid House*, 1994: 128–9)

The first speaker creates solidarity by addressing Boab in his own variety. But, when Boab challenges God's identity, he switches into the standard, thus proving his credentials. Code switching is used here to mark a change in the relations between the characters. The association between power and the standard language is still strong: Boab – and probably the reader – expect God to speak standard English. This kind of code switching is 'metaphorical' switching (see Fasold 1987: 194). The exchange thus serves as an oblique comment on the sociolinguistic attitudes of the society depicted. Readers may be puzzled, even antagonised, by the use of the vernacular.

5.3 METHODS OF ANALYSIS

The terminology and approach taken here is based on Leech and Short (1981; Short 1996 also offers a very clear account). The term discourse is used to cover both speech and thought representations, except when it is necessary to distinguish between them. The representation of speech in fictional discourse is best seen as organised on a cline of increasing narratorial involvement, from a range of ways of rendering speech and thought to the narrator's report of speech/thought act (NRSA/NRTA), where the narrator indicates that a speech or thought act has taken place, and possibly gives some indication of its contents, without any commitment to citing or echoing the words purportedly used.

5.3.1 Free direct discourse

Free direct discourse (FDD) is characterised by the absence of reporting verbs and quotation marks, and hence the absence of any overt trace of the narrator's presence. The text purportedly represents exactly what the character 'said' or thought:

> You believed this?
> Everyone believed it, even though no one had ever seen it. No one living in our village anyway. (Alice Walker, *Possessing the Secret of Joy*, 1992/1993: 113)

In practice, many would accept as a case of FDD a clause with a reporting verb. 'Pure' FDD, without a reporting verb, is liable to be misconstrued: in the example above, for instance, one might wonder whether the second sentence represents the character's thoughts, rather than her reply to the question, since it is a first-person narrative, moving freely between the thoughts, actions and utterances of the narrator. Free direct thought (FDT) purportedly comes straight from the character's mind (one is, of course, always aware of the fact that a narrator has examined the character's mind and determined exactly how much to reproduce: it is, in fact, a thoroughly 'omniscient' mode of proceeding).

> The bishop's a fair man, he thought; as he put one muddy foot in front of the other. The bishop's a just man, is he? Well, perhaps so. Perhaps he may be. Perhaps fairness abounds. (Hilary Mantel, *Fludd*, 1989/1990: 73)

Free direct discourse often has a reporting clause, in order to make clear its status, as in this example. But the character is reflecting on what someone else has said to him: 'A very fair man, His Grace, a very just man . . .' (71). So her speech is embedded in his, as he thinks it over. The situation can become more complex when there are layers of embedded discourse:

> 'So I didn't think anything of it,' Karen said later. 'I thought she must've tracked in some mud. I didn't stop to think, Where would you get down to mud with all this snow on the ground?' (Alice Munro, 'Fits', 1996/1997: 285)

Here a character is telling a story, and adds a FDT clause commenting on her own thought processes, or the lack of them. Short (1988: 71) argues that there is no principled method to distinguish between direct speech and free direct speech. The examples considered here seem to support this view.

5.3.2 Direct discourse

Direct discourse (DD) is normally marked by quotation marks and the presence of a reporting verb (such as *said, thought*).

> 'You're a rotten driver,' I protested. 'Either you ought to be more careful, or you oughtn't to drive at all.'
> 'I am careful.'
> 'No, you're not.'

'Well, other people are,' she said lightly.
'What's that got to do with it?'
'They'll keep out of my way' she insisted. 'It takes two to make an accident.'
                    (Fitzgerald, *The Great Gatsby*, 1926/1962: 65)

The motivation for using direct discourse may be to lend an air of verisimilitude, and increase variety in a text; it is also a prime means of characterisation. The choice of lexis, and the grammatical options chosen by the character may be indices of social situation, background, education, interests and so on. In general terms, it seems likely that novelists use direct discourse for what they consider to be the more significant utterances, while relegating the less important to indirect discourse, with its potential for summarising and brevity, or simply using NRSA/NRTA to report that a speech or thought act has taken place. However, the practice of individuals varies enormously, so it is probably best to see the choice of discourse type as a purely stylistic one.

Fictional dialogue is rarely realistic. Indeed, until the advent of tape recorders, most people probably had no idea of the hesitations, false starts, incomplete sentences and unclear references that characterise the spoken language, which is context dependent and often addressed to interlocutors who can supply much of the meaning. Further, much of our everyday conversation is boring except (perhaps) to the participants. A degree of artistry is therefore required even when a passage of dialogue is more or less unmediated by narratorial comment. It must contrive to suggest naturalism, without the reality:

'I'm dying to see what Derek's landed himself with,' said Lili.
'You'll see them at the wedding,' said my mother.
'It's not the same,' said Lili. 'I want to see their little nest.'
                    (Ellis, *The Clothes in the Wardrobe*, 1987/1989: 112)

A minor use of direct discourse occurs when it is not attributed to any specific speaker, but rather is used to characterise a whole class of people. (This is comparable to the use, discussed by Short (1988) of apparent DD in newspapers, when an attitude, rather than any words likely to have been spoken, is used.) Chafe (1994: 216) notes that the use of direct discourse attributed to a number of people occurs in the spoken language – perhaps most often when we are reporting, in the manner of a Greek chorus, on the reaction of our friends: for example, *'You are a fool' everyone told me.* This occurs occasionally in fictional discourse too. When the narrator is describing the kind of woman Miss Brodie is, and setting her character in the context of her time, we are told that most people were opinionated and argumentative. Their views were aired in local shops and similar meeting places: '*I tell you this, Mr Geddes, birth control is the only answer to the problems of the working class...*'(Spark, *The Prime of Miss Jean Brodie*, 1961/1965: 43). Using direct discourse rather than some form of indirect discourse for such purposes conveys a greater sense of immediacy, and perhaps stresses the importance of what is said. So, while it may lack in verisimilitude, it adds to the emotive impact. This is presumably why Woolf sometimes used

DD to convey what a character is thinking – and may or may not have said – while a remark which clearly must have occurred is relegated to indirect speech:

> 'Nature has but little clay,' said Mr Bankes once, hearing her voice on the telephone, and much moved by it, though she was only telling a fact about a train, 'like that of which she moulded you.' . . . Yes, he would catch the 10.30 at Euston.
> (*To the Lighthouse*, 1927/1964: 35)

It is a feature of Woolf's style to use DD to mark the emotions of a character, while using indirect discourse for what must have been spoken – details about train time-tables in this case – because it is of less significance to the speaker.

5.3.3 Indirect discourse

Novels are not plays, and more than direct discourse is required. Most novelists use a range of techniques to report the speech of characters. All forms of indirect discourse are characterised by the back-shifting of tense in the reported clause: thus the present tense becomes the past, the past tense the past perfect. Other deictics are also normally shifted in indirect discourse, so that pronouns are shifted: *you* becomes *he/she*; proximal adverbs such as *now* become *then*; *here* is replaced by *there* and so on. The reported elements are, prototypically, embedded in a subordinate clause introduced by *that*.

There are many complexities in the area of direct and indirect discourse. That difficulties can occur in the interpretation of indirect discourse is exemplified by a cover of *Private Eye* (20 November 1992) in which Mr Hurd, then Foreign Secretary, is seen advising the Prime Minister: *Just say 'I knew nothing about it.'* The hapless Mr Major responds with *Mr Hurd knew nothing about it*. The confusion here is between 'using' a term (that is, employing it with referential meaning in discourse) and 'mentioning' it. 'Mention' is any metalingual use of a word: for example, defining it. In speech intonation marks a distinction between *Just say I knew nothing about it* and the 'mention' intended by Mr Hurd in the *Private Eye* cover, just as quotation marks indicate the distinction in written texts. If, in direct speech, we 'use' words, in indirect discourse they are 'mentioned'. In other words, indirect speech is a reflexive use of language (Lyons 1969: 202; Lucy 1993: 2).

The focus here is on the various forms of indirect discourse, the ways in which they are used and the interpretive problems they present. They contribute to giving fictional discourse complex layers of meaning, and they can generate implicatures when combined with the information we derive from the narrator's discourse.

5.3.4 Free indirect discourse

Free indirect discourse (FID) is closer to direct discourse than indirect discourse: reporting verbs are optional, so that the speech or thought may be placed in the main clause. Simpson (1993) points out that a test to identify a free indirect form is to transpose it into the direct form. The tense is normally back-shifted, as are pronouns, but other deictics are often anchored in the speaker. Free indirect discourse is often marked by the use of exclamation marks and the occurrence of slang or colloquialisms that are characteristic of the speaker rather than the narrator. It is a fusion of two voices and two perspectives, that of the narratorial reporting voice and that of the character, a feature captured in Pascal's title *The Dual Voice* (1977). It is, of course, an example of Bakhtin's hybrid discourse (considered in Chapter 7). Free indirect discourse is often contextualised by the narrator. A major effect of using varieties of indirect discourse is to problematise the text: it is not always straightforward to decide when the voice of the character leaves off and the narrator's takes over: this is a potent source of complexity and irony in discourse. A character's idiolect may be used to suggest which portions of a passage in indirect speech are narratorial, and which emanate from the character. This is the account of a telephone conversation between someone in a hotel lobby and a resident: *The sleepy voice became gradually enthusiastic. Well, how was Gordy old boy! Well, he certainly was surprised and tickled! Would Gordy come right up, for Pete's sake!* (Fitzgerald, 'May Day', in *The Diamond as Big as the Ritz and other Stories*, 1920/1962: 32). Here the first sentence is narratorial, the second and third move into FIT. The word order is the same as it would be in direct speech. The informal lexis and the potentially FDD *for Pete's sake* strengthen the association with the character's voice, and indicate his thought processes. The use of characters' idiolect in passages of FIT is a way of indicating change in focalisation; while the present passage is perhaps too short to demonstrate idiolectal features of the character, the lexis is clearly closer to that of the character than the narrator's elsewhere in the text. Chafe (1994: 222) points out that, contrary to the normal assumption that FIT is part of written language only, it does occur, albeit rarely, in the spoken language.

5.3.5 Indirect discourse

Indirect discourse is the canonical form of reported speech. The narrator's presence is clearly indicated by the back-shifted verbs and the transposition of all deictics to their distal counterparts. The citation of the words actually used is optional; it is often heavily summarising: *After this I got embraced, told to wear flannel, be sure to write often, and so on* (Conrad, *Heart of Darkness*, 1902/1983: 39). It need not confine itself to a close verbal counterpart of the words purportedly spoken, and may encode elements of the reporter's attitude to the matter: *Her first husband, the Frenchman, had been given to boasting obscurely about his distant antecedents without disclosing precisely who these were* (Ellis, *The 27th Kingdom*, 1982: 50).

Since in fiction there is no way in which one can test the accuracy of the indirect speech in relation to the original it purports to represent, the difficulties that arise in the real world concerning the relationship between direct and reported speech do not arise. In journalism, the use of quotation marks is no guarantee that the words so enclosed emanated from the speaker: quotation marks are used somewhat indiscriminately by the press, just as the record of Hansard is far from being an accurate reflection of the words used. Speakers are allowed to 'tidy up' their grammar, so slips of the tongue and solecisms disappear from the record (Short 1988). The motivation for using direct discourse here, as no doubt often also in fiction, is to lend an air of verisimilitude, and increase the interest of the text. In general terms, it seems likely that novelists use direct discourse for what they consider to be the more significant utterances, while relegating the less important to indirect discourse, with its potential for summarising and brevity.

Unless a character within the fiction clearly misrepresents another's utterance, one has to take it that the reported speech is a more or less accurate reproduction of the (hypothetical) underlying direct discourse.

> He said much of his earnest desire of their living in the most sociable terms with his family, and pressed them so cordially to dine at Baron Park every day till they were better settled at home, that, though his entreaties were carried to a point of perseverance beyond civility, they could not give offence. (Jane Austen, *Sense and Sensibility*, 1811/1961: 63)

The first sentence is characteristically summarising. The narrator here adds comments that suggest the social norms of the characters have been broached; these attitudes may well be shared by the narrator. This brief example suggests why the reproduction of speech is a teasingly grey area in interpreting fictional discourse.

The following passage exemplifies some of the complexities that may be found:

> We must all be cut out for what we do, he thought. However you make your living is where your talent lies. He had sold vitality, in one form or another, all his life and when your affections are not too involved you give much better value for the money. He had found that out but he would never write that now, either. No, he would not write that, though it was well worth writing. (Hemingway, 'The Snows of Kilimanjaro', 1939/1964: 450)

This passage comes from a text which, until the death of the protagonist, is presented almost entirely from within his consciousness, except for a brief introduction and reporting verbs. The first sentence here is clearly FDT; the second also (bearing in mind Hemingway's characteristic instability in the use of personal pronouns, and the absence of an impersonal pronoun in most varieties of English, which would simplify matters here). At first blush the third sentence seems to begin with a narratorial comment, but when the third person changes to the second it seems most likely that this is still FIT. Sentences four and five, particularly with the *either* at the end of the fourth and the initial *no* in the fifth, suggest that we are here following the protagonist's mental argument. So, despite the variety of pronouns, it can all be accounted for as FIT.

Leech and Short argue that while the norm for reporting speech is direct discourse, the norm for reporting thought is indirect thought, because thoughts are not known to anyone but the thinker (outside of fictions). In addition, they need not be verbalised, so indirect thought, which is essentially the narrator's verbalisation of a character's thoughts, must be regarded as the norm. Any movement toward FIT, which is closer to the character, and is likely to include more attitudinal markers, is in a sense more artificial (1981: 345). Despite the basic impossibility of direct thought, Leech and Short note that direct thought is used regularly; they argue that FIT, being less artificial, is a natural development. It avoids the danger of the silent soliloquy. It also maintains the tense of the narrative and, perhaps most importantly, allows the dual perspective of narrator and character to co-exist within a sentence. Since this feature is one of the most important aspects of fictional prose, it seems likely that it has some bearing on the choice of FIT.

5.4 NARRATOR'S REPORT OF SPEECH/THOUGHT ACT

Finally, in narrator's report of a speech or thought act (NRSA/NRTA) the narrator reports that a speech or thought act has occurred, without necessarily indicating the words used: it can be heavily summarising. A character's thought may be indicated: *He was an old man, he realised* (Brown, 'The Two Fiddlers', 1974: 21). Or a speech act may be reported: *The lord ordered a steward to bring some refreshments to the musician* ('The Two Fiddlers', 1974: 16). There are also cases which should probably be described as NRTA, but where the narrator echoes some of the idiolectal features attributable to characters, the effect is comparable to FIT in the intimacy with the character that is promoted. Near the beginning of Lodge's *Changing Places* the narrator introduces the protagonists in the present tense. This paragraph begins with a description of the situation, moves into NTRA and (very smoothly, on account of the tense) then to FDT:

> While he is on the ground, preparing for his journey, he thinks of flying with exhilaration . . . when he, and the other passengers, are seated, well-being returns. The seats are so remarkably comfortable that one feels quite content to stay put, but it is reassuring that the aisle is free should one wish to walk up it. There is soothing music playing. The lighting is restful. (Lodge 1975/1979: 9)

The shift into FDT is marked by the pronoun *one* and by adjectives – *remarkably, soothing, restful* – that have an interpersonal function (Halliday 1985). That is, they do not help to identify the referent, but indicate the speaker's attitude toward it.

5.5 CONCLUSION

The prime motivation for the use of direct discourse is that it seems to allow the reader direct contact with the character. However, since it is rarely wholly unmediated, there are opportunities even here to allow for two perspectives – even a reporting clause can allow the narrator to indicate the character's attitude to the conversation. The varieties of free indirect discourse are interesting because of the mingling of perspectives the technique permits. This topic is further developed below, in considering psychonarration (see Chapter 10). Since the interest of novelists seems to have moved from pure narrative events to the depiction of the states of mind and motivation of their creatures, the various methods of speech and thought presentation are increasingly used, in a whole variety of ways.

In the next chapter I will consider the contribution that politeness theory can make: most obviously in direct discourse, but also more broadly in the establishment of relations between narrator and reader.

Chapter 6

Politeness and Literary Discourse

6.1 POLITENESS THEORIES

I will now briefly review two of the most useful politeness theories, noting that they were developed to account for face-to-face interactions, not literary discourse. The relevance of such theories to dialogue between characters in fiction is obvious; its relevance to the communicative flow between narrator and reader is less clear, but I shall try to show that, in spite of the fact that the invitation to read anything can be regarded as an imposition, and so inherently impolite, politeness does have a role here.

6.2 BROWN AND LEVINSON'S POLITENESS THEORY

Brown and Levinson (1987) develop a widely accepted theory of politeness, which they consider is cross-culturally valid. Briefly, it holds that people are motivated by their need to maintain their 'face' (in the sociological sense, developed by Goffman 1967): the need to be approved of by others, and to maintain a sense of self-worth. Brown and Levinson consider that 'face' has two aspects:

1. Negative face: the right to freedom of action and freedom from imposition.
2. Positive face: the need to be appreciated by others, and to maintain a positive self-image.

Positive and negative face needs can readily conflict. For example, if you ask me for a loan, you are threatening my negative face; if I make the loan, I am maintaining my positive face, at the expense of my pocket. If you decide not to ask for the loan and, for want of £5, are compelled to walk home and catch a cold, I may be most upset, since you have implied that we are not friends, and thus damaged my positive face. These conflicts explain why we engage in all sorts of redressive strategies (for a full account, see Brown and Levinson). At one extreme, we avoid the face threatening act (FTA) – as when a loan is not requested. Or a variety of indirect hinting strategies may be employed. You may comment on the inclement weather, and remark that you have no money for a taxi. You may remind me of our friendship (for example, by using a term of endearment or nickname), or otherwise signal that we are members of the same social group. Politeness strategies explain why it is that we can (in English) use the imperative when we are making an inherently polite offer – *have a sherry* whereas when we are making a request we are conventionally indirect – *can you pass the salt.*

The details of Brown and Levinson's exhaustive analysis of the ways in which we manage to appear polite and still get our own way need not be considered here. But it should be noted that certain topics, such as metaphor and irony, of great significance to literary discourse, can be considered in the light of politeness phenomena, as will be discussed below.

6.3 LEECH'S POLITENESS

Another method of approaching politeness was developed by Leech (1983: 81): 'minimize (other things being equal) the expression of impolite beliefs' and 'maximize (other things being equal) the expression of polite beliefs.' To this politeness principle he attaches a number of maxims (such as modesty, tact, approbation, sympathy, generosity, agreement). Politeness in this model is essentially a scalar phenomenon: the degree of imposition on the hearer will normally condition the degree of indirectness, mitigation or other politeness marker from the speaker. Thus, *Answer the phone* is less polite than a request. Of course, much depends on the relationship between the interlocutors; we can be more direct with intimates. If the hearer is aware that it is impossible for the speaker to answer the phone, the imperative might not be considered inappropriate. A difficulty with his analysis is that it seems to lead to a proliferation of maxims on an *ad hoc* basis (as Thomas 1995 notes). One of his suggestions is that there may be an interest principle, which would explain why we use hyperbole (overstatement) and litotes (understatement). These can be considered to be part of politeness: if I am telling a story, and grossly over or understate the reactions of the participants, this may marginally increase the interest of the narrative. This is quite common in oral stories: expressions like *I nearly died* can of course refer to an unfortunate incident during surgery, but they are more likely to convey an attitude to events in the narrative. So, when a young woman has a dancing partner she dislikes, the narrator says *The moment of her release from him was extacy* (Austen, *Pride and Prejudice*, 1813/1972: 133). The motivation for saying *not bad* or *not uninteresting* when one means that it was excellent (or very bad) or most interesting, may be, as Leech suggests, a counterweight to hyperbole, and guarantee that the speaker is observing the CP. Litotes was very characteristic of Old English poetry; the *Beowulf* poet tells of the founder of the Danish royal line, who was a foundling. On his death, he was given a ship funeral, laden with no fewer gifts and treasures than he had when he arrived: that is, it was laden with a great many more.

A member of a group performing at the Edinburgh Fringe is asked about the reviews: *'Not great,' Charles Collins admitted. 'We've only had four,' he went on, knowing if he didn't say it someone else would. 'They weren't exactly complimentary'* (Rankin, 'A Good Hanging', 1992/1998: 114). It is clear that the reviews must have been appalling. So why not say so? *Amour-propre,* perhaps. The speaker is both author and director of the failed play. It can hardly be to spare the feelings of his companions, who know the situation. But mitigating devices, in such circumstances, might be accounted a politeness phenomenon.

6.4 POLITENESS AND LITERARY DISCOURSE

Having considered the general theories of politeness, which were developed to account for conversational interactions, I turn to the issue of the extent to which they may be applicable to literary discourse (cf. Sell 1991).

There is an inherent impoliteness in being invited to read a book. It is an imposition, which threatens our negative face. It makes demands upon our time, and, as Cook (1994) suggests (see Chapter 3), it may seek to overturn our schemata, to change our minds about things we may hold dear. It may expose us to uncomfortable views of the world, show us the perspective of people with whom we profoundly disagree. We note that in ordinary interactions, speakers usually ask permission in some way if they are to hold the floor for some time by telling a story because it interrupts the normal turn-taking of conversation, and, as Labov's analysis of natural narratives shows, the audience is aware of the imposition, and speakers try to minimise it (see Chapter 3). The evaluative devices considered by Labov are clearly matters of interpersonal rhetoric and, generally speaking, attend to the reader's positive face, in the attempt to make the text clear, interesting, and indicating what is of particular interest.

6.4.1 Politeness: Narrator and Reader Level

Politeness needs to be considered on different levels of narrative organisation. On the level of character-to-character interaction, the normal conventions of politeness apply and will be exemplified below. The situation is slightly different, and more complex, on the higher level of author/narrator and reader. Here the interaction is essentially one-way: our only recourse if we do not like something is to stop reading, as Wodehouse points out: he must engage his readers' interest, lest *people throw him aside and go out to picture palaces* (*A Damsel in Distress*, 1919/1961: 5). Wodehouse here acknowledges that readers may regard the act of reading as an imposition. In principle, telling or writing a story can be regarded as an FTA: we are expected to yield the floor, or give up our time, to attend to someone else. Arguably, our decision to read a novel is motivated by interest, admiration for an author, perhaps a wish to pass the time or, in an academic situation, compulsion. In that case, it can hardly count as an FTA. Some authors are sensitive to the potentially FTA of narration: writers like Fielding attempt to establish a relationship with the reader, and mark the end of the novel with a formal parting. He points out (*Tom Jones*, 1749/1973 XVIII: 1) that fellow-travellers on a stagecoach frequently make up any quarrels, secure in the knowledge that they are unlikely to meet again. Such formality is more commonly found in eighteenth-century fiction than in modern novels. On the other hand, he engages in a major FTA in the introduction to Book X. Ostensibly offering instructions to readers on matters of characterisation, he accuses them of not having enough Latin to read Virgil (and promptly quotes Juvenal, and translates it in a footnote). Throughout, the reader is addressed as *thou, my good reptile* (by this date *thou* is used only to inferiors). Only at the end of the chapter does he return to the polite term of address: *you, my friend*. All this shows a total disregard for the reader's positive face, until some restitution is made at the end.

A very serious type of FTA that occurs on the authorial or narratorial level lies in the choice of topic. Many fictions cause offence to some readers: an extreme example is Salman Rushdie's *Satanic Verses*, which led to a *fatwa* being pronounced against him. A less extreme example is Nabokov's *Lolita*, where the subject matter is also offensive to some readers. Joyce experienced great difficulties in getting *Dubliners* published: it was deemed so offensive that a printer destroyed the plates. There is a relationship between reader and writer: we may be offended by certain topics, as recurrent demands for censorship show. When the Scottish novelists James Kelman and Irvine Welsh were published, it was clear that many English readers felt that writing in their dialects were inherently FTAs.

The norms and knowledge required to process a text also change over time. This can result in problems for the reader not foreseen by the author. Obvious examples are quotations from Latin, which until the post-war changes in British education could be assumed to be understood by most readers; understanding Latin is not even likely to have been a marker of in-group identity, and so promote solidarity with the reader. Nowadays, it is quite likely that the reader will not understand it, so it may be interpreted as an FTA. (This is a case where the implied reader and the real reader are at some distance from each other – see Chapter 1.) Much the same applies to quotations (or intertextuality), or echoes of other literary works. The reader who misses them is at a disadvantage, and, once apprised of the error, may well feel his positive face has suffered. For example, in Lodge's *Changing Places* (1975/1978) an American professor, on an exchange to an English university, finds a book on novel-writing belonging to the lecturer he has exchanged with. The book, called *Let's Write a Novel*, belongs to a series that includes *Let's Weave a Rug* and similar self-help titles: 'Every novel must tell a story' it began. 'Oh, dear, yes,' Morris commented sardonically. (1978: 87). The *sardonically* may puzzle a reader who does not pick up the echo of *Yes – oh dear yes – the novel tells a story*, from Forster's *Aspects of the Novel*. In Lawrence's 'Tickets, Please' there are a number of intertextual elements. One of them tells us that the philandering ticket inspector leaves one girl for *pastures new*. The echo of Lycidas may not seem particularly significant (a reader unfamiliar with Milton might notice only the inversion of the normal order of noun and adjective), but it points to the theme of the story (essentially a retelling of Dionysiac rituals, with a young man torn up by the women) by stressing the difference between the idyllic pastoral past (!) and the present.

So far as the linguistic organisation of a text is concerned, certain figures of speech can constitute an FTA. Leech (1983) argues that irony is used to convey an offensive remark without (on the surface level at least) violating his politeness principle. In other words, it appears to attend to the hearer's positive face, while conveying a negative comment. This is a narrow view of irony, implying that one means the opposite of what one says. But irony can be far more subtle than that. It will be considered more fully in Chapter 8, but in the context of politeness, it is worth noting that irony is potentially face threatening in a number of ways: it requires extra processing effort, and if readers miss it and it is subsequently drawn to their attention, embarrassment and a sense of exclusion are the likely consequence. The knowledge that we are all occasionally gulled does nothing to ease the pain. Metaphor poses comparable problems. Both figures can promote distancing or solidarity – as is the case with many politeness strategies, as we have seen. The trade-off between performing an FTA which may signal that we are on intimate or at least friendly terms with our interlocutor has to be balanced against the possible offence caused. Any flouting of Grice's maxims may have this effect. (Sell (1991) argues that the co-operative principle is inherently polite.) One of the problems created by metaphor and irony is similar to the problems potentially activated by a decision to over- or under-specify. As we saw when considering schema theory (see Chapter 3), to under-specify risks losing the audience, while over-specifying may imply a lack of trust in the intelligence of the interlocutor. This applies equally to metaphor and irony.

Another potential FTA arises as a result of the choice of method of narration. To begin a narrative *in medias res* is commonplace, but some readers may be irritated by it, rather than intrigued, and so regard it as an FTA. Many readers enjoy the challenge of very problematic styles, such as the use of FID, where it is often difficult to disentangle the views of character and narrator. Even more difficult are some novels, or passages, in the so-called 'stream of consciousness' technique. These issues are considered below in the context of psychonarration. But in each case, the reader suffers the imposition of being made to work much harder to discover the 'meaning' of the text. A novel such as Faulkner's *As I Lay Dying* requires the reader to reconstruct a narrative from the actions and thoughts of the characters. These techniques tease the reader, who either rises to the challenge or, as Wodehouse suggests, goes to a picture palace.

6.5 POLITENESS: CHARACTER-TO-CHARACTER LEVEL

6.5.1 Polite interactions

Dialogue containing inherently polite interactions is not particularly easy to find, perhaps because it is not very interesting:

> 'Wouldn't you like some more broth?' the woman asked him now.
> 'No, thank you very much. It is awfully good.'
> (Hemingway, 'The Snows of Kilimanjaro', 1939/1964: 458)

Quite often such dialogue is relegated to a combination of NRSA or FIS with perhaps one fragment of DD. In this example, we note that an offer (inherently polite) is made; the refusal is softened by praise, because it potentially affronts the positive face of the speaker.

6.5.2 Quarrels

The same characters involved in the last dialogue are not always so polite to each other. As they are (apparently) married, one can argue that impolite dialogue is not only naturalistic, but promotes or maintains intimacy.

'. . . You can't die if you don't give up.'
'Where did you read that? You're such a bloody fool.'
                    (Hemingway, 'The Snows of Kilimanjaro', 1939/1964: 444)

Both participants are bald on record, and the second is clearly an affront to the positive face of the addressee. It is unlikely to be used except where the interactants are intimates, or there is a strongly asymmetrical relationship.

Another interesting example of an argument (also in a domestic context) involves three old people:

'. . . Cremation is best.'[1]
'I do so agree with you,' said Charmian sleepily.[2]
'No, you do *not* agree with me,' he said. 'RCs are not allowed to be cremated.'[3]
'I mean, I'm sure you are right, Eric dear.'[4]
'I am not Eric,' said Godfrey. 'You are not sure I'm right. Ask Mrs Anthony, she'll tell you that RCs are against cremation.' He opened the door and bawled for Mrs Anthony. She came in with a sigh.[5]
'Mrs Anthony, you're a Roman Catholic aren't you?' said Godfrey.[6]
'That's right. I've got something on the stove.'[7]
'Do you believe in cremation?'[8]
'Well,' she said, 'I don't really much like the idea of being shoved away quick like that. I feel somehow it's sort of – '[9]
'It isn't a matter of how you feel, it's a question of what your Church says you've not got to do. Your Church says you must not be cremated, that's the point.'[10]
'Well, as I say, Mr Colston, I don't really fancy the idea – '[11]
'*Fancy the idea* . . . It is not a question of what you fancy. You have no choice in the matter, do you see?'[12]

. . .

'I see, Mr Colston. I've got something on the stove.'[13]
'I believe in cremation but you don't – Charmian, you disapprove of cremation, you understand . . .'[14]
'Very well, Godfrey.'[15]
'And you too, Mrs Anthony.'[16]
'OK, Mr Colston.'[17]
'On principle,' said Godfrey.[18]
'That's right,' said Mrs Anthony and disappeared.[19]
                        (Spark, *Memento Mori*, 1959/1961: 32–3)

This remarkable argument between an old man, his wife and cook suggests that Culpeper et al. (2003) are right to suggest that naked aggression is not accountable for under Brown and Levinson's analysis of politeness. We do not have an example of bald on record strategy, but what in the playground would be called an attempt to pick a fight. Perhaps most notable is the fact that neither of the women is, apparently, interested in the discussion. Charmian offers agreement with the proposition (and the narrator notes her sleepiness, a possible implicature is that she is not interested in the topic). Godfrey responds most aggressively, contradicting her. The social relationships are asymmetrical: Godfrey controls the topic, the turns, and interrupts (see O'Donnell 1990), while the women are polite throughout.

Part of the differences between the interlocutors here may be accounted for by different 'styles'. A good deal of research suggests that, typically, women use mitigating devices to reduce the impact of disagreement. Arguably, this is a reflection of an inferior position, as is the case here when Mrs Anthony uses *well* to preface her comments at sentences 9 and 11. Similarly, she uses other down-toners such as *really* (sentences 9 and 11) and *sort of* (sentence 9) (see Coates 1988). Terms of this type may be accounted for on the grounds that they attend to the 'face' wants of the interlocutor, softening potential areas of disagreement, so promoting social harmony. Mrs Anthony has the additional advantage of having work to attend to, which she uses to try to end the conversation. Charmian's tactics are somewhat different: she uses emphatic *so* (the so-called feminine intensive) at sentence 2; at 4 she says *I'm sure you are right. Sure* expresses epistemic modality; it is commonly used to suggest that one is not certain at all (see the discussion in Chapter 4). Charmian's tactics, like Mrs Anthony's, seem designed to keep the domestic peace and attend to relations with her husband, who is intent on being as abrasive as possible. At sentence 14 he abandons logic when he says *I believe in cremation but you don't . . . you disapprove of cremation.* Cremation exists: it is not a matter of belief. Further, no human can tell another what they think, or approve of. This abuse of epistemic modality is not uncommon amongst first-person narrators; it is perhaps less common in conversation (see Chapter 4).

Godfrey's contributions are remarkable for the series of FTAs in which he engages: in sentence 3 he aggressively contradicts Charmian, so threatening her positive and negative faces: she is allowed no self-determination, and is not even allowed to know what she thinks. At sentence 5 he contradicts her (accurately, the first time), but without any justification for the second. Again, her positive and negative faces are threatened. When Mrs Anthony is summoned from the kitchen, he manages to affront her positive and negative faces (sentences 10 and 12) by interrupting and contradicting her. This is an altogether remarkable set of utterances, which reminds us that the domestic interior is the most likely cockpit for such interactions. Politeness theory tells us that it is because, in that secure environment, we can engage in banter, exaggeration and insult to show our basic solidarity. That hardly seems to be the case here. Vuchinich (1990) suggests that one of the possible ends of domestic conflicts is submission, which appears to be what is happening here. The difficulty with this interpretation is that neither of the women appears to be interested in the topic: one can argue that they in fact win, since the topic is shelved.

A different type of verbal aggression is found here: '*How is the beautiful red-faced*

Mr Wilson? Are you feeling better, Francis, my pearl?' (Hemingway, 'The Short Happy Life of Francis Macomber', 1939/1964: 417). Mrs Macomber, who has seen her husband run away from a lion he was supposed to shoot, and has earlier told Mr Wilson that he has a red face, addresses both men, and is clearly impolite to both. The comment to her husband is easier to deal with: she clearly does not see him as a pearl, so an apparently polite term is an FTA. (It is an example of hyperbole, or gross overstatement of the maxim of quality.) She means just the opposite of what she says (Leech calls this irony.) The case of Wilson is a little different. The third-person form of address is distancing. In the past, it might be regarded as an ultra-polite form. But, as Brown and Levinson point out (1987: 230), honorific and similar terms can degrade into terms of intimacy or even contempt. That seems to be the case here. We note that *beautiful* used for Wilson and the appositive *my pearl* seem inappropriate for male addressees.

6.6 CONCLUSION

On character-to-character level interaction, we are in the same realm as considered by the theoreticians of politeness. Superficial violations of politeness may lead to more interesting discourse, for example when Leech's interest principle is involved. In the outer levels, where the narrator addresses readers, politeness is clearly also at work, creating, maintaining or destabilising relations with the readers.

The next chapter considers another approach to the relationship between interlocutors, as I will look at relevance theory. I will argue that a major contribution it makes to the study of literary language lies in its approach to impolite utterances, such as irony.

Chapter 7

Relevance and Echoic Discourse

7.1 INTRODUCTION

Relevance theory was developed by Sperber and Wilson (1986/1995). An accessible account of their theory is to be found in Blakemore (1992). It is a cognitive theory, arising from their dissatisfaction with Grice's co-operative principle. Their criticism is essentially that to search an utterance for meanings which might be implicated gives excessive freedom of interpretation, since no bounds are set on the implicatures which might be generated. They develop a cognitive theory, which holds that only the maxim of relation (relevance) is necessary. This is re-defined in the second edition as follows:

> a. The ostensive stimulus is relevant enough for it to be worth the addressee's effort to process it.
> b. The ostensive stimulus is the most relevant one compatible with the communicator's abilities and preferences. (1995: 270)

They consider that any communicative act carries the presumption of its own relevance.

7.2 DEFINITIONS

Before proceeding further it may be helpful to define some of the terms used by Sperber and Wilson.

Ostensive stimulus: One emanating from a sentient being whose intention is to inform or communicate. *An ostensive act of communication automatically communicates a presumption of relevance* (1995: 156). This need not, of course, be encoded in language. Ostensive stimuli include pointing, looking fixedly at something, or away from it, raising an eyebrow and so on. A cat that looks indignantly at the food on its plate, and then walks across to the cupboard where cat food is kept, is engaging in an ostensive stimulus.

Logical entries: These are small, finite and relatively constant across speakers and time. A logical entry can be complete. For example, a learner will show that she has mastered the logical entries for *know* and *think* by using the words appropriately.

Encyclopaedic entries: These include information about factual assumptions, knowledge of the world, and what are elsewhere called schemata, frames, prototypes and scripts. An encyclopaedic entry is open ended, and will vary across speakers and time. Speakers do not necessarily share the same information (for example, in the world of pedigree cats, a distinction is drawn between Foreign and Oriental cats). Both the logical entry and encyclopaedic entries are activated as appropriate in the interpretation of an utterance.

Explicature: *A combination of linguistically encoded and contextually inferred conceptual features* (Sperber and Wilson 1995: 182). The greater the reliance on what is linguistically encoded, the more explicit the message. In their example, *It will get cold* will tell the hearer that there is someone in the house, who has spoken, and has made a prediction. If the speaker is cooking, and it is dinner time, the hearer will interpret *it* as a reference to the food. These (and others) are explicatures of the utterance. The **implicature** is that the cook wants the hearer to come at once. Other implicatures may arise from the tone of voice. One may note that if we eavesdrop on conversations at a bus stop, we may be able to access the explicatures, but are less likely to access the implicatures.

Implicature: those elements of a message that are not encoded directly, but whose recovery is based on the assumption that the hearer will be able to make the appropriate inferences. If some such assumptions were not made, communication would be long-winded and clumsy. The speaker is not wholly responsible for the implicatures which a hearer may derive from a message; the more oblique the communication, the more is left to the audience to recover. In the example above a fairly strong implicature is that the cook wants people to come and eat, but there may be other, weaker implicatures that may depend upon the relationship between the people; there may be an implied threat about future cooking arrangements, for instance.

7.3 RELEVANT COMMUNICATION

For an utterance to be relevant, it requires only that it make some change in the hearer's cognitive environment. (So if you tell me something I already know, in this view it fails to be relevant. However, Sperber and Wilson do not allow for the possibility that I may appreciate your interest in me and my concerns, and so perceive it as relevant.) If a change in the cognitive environment occurs, it is worthy of attention and as much processing effort as the hearer judges necessary to derive appropriate rewards. Communication is seen as the joint responsibility of speaker and hearer: the theory assumes that the speaker will encode the message in such a way as to make it relevant to the hearer. The implicatures the hearer derives from it are her own responsibility, and not wholly predictable by the speaker. However, if the hearer derives an implicature that the speaker could not have foreseen, it cannot be consistent with the principle of relevance. They also consider that ambiguity leads to a failure of communication. If two different interpretations of an utterance come simultaneously to the hearer's mind, and both are consistent with the principle of relevance, there is no way of choosing between them, and communication fails (1995: 169).

Thus, any act of communication implies that it is worth the hearer's attention: it carries with it an automatic presumption of its relevance. (The fact that when we do not see the point of an utterance, we challenge its relevance suggests that there is some truth in this. Comments like *why did you say that?* or *what's the point?* are common.) Relevance theory further assumes that the less processing effort required, the more relevant it is assumed to be (Wilson and Sperber 1989: 109). This view has been modified in the second edition of their book. They now consider that the encoder of the message may consider the amount of effort she has to put in to the utterance, and may not minimise the hearer's effort. This need not be for reasons of perversity; it is clear that we do not always speak with perfect clarity, or convey our meanings with absolute precision. Having cognitive effects in a given context is a necessary and sufficient condition for relevance. It is a matter of degree, and the degree of relevance will depend on the amount of processing time and effort needed (the input) in relation to the output: the number of contextual implicatures that can be drawn. If two utterances take the same amount of processing, the one with most cognitive effects will be judged the more relevant. So there is a laziness principle at work: the assumption is that the less effort required for maximal rewards, the greater the degree of relevance. When an utterance is made in a particular context, it will generate a number of implicatures, some stronger than others. A strong implicature amounts to little more than the propositional content of an utterance. Much will depend, in spoken language, on paralinguistic features such as intonation, facial expression and so on. But some utterances may communicate only an indeterminate set of assumptions which may not be endorsed by the speaker. For instance, if my husband says he will not be home for dinner, what is explicit is that he will not be at dinner. His tone of voice and expression may generate a series of weaker implicatures: he may or may not be looking forward to his evening. He may be aware that his announcement could result in a change of menu; that I might make other arrangements for the evening. The possibility that I might choose to cook my favourite meal, which he dislikes, might occur to him as an implicature I might access. What could not be part of his communicative intention (and hence not part of a relevance theoretic approach) would be that I would be free to invite my (secret) lover for the evening. More or fewer of these implicatures will be activated by the hearer according to the situation. Thus, what is asserted in an utterance is strongly communicated. But a number of much more weakly communicated implicatures may also be generated. These will depend on the relations between speakers and other contextual features. We are not always explicit in what we say:

(*Lady Constance*) '. . . I discovered her with a young man in a tweed coat and flannel knickerbockers. They were kissing one another in the summerhouse.'

Lord Emsworth clicked his tongue.

'Ought to have been out in the sunshine,' he said, disapprovingly. (Wodehouse, *Lord Emsworth and Others*, 1937/1966: 15)

This passage was considered above (in Chapter 2), as an instance of the misfiring of an illocutionary act. Relevance theory looks at Lady Constance's utterance and notes that it is fairly explicit. The hearer has to supply referents for *her, a young man* is presumably unknown to the speaker (hence the use of the indefinite article); the use of the word *discover* may, but need not, suggest the unexpected. Sperber and Wilson consider that the hearer will make the following assumptions:

1. The speaker is optimally relevant.
2. She has said that two people were kissing each other in the summerhouse.
3. She believes this to be true.
4. It is true.

These they call the explicatures of her utterance. What remains is why she chose to say this. At the beginning of this conversation, Lady Constance has reminded Lord Emsworth that their niece is having an affair with a young man whom she considers undesirable. No doubt she intends him to access a range of implicatures including her distress, her attitude to her niece and the young man, and probably that, as head of the family he should put a stop to the relationship. Her use of the indefinite article in referring to the young man is unhelpful: he is, of course, the undesirable suitor she has already referred to.

7.4 IMPLICATURE AND LITERARY TEXTS

Arguably, in reading a literary text we are disposed to pursue possible implicatures, many of which will be very weak. While Sperber and Wilson accept that one may feel increasingly rewarded as one pursues ever weaker implicatures, the speaker cannot assume that we would be prepared to expend so much effort. Therefore, there comes a moment when the weakest of implicatures cannot be reckoned to be part of the intended message. This aspect of their theory causes some difficulties in the interpretation of literary texts, where it is widely felt that the more implicatures that can be derived, the more rewarding the text is. (Indeed, it seems almost institutionalised in university literature departments that the more meanings a student derives from a text, the better the student.) Pilkington (1991, 1996, 2000) considers literary texts, and is clearly prepared to allow for major searches for weak implicatures; he notes how interconnected textual features contribute mutually to encourage the search. In other words, the densely textured discourse of literary texts will encourage us to look for implicatures more actively than if we are reading a newspaper, or participating in a banal conversation. Blakemore (1993) argues cogently that the reader is responsible for accessing and interpreting weak implicatures. These enrich the reading, but they must be consistent with the principle of relevance. Such weak implicatures are not endorsed by the speaker, but are, so to speak, licit. The variety of encyclopaedic knowledge that individuals bring to reading will affect the implicatures they derive, and their assessment of them. Hence the more we bring to a text, the richer our interpretation may be.

Different readers will access different implicatures. This explains how it is that readers can differ in their interpretations, though, according to relevance theory, they will not differ in their broad assessment of the 'meaning' of an utterance. For example, if we consider Cope's 'Reading Scheme' discussed above (in Chapter 3), a child reader would understand the text, accompanying the pictures implied by the title, as essentially descriptive of the pictures. An adult reader would probably access a series of implicatures, and read it as the narrative of a commonplace adultery. One implicature the reader might derive is that Cope, by lightening the load of reading tedious books to small children, is communicating her technical expertise to an appreciative audience.

7.5 CONTEXT

Context is one area where relevance theory differs sharply from other theories. Sperber and Wilson define context as the set of premises used to interpret an utterance (1995: 15). They consider that context is a construct which is largely under the control of the hearer, starting with the assumption that the utterance is relevant. It is a psychological construct, a subset of the hearer's assumptions about the world. They note that these assumptions need not be accurate to affect interpretation of the utterance. Unlike some other definitions of context (1995: 137–42), it is not limited to the immediately preceding discourse and the physical environment of the interlocutors. Context will include any encyclopaedic knowledge that may be necessary to process the utterance, including scientific knowledge, religious attitudes and cultural knowledge; in fact anything which may affect an individual's interpretation of an utterance. This kind of knowledge, unlike logical knowledge and lexical and grammatical knowledge, which are in principle finite, will vary from one person to another, and change over time. This is a partial explanation of why interpretations of literary (and other) texts vary (1995: 87). Sperber and Wilson's definition of context shares certain elements with schema theory, which holds that we have prototypical 'scripts' or 'schemata' which allow us to fill out the information supplied in a text with our background knowledge. Mentioning a taxi driver will evoke a different schema than if a 'driver' were referred to alone. Taxi drivers ply for hire, driver and passenger probably do not know each other, and may or may not speak during the journey; the taxi driver (it is assumed) knows where he is going; other drivers may not. The type of car may also differ according to whether it is a taxi or a private car. We therefore choose a context that makes maximal sense of an utterance, given our assumption that the speaker intended meaningful communication and process as far as is necessary for us to feel adequately rewarded for the effort expended. Relevance theory holds that it is not licit to go beyond that stage in interpreting an utterance. One of the major limitations of relevance theory is that their examples rarely extend beyond a single dyadic interchange. No attempt is made to refer to the much more nuanced studies of context (see above, Chapter 1). In particular, Werth's (1999) study of context, showing how it develops during the processing of a text, is far more valuable. He sees it as a discoursal phenomenon, in which the preceding text is a main driver in the creation and maintenance of context.

For an example of a relevance approach to context, consider the following, taken from 'Observer', the diary column of the *Financial Times* (27 October, 1997). It begins with a short paragraph pointing out that to delete a file from a computer's hard disk does not permanently erase it until it is overwritten by a subsequent file.

> More than a bit embarrassing now the courts have taken to collecting hard disks as evidence. Now American professor and author George Friedman has come up with an answer: his 'Shredder' software guarantees to exterminate deleted files for good. He's already taken the first order for this clever but inexpensive gizmo – from a law firm in Little Rock, Arkansas.

No context is given other than that supplied above. A Martian reader might well be puzzled by this note: why should anyone other than the manufacturer of the software care who placed the first order? 'Observer' is fond of humorous anecdotes; often they are very pointed. In order to understand his comment, we need to know at least the following:

1. President and Mrs Clinton were both members of law firms in Little Rock.
2. Law firms use computers.
3. Both have been accused of attempting to conceal their involvement in certain financial dealings in Little Rock (the Whitewater affair).

A possible implicature is that the Clintons would be interested in this software. If this interpretation (or something like it) is not adopted, the story seems fairly point-less. It is perhaps worth noting that, as a journal with an international readership, the *Financial Times* is normally explicit in its system of reference. Tony Blair, for example, is identified as the British Prime Minister. It is only 'Observer' who is allowed to make such demands on the contextual knowledge and inferencing skills of his readers. In fact, the amount of processing required is not great since most readers probably have limited knowledge of Little Rock, so the salient interpretation will spring to mind; the case might be very different if readers had considerable knowledge of the town. On the other hand, readers in Arkansas might simply react with pleasure to know that someone in their state was at the forefront of technology. Thus, context and encyclopaedic knowledge together supply the information needed to make the article relevant. The implied reader is clearly important when writing such a note, in considering what needs to be spelt out, and what can be assumed in the way of encyclopaedic knowledge, especially bearing in mind that teasing implic-atures are more fun than an explicit statement. 'Observer' hopes to entertain, as well as enlighten.

In this case at least, Sperber and Wilson's account of context seems most useful. The assumption is that the reader will draw on encyclopaedic knowledge, will prob-ably be aware that the Clintons come from Little Rock; they probably do not know much about law firms there other than those in which the Clintons were partners. Thus the place name is sufficient to trigger an array of information which is relevant to the interpretation. One might note in passing the speed with which this information is processed: readers do not expect to have to puzzle over 'Observer' and similar columns. It is almost like a word-association test: Little Rock will suggest 'Clinton', certainly with the supporting reference to law firms.

The context of literary discourse is not usually so opaque, though it is often created by similarly slight touches. It is usually assumed that a literary text is self-standing: it must supply all the contextual references required for its interpretation (but see Chapter 3 and the discussion of paratextual elements). The first paragraphs of a fiction usually serve to orient the reader into the fictional world by various means (see Chapter 1 for a discussion of the implications of the role of the definite and indefinite article). Beyond the first sentence, the main source of context is the developing text itself, together with whatever encyclopaedic knowledge we need to process it.

7.6 ECHOIC LANGUAGE

Sperber and Wilson argue that, in interpreting ordinary assertions, we pay attention to the propositional form. However, language can be used in other ways as well: an utterance can be used to represent what it resembles (metalingual use). If you ask me what John said and I reply *I'll tell you later* you may be uncertain as to whether I am quoting his words ('mentioning them': that is, a metalingual use) or making an assertion: that I will inform you at some subsequent time. That is, I may 'echo' what John said (quotation), as well as paraphrasing it in indirect discourse: *he said that he would tell me later.*

Sperber and Wilson argue that this is a commonplace in language use (and in other communicative behaviour: we can point at something instead of naming it). Their account of irony also depends upon echoic language use (see Chapter 8). It should be noted that Bakhtin's heteroglossia is, in part, an example of echoic language use which encompasses free indirect discourse.

Relevance theory is essentially a cognitive theory, and as such its validity must ultimately be judged by psycholinguists. However, in contrast to Grice's co-operative principle, which may not be generalisable across cultures or at the very least is interpreted differently by different societies, Sperber and Wilson's theory proposes an analysis of cognition which would be universally valid. Degrees of indirection – that is, the predisposition of societies to expect more or less explicit utterances – may vary cross-culturally, in much the same way as politeness phenomena have different manifestations in different cultures. Japanese readers, trained in the interpretation of haiku, may find English lyrics painfully explicit. From the perspective adopted here, it seems that Relevance theory has a contribution to make to the study of literary discourse. The concept of arrays of weak implicatures suggests how it is that readers come to different interpretations of a text, and why some readers are more competent than others. Readers differ in their encyclopaedic knowledge, and in their ability to remember and connect various parts of the text and so generate different numbers of implicatures. They also differ in the effort they are prepared to make in reading a text. Its view of context, in particular the kind of information taken into account in processing discourse, is limited owing to its failure to take into account the whole communicative framework, especially the preceding and following discourse, which is particularly significant for literary texts.

7.7 POETIC EFFECTS

This is the (unhappy) term relevance theoreticians use to describe utterances which derive their effects from a wide range of relatively weak implicatures (Sperber and Wilson 1995: 222). In their account, metaphor is interpreted in this way: it is a less faithful form of expressing the speaker's thoughts, but it generates many implicatures, which are to a large extent under the control of the hearer, who will pursue them as long as she is deriving an appropriate reward in terms of weak implicatures. Note that the weaker implicatures cannot be taken to be endorsed by the speaker: they are essentially the responsibility of the hearer. Their effect derives in part from the reliance placed on the hearer to pursue the implicatures; the suggestion that speaker and hearer share a good deal of knowledge and background, so that empathy is increased if things are implied rather than spelled out. This is interestingly close to Cooper's suggestion that one of the effects of metaphor is to promote a sense of shared attitudes and intimacy (see Chapter 8). We are flattered by the assumption that we are capable of following and developing the speaker's thoughts. Sperber and Wilson suggest that common effects rather than common knowledge are important here.

7.8 'GARDEN PATH' UTTERANCES

Some utterances are deceptive, in that the first obvious interpretation may not be the correct one (that is, we are led down the garden path to an unexpected place). This often applies to jokes (see Grundy 1995: 141–9), and is characteristic of irony (Sperber and Wilson 1995: 242). Language games abound (see Halliday 1978). In these cases, it is assumed that the extra rewards compensate for the effort involved. Sperber and Wilson assume that irony is intended to ridicule the opinion echoed: it is a mocking form of discourse. They rightly argue that irony does not consist of saying the opposite of what one means, but only of suggesting greater or lesser distance or distaste from the opinion expressed.

7.9 LIMITATIONS OF RELEVANCE THEORY

One of relevance theory's limitations is the insistence that the first relevant interpretation to come to mind must be the one intended by the speaker. Therefore ambiguities are excluded, as a failure to communicate successfully (1995: 169), supposing that two different interpretations are accessed simultaneously. Ambiguities are, however, common in literary discourse (as well as in the spoken language, where they may also be intentional – the intent often being to amuse). Ambiguity must be taken into account in interpretation. Relevance theoreticians might argue that they do not come to mind simultaneously and furthermore that they are not necessarily ambiguities, but rather slightly different ways of interpreting something, which might therefore be explained as simply generating possible implicatures. While relevance theory does allow for the pursuit of implicatures or 'poetic effects', one of its limitations is that its proponents do not seem ready to allow for the rather jokey uses of language that are prevalent in the playground as well as in literature:

> [h]aving found an interpretation consistent with the principle of relevance – an interpretation (which may itself be very rich and very vague) which the writer might have thought of as an adequate repayment for the reader's effort – why not go on and look for ever richer interpretations and reverberations? If we are right, and considerations of relevance lie at the heart of verbal communication, such searches go beyond the domain of communication proper. Though the writer might have *wished* to communicate more than the first interpretation tested and found consistent with the principle of relevance, she cannot have rationally *intended* to. (Wilson and Sperber 1989: 116)

While it is now conventional wisdom to assert that literary discourse does not differ linguistically in essentials from non-literary discourse, since both exploit the language of the time, it is also the case that the reading of literary texts does seem to differ from the reading and interpretation of non-literary discourse (see Thorne (1988), cited in Chapter 2 above). This means, in relevance terms, that readers are more prepared to access a great range of weak implicatures. As we have seen (Chapter 1), reading literary works differs from the canonical situation in obvious ways: the immediate absence of an audience influences the writing process; the audience is (usually) unknown to the author. Furthermore, readers are a disparate lot, who may bring different elements of encyclopaedic knowledge to the interpretation of a text, particularly if there is a large temporal gap between composition and reading. So readers are likely to access different implicatures, which results in different interpretations of a text. Pilkington (1991) argues for a reading of poetry along lines very similar to Thorne's, suggesting that readers of poetry expect to access a very large range of weak implicatures in arriving at an interpretation. He therefore considers that a good poem, like a good metaphor, cannot be paraphrased: different readers will assign different weight to the implicatures they assess. It is not a case, as he points out, of alternative readings, rather of more or less rich ones.

7.10 CODE SWITCHING AND RELEVANCE THEORY

Relevance theory has nothing to say about code switching; it has no interest in discoursal features, but it can have something to say about the phenomenon. If it is a generalisable theory, then it should be able to contribute to the study of all communicative features of discourse. Code switching is commonplace: in the complex contemporary social world it seems most likely that almost all of us are members of over-lapping speech communities, which may be differentiated by lexis, pronunciation, forms of address or any other distinguishing feature. We therefore adjust our mode of speech to our interlocutors, the situation and the topic being discussed (see Fasold 1990: 40). For those within the communicative situation, of course, code switching may be perceived as promoting solidarity, and this reaction will presumably be shared by readers who come from the same community, though the promotion of solidarity often carries with it the exclusion of others.

Code switching, or the use of dialect (or a foreign language) in fiction, is intermittently fashionable, whether in the marking of non-standard pronunciation or the use of dialect words which may be unfamiliar to most readers. Relevance theoreticians must assume that such use of dialect is motivated, and contributes to the meaning of an utterance through the generation of weak implicatures. This may seem counter-intuitive, particularly if readers are struggling to come to terms with a dialect with which we may not be familiar (see Toolan 1992). We may therefore feel excluded or perhaps attracted by the strangeness. Phoneticians may regret the imprecision of nov-elists; the use of dialect words may cause processing difficulties. Irritation is a pos-sible reaction if we are unfamiliar with the dialect. Even if the reader is a speaker of the dialect, literacy is based on standard spellings, and therefore processing difficul-ties are apt to occur: even a speaker who says *ooirs* when she reads *hours* is likely to be temporarily taken aback by the spelling. On the other hand, there is no doubt that use of dialect may change our cognitive environment: in that sense it is educational, and relevant. In relevance theoretic terms, code switching may be argued to have an effect analogous to implicatures, metaphor and such devices, in generating a range of more or less weak implicatures; like metaphor, the use of dialect may promote a sense of community, of being members of an in-group who can appreciate its effects. The use of dialect can contribute to situating the narratorial voice, or that of the char-acters. All of these will be more or less weak implicatures, which may be strength-ened by other elements in the text. Code switching will most likely have the effect of promoting solidarity with some readers, while possibly alienating others. So the effect of verisimilitude must be weighed against the possible disadvantages.

The use of dialect works in at least two ways: it serves to characterise or identify the narrator or character sociolinguistically, but readers may react in unpredictable ways, partly on account of the dialect chosen, and perhaps with our familiarity (or ignorance) of it. It makes the reader consider why a particular encoding has been chosen, and what effects it might have. If it is used successfully, readers will feel ade-quately rewarded for the undoubted extra processing effort involved. Dialects vary of course in their accessibility: stage 'Mummerset' was so commonly used that audi-ences presumably became accustomed to it, just as Estuary English is very familiar to British audiences now. Similarly, conventional representations of American English occur very commonly. In one of Welsh's short stories, a redundant worker from Edinburgh tells of taking his family to Disneyland. His daughter is frightened by a man dressed as a bear; an altercation ensues; the police come: *they sais tae ays: Whit's the fucking score here, mate, bit likesay American, ken?* ('Disnae Matter', 1994:

119). He makes no attempt to reproduce American dialect except at the end: *Thanks a lot, buddy. Have a nice day.* This string of fixed collocations does no more than lend local colour; its triteness does not impose processing difficulties on the reader (though the rest of the story may well). From a relevance perspective, the question must be whether the undoubted additional processing effort required for most readers of this text is sufficiently rewarded by cognitive effects. No doubt individuals will differ in their reactions, their ability to decode the text, and the amount of effort (for example, buying a dictionary) they are prepared to put in. This applies to any heavy use of dialect in fiction: if it is a familiar variety, not much trouble will ensue, but some readers have difficulty with some Scott novels, though they are less likely to experience many problems with Dickens.

The use of dialect may contribute to characterisation, as well as situating characters sociolinguistically, as in the examples above. It can be used most economically to suggest a much wider cultural context, relevant to the interpretation of the fiction. In Golding's *Lord of the Flies*, Piggy is instantly recognisable as an outsider by virtue of his substandard English:

> 'My auntie told me not to run,' he explained, 'on account of my asthma.'
> 'Ass-mar?'
> 'That's right. Can't catch me breath.'

> (1954/1958: 14)

As the novel develops, Piggy emerges as one of the most intelligent of the boys, but he is rarely taken seriously, largely because of his social class and weight. Ralph, who becomes leader, speaks the standard language; his father is a naval officer. Another of the characters is head chorister. When he and his choir meet the other children:

> 'We got most names' said Piggy. 'Got 'em just now.'
> 'Kids' names,' said Merridew. 'Why should I be Jack? I'm Merridew.'

> (1954/1958: 28)

Thus the class system of England is re-created on the island in microcosm. Certainly in *Lord of the Flies* sociolects are used as a shorthand way of identifying the backgrounds of characters who soon lose or abandon their clothes and other obvious marks of social identity. Chambers notes that *stereotypes can be triggered by the presence of one stigmatized variant in forty seconds of speech* (1995: 252). One may note, parenthetically, that such a finding suggests that it is not wholly inappropriate to identify idiolectal features of fictional characters on the basis of the slender evidence available.

From a relevance perspective, the use of dialect seems to create a range of more or less weak implicatures, some of which affect our assessment of the characters in terms of their education and social situation, and thus are comparable to the kind of contextual information we gather automatically in spoken interactions. Code switching can also indicate the kind of situation involved. On the other hand, the processing effort involved is substantially greater than for reading the standard language: authors must assume that the effects they invite their readers to access will compensate for the extra expenditure of time and effort; as Sperber and Wilson note, if there is deliberate obscurity, the hearer may doubt whether genuine communication was intended. That point is clearly relevant to literary discourse in general: some poems are very obscure, though the argument is that the cognitive effects they offer will ultimately be rewarding. Some novels, such as *Finnegans Wake*, may fall into the same category for many readers.

7.11 CRITICISMS OF RELEVANCE THEORY

Amongst the criticisms of relevance theory is the absence of any significant attention to the social context in which language use is situated (cf. Mey 1994). Goatly poses the question 'relevant to what?' (1997: 148), arguing from a Hallidayan perspective that discourse takes place within a social space, and its relevance and interpretation are closely linked to genres and social situation. Goatly also argues strongly against the implied assumption in relevance theory that we converse (or write) only to exchange information. But of course this is not true: language games, storytelling, lying are all commonplace. Riddling begins in the playground. Sperber and Wilson's examples (like Grice's) are made up; usually the interactions are very short. This does not reflect the realities of everyday conversation, where the direction of discussion, turn taking, and so on are negotiated between speakers. They ignore sociocultural variation.

Werth (1999) is highly critical of relevance theory on two principal, but related grounds. One is the very limited view of context it adopts, which does not take into account the discourse in which (in the real world, though not in the examples used) linguistic exchanges take place. He argues that the principle of relevance requires that only new information (which changes our cognitive environment, in their terms) is relevant. Werth's view is that as a discourse develops (whether written or spoken), there is a shifting common ground between the interlocutors, which affects the ongoing interpretation of the text. Context is an ever-rolling stream, which is adjusted as the discourse develops. His other stricture is that they do not sufficiently take into account the hearer's knowledge in their model. Accessing our knowledge base is, in his view, text driven.

There is no doubt, I think, that relevance theory's rejection of free-wheeling deconstructive activities is welcome. The difficulty arises in deciding how many weak implicatures are, in this perspective, licit. Since a number of scholars interested in literature have adopted a relevance approach, some of the strictures raised against the theory have been addressed – or at least, the interpretations of relevance theory offered – have been loosened. Pilkington, for example, is interested in literary texts, and takes full account of the whole text in assessing the relevance of an utterance (1996, 2000). But, Sperber and Wilson's theory fails to consider sufficiently the different aims and interests of readers as opposed to interactants in spoken discourse. The analysis of echoic language is particularly fruitful. In this respect it is closely similar to Bakhtin in his study of hybrid discourse and heteroglossia, which I shall consider now.

7.12 BAKHTIN'S ANALYSIS OF ECHOIC LANGUAGE

The Russian scholar Bakhtin (1895–1975) made a substantial contribution to the study of language (for a useful overview of his life and work, see Clark and Holquist 1984, Holquist 1990). He has, in effect, a sociolinguistic perspective that illuminates much literary discourse. I will therefore consider aspects of his theories here, though I will avoid most of his terminology. Of particular interest is his contribution to the study of the language of fiction. He was particularly interested in the mingling of voices in fiction, including the effects of the interplay between the language of characters and narrator, which arises partly from the exploitation of the various forms of indirect discourse. He was also concerned to promote respect for the varieties of language displayed in such texts.

For Bakhtin meaning in language is context-bound, and can only be interpreted and understood within its context. This is a firmly pragmatic approach to discourse. Bakhtin's philosophy of language is wholly opposed to any attempt to 'purify the dialect of the tribe'. On the contrary (possibly because of the repressive regimes under which he lived), he gloried in the diversity of language, arguing that there are two opposing forces at work: the centripetal or unifying, and the centrifugal, which reflects the variety of speakers, experiences and historical periods encoded in language. Language is not unitary, existing to convey a single, unique meaning, but reflects the variety of social experiences in which it is rooted. He considers that every utterance anticipates a reply (and prepares itself to react to it), so that language is inherently dialogic (1981: 280). This 'dialogue' is conceived of as taking place across time, as well as in the immediate context of the utterance. Thus language is understood to be 'trailing clouds of glory', carrying with it the experiences of the past, as well as having present relevance. Furthermore, an utterance can only be understood in the context in which it is uttered: context changes the meaning of linguistic tokens. For example, the beginning of Lodge's *Small World* (1984/1985) is a translation of the beginning of *The Canterbury Tales*, a paean to spring. The translation is close to the original, including words like *engendered, zephyr, dulcet* which are perhaps unpredictable items in their new context. The narrator then points out that, just as in the Middle Ages, in spring people want to go on pilgrimages: *Only, these days, professional people call them conferences* (1985: 9). The similarities between conferences and pilgrimages are explored: both afford all *the pleasures and diversions of travel while appearing to be bent on self-improvement* (1985: 9). They both have penitential aspects (conferences papers); both bring together people who do not like each other, as well as old friends, and so on. This use of the very famous beginning of an English poem on one level links two different text types, suggests some of their differences, and implicitly invites us to consider the continuity of English culture (however much its superficial manifestations may change).

Bakhtin considers that natural language is highly variable; it reflects the different world views of individuals, their different experiences and interpretations of their experiences. In this respect, Bakhtin may be described as holding to a weak Whorfian position, in that he accepts that our language reflects the way we view the world

(1981: 333). He contrasts this natural situation of language with what he terms unifying language, which is essentially the standard language. He is opposed to standardisation, beyond what is required for mutual comprehension (this is a view that most sociolinguists would share). Virtually all language use will include heterogeneous elements within a matrix of the standard, with rare exceptions such as certain forms of official documents, and legal and some scientific discourse. These are amongst the most rigorously controlled genres. The language of fiction is perhaps the freest, able to reflect the societies depicted. Taste is (or was) the only serious constraint operating on a novelist. Novelists are freer than we are in ordinary conversation, since they need not fear offending their interlocutor: the offended can simply stop reading.

I do not propose to employ all of Bakhtin's terminology here; rather, I have attempted to translate it into contemporary linguistic terminology, and hope that clarity has increased as a result without distorting his ideas. However, two crucial terms require to be discussed.

7.13 HETEROGLOSSIA

This is identified as the defining feature of novelistic discourse, as well as being characteristic of ordinary language use. It is essentially the combination of registers, sociolects, idiolects, professional jargons (or technical language), parody, genre (in both the linguistic and literary senses); the distinctive language of different generations, and diachronic changes in language (1981: 262, 321). The example from Lodge's *Small World* is an example of heteroglossia. Within fictional discourse, the interplay between narratorial language and that of the characters, with their different perceptions and world views is a prime source of heteroglossia. In Mantel's *Fludd* the uneducated housekeeper of the parish priest picks up his habit of referring to members of the Bishop's household as *sycophants*. She *supposed they were a kind of deacon* (1989/1990: 5). So too the children in the convent school are terrified by the *Equipment* (1989/1990: 114). That is what the Mother Superior calls it. It is no more than the kind of gymnastic equipment to be found in most schools, but these deprived children are used to no more than bouncing about on rubber mats. These words, from registers unfamiliar to those exposed to them, indicate to the reader the limited education of the characters; in the case of *sycophants*, it gives early warning of the conflict between the priest and his Bishop. The children probably think *equipment* is a technical term for parallel bars and the like. More interestingly, one of the nuns tells the curate that she has a dispensation permitting her to wear Wellington boots. This is glossed: *a special permission* (1989/1990: 79). This is clearly a politeness strategy – the narrator fears that readers may not know what a dispensation is. But in the next sentence, the nun says she has applied for a dispensation for a *rainmate*. Readers probably know what that is, but the curate does not, and has to ask. Here the range of lects available to different members of society is underlined. But the narrator is not always co-operative. In the same passage, the curate reflects on alchemy: *this is the spagyric art; this is the Alchemical Wedding*. No doubt it enhances the mystery of alchemy that we have to have recourse to a major dictionary to discover that *spagyric* means alchemy. These examples suggest the range of registers available to us: most of us are not masters of many of them. The complexity and multifarious nature of society is adumbrated by these means.

Bakhtin notes the way in which the discourse of the narrator may be affected – even infected – by that of the characters (see Bakhtin 1981: 315). Bakhtin (1984) calls this kind of 'appropriation' of the language of a character, or a social group, *stylisation*. This feature is prominent in the language of *The Prime of Miss Jean Brodie* (Spark: 1961/1965), a novel charting the development of Miss Brodie's pupils. Their development is, in part, marked by their developing language. The narrator sometimes echoes the language or vision associated with the child characters. When the girls begin to study science in the secondary school: '*You still keep up with Miss Brodie?' said Miss Mackay, with a gleaming smile. She had new teeth* (1961/1965: 115). Spark does not usually indulge in reporting clauses of this type. The narrator here echoes not only the sharp-eyed observations of her child characters, but the language of toothpaste advertisements, and fiction for schoolgirls (these girls write their own stories too.) Nash (1990) notes the use of such reporting clauses in popular fiction, where, he suggests, they serve to lend a spurious air of interest to trite situations. All of this makes the narratorial voice as elusive as quicksilver: the reader has to be very alert to situate herself within the text. This is one of the prime effects of heteroglossic discourse. The narrator's use of this trite reporting clause thus reverberates in a number of ways for the alert reader.

One of the effects of heteroglossia in this novel is that it conveys the process of acquiring and accommodating new ideas (in this respect it is not unlike metaphor). The following passage is part of a letter purportedly written by two of Miss Brodie's pupils, approaching the end of their primary school education under Miss Brodie:

> Intimacy has never taken place with him.[1] He is married to another.[2] One day in the art room we melted into each other's arms and knew the truth.[3] But I was proud of giving myself to you when you came and took me in the bracken on Arthur's Seat while the storm raged about us.[4] If I am in a certain condition I shall place the infant in the care of a worthy shepherd and his wife, and we can discuss it calmly as platonic acquaintances.[5] I may permit misconduct to occur again from time to time as an outlet because I am in my Prime.[6] We can also have many a breezy day in the fishing boat at sea.[7] (Spark 1961/1965: 73)

The text reflects the various linguistic influences on the children as they become interested in sexual matters. They are hampered by a shortage of hard facts; their language reveals the sources available to them. The register of police reports in the papers, to which the girls had access is echoed in sentences 1 and 6; the world of the folk tale (sentence 5), and the language of romantic fiction (sentences 3 and 4) are also used. The result is a most unlikely love letter, but one which offers insights into the children's view of the adult world.

The ignorance of the girls is reflected in the incongruous mixing of inappropriate registers in a letter which purports to be between two lovers. The text thus reflects various sociolects in society, a heteroglossia which shows the different attitudes to extramarital sex (depending on whether we are reading the police reports of the 1930s, folk tales, romantic fiction and so on); all of these are of course a world away from the language lovers use. It is perhaps worth noting here that the children have not yet developed idiolects: rather their language is (appropriately) shown in development throughout the novel.

One of the most extreme forms of heteroglossia represents what Halliday (1978) terms an anti-language. Anti-languages develop in places like the underworld, prisons and schools where a subculture's values are in opposition to those of the rest of society; they are the result of the resocialisation of the members. They reflect counter-reality, in opposition to established norms. They have some of the same functions as jargons, and terms of art of any profession. Halliday suggests that the language of literature is itself an anti-language, since it contributes to the social discourse of society, whether by reinforcing existing models or offering a different one. Literature is involved in the creation of an alternative reality, which is one of the functions of an anti-language. He also notes that a feature of anti-languages is the selection of meanings to be exchanged. I take that to mean that both anti-languages and literature create contexts in which particular values and meanings are encoded.

7.14 HYBRID DISCOURSE

This is the other term used by Bakhtin that requires comment. It is defined as:

> A mixture of two social languages within the limits of a single utterance, an encounter, within the arena of an utterance, between two different linguistic consciousnesses, separated from one another by an epoch, by social differentiation or by some other factor . . . [it is] the mixture of two *individualized* language consciousnesses . . . the individual, representing authorial consciousness and will . . . and the individualized linguistic consciousness and will of the character represented, on the other. (1981: 358–9)

Bakhtin also describes it as:

> an utterance that belongs, by its grammatical [syntactic] and compositional markers, to a single speaker, but that actually contains mixed within it two utterances, two speech manners, two styles, two 'languages', two semantic and axiological belief systems. (1981: 304)

At least two phenomena would seem to be included in this definition. One is free indirect discourse in all its forms, which results in the mingling of the narrator's and character discourse; the other is the combination of sociolects reflecting the society of the fiction. It sounds as though hybrid discourse is a higher-level operation, while heteroglossia is the mechanism whereby it manifests itself in texts.

Thus in hybrid discourse the co-presence of two language systems is found (1981: 360). This can happen when the narrator temporarily aligns himself with 'general opinion', or with the attitudes of characters within the fiction. The first sentence of *Pride and Prejudice* is an example of the former: *It is a truth universally acknowledged that a single man in possession of a good fortune, must be in want of a wife* (1813/1972: 51). Austen echoes the thoughts of a whole class of people (mothers whose daughters need to be provided for), some of whom appear in the novel.

The narratorial voice in Lawrence's 'Tickets, Please' aligns itself with the views of characters in the fiction when, as a description of the protagonist we are told, *Therefore the inspectors are of the right age, and one, the chief, is also good-looking* (1922/1995: 36). Here we encounter a shift from a slightly ironic and distant narrator to one who adopts the perspective of the girl conductors: it is their judgement that the inspector is of the *right age*. One of the results of this is that the distance between narrator and characters fluctuates, which in turn causes a changing relationship between reader and narrator. There are constant realignments of perspective and attitudes to be balanced. Since the instability in the narratorial voice that this creates means that we cannot always be absolutely certain of the views it encodes, one of the consequences is a distancing, or doubling, of the perspectives encoded within even a single sentence or clause. There are thus two consciousnesses encoded within a single utterance, which must therefore be doubly interpreted. It should be noted that these consciousnesses need not refer to individuals only: in the Lawrence example the reference is either to Annie, who will have an affair with the protagonist, or the whole group of girls who compete for the inspector's attention. Often such combinations of perspectives have the effect of undercutting the views of the characters, or the group opinion echoed, and are therefore a fruitful source of irony.

Similarly:

> The Royal and Northwestern Hotel had been designed by a pupil of Sir Gilbert Scott in a moment of absent-mindedness, and when Roisin O'Halloran entered its portals she felt uneasily at home . . . 'Like church,' she whispered. The foyer had a marmoreal chill. Behind a mahogany desk, curiously carved, proportioned like an altar . . . (Mantel, *Fludd*, 1989/1990: 163)

The narrator comments ironically on the architecture, then shows the naïvety of the character. The duality of perspectives is clear, though here the views of character and narrator are in agreement – it is their knowledge of the world which separates them.

An element of hybrid discourse can be introduced by a single word, with the blending of two perspectives within a sentence. That is, it is essentially echoic. For Bakhtin such discourse is 'double accented' (1981: 304). For example, *It grew light and Claudia lay for a while watching a lot of very pointless birds taking off from the tree outside her window* . . . (Ellis, *The Other Side of the Fire*, 1983/1985: 37). Here, embedded in narratorial description, the adjective *pointless* suggests the dyspeptic views of the character. Non-restrictive modifiers often serve such a purpose.

The other discourse feature that seems to be referred to as 'hybrid' is free indirect discourse, which also mingles the language of character and narrator in a complex fusion which is sometimes very difficult to disentangle. It is used to much the same effect as the realignment of the narrator's perceptions with that of the characters considered above. In the case of FID, the duality of voice is obvious, though it is not always clear precisely where demarcation between narrator and character should be placed. Consider the following:

> Valentine said nothing.[1] There was really very little that the bereaved could say to each other, since trouble shared was trouble doubled.[2] She contained her sorrow and observed her father doing the same: nothing but a vessel, an instrument for grief, denied all other purpose, so full was he.[3] Of course he had died, his structure inadequate to the destructive forces within him. Valentine had not shared the gloomy view people had taken of his demise.[4] To her he seemed to have fulfilled a role more nearly and precisely than others called to less harrowing modes of being.[5] He would have come to himself in a dark garden, cool with the mists of morning, to hear his name being spoken.[6] Of Joan she was less sure.[7] Joan had been naughty – reckless and insouciant.[8] She might be trapped in the light, the light that permits no shadow.[9] And yet in the course of whatever passes for time in Heaven and Hell, all would be resolved, since the good deserve that the bad should be forgiven, the nature of goodness being to love.[10] (Ellis, *The 27th Kingdom*, 1982: 48)

The presence of *verba sentiendi* (*observed, had not shared, seemed*) are indices of NRTA; but for the rest it is not easy to distinguish between the voices of narrator and character. In sentence 3, one can argue that following the colon we shift into FIT. Sentence 6 is FIT; sentence 7 possibly, though it could be narratorial. The rest seems to me to be clearly FIT. This passage illustrates the difficulty of identifying the voices in texts of this sort: the resulting instability places heavy interpretive burdens on the reader.

Varieties of free direct and indirect discourse have been considered above; it is therefore sufficient to note here that it is one of the features of texts that contribute to hybrid discourse. One of the points about FID is that it has an echoic element: the result is again instability in the discourse of the fiction, with consequent interpretive doubts for the reader, who may be uncertain whether to attribute elements to narrator or character. Clear examples of heteroglossia are found in indirect discourse, particularly in free indirect forms where the voices of character and narrator are inextricably blended. The juxtaposition of two perspectives in FID is likely to give rise to irony.

It should be noted that not all cases of hybrid discourse exhibit heteroglossia:

> Had there been an axe handy, a poker, or any weapon that would have gashed a hole in his father's breast and killed him, there and then, James would have seized it. Such were the extremes of emotion that Mr Ramsay excited in his children's breasts by his mere presence; standing, as now, lean as a knife, narrow as the blade of one, grinning sarcastically, not only with the pleasure of disillusioning his son and casting ridicule upon his wife, who was ten thousand times better than he was (James thought), but also with some secret conceit at his own accuracy of judgement. What he said was true. It was always true. He was incapable of untruth; never tampered with a fact; never altered a disagreeable word to suit the pleasure

or convenience of any mortal being, least of all of his own children, who, sprung from his loins, should be aware from childhood that life is difficult; facts uncompromising; and the passage to that fabled land where our brightest hopes are extinguished, our frail barks founder in darkness (here Mr Ramsay would straighten his back and narrow his little blue eyes upon the horizon), one that needs, above all, courage, truth, and the power to endure. (Woolf, *To the Lighthouse*, 1927/1964: 6)

This passage comes from the beginning of the novel. It begins with NRTA of a small boy's rage against his father. It is far from the language one might expect of a six-year-old until the hyperbolic *ten thousand times better than he was*, which is of course FIT. Small children do not think of their mother as someone's wife, so that is clearly narratorial. The remarkable thing about this passage (which is characteristic of Woolf's style) is the sudden shift into another character's mind immediately after this. It begins with a narratorial comment, but the rest of the paragraph is best seen as FIT. It is characterised by the rather over-blown rhetoric which Ramsay seems to use to himself – it is not like his spoken language, but he is given to seeing himself as engaged in a dangerous enterprise. The narrator resumes temporarily in the parenthetic comment that interrupts Ramsay's reflections just before the end of the passage (*would* shows that this is a regular pattern of Ramsay's thoughts). From this passage, or indeed from the novel as a whole, one cannot identify idiolectal traits of the characters (except for the cleaning ladies in the central section 'Time Passes' which are marked by departures from standard grammatical norms). The sudden shift from one character's thoughts to those of another is potentially unsettling to the reader, and inherently impolite in its challenge to our understanding: most people say that they read Woolf rather more slowly than other novelists. On the other hand, the technique lends smoothness to the text, as it moves subtly from one mind to another. The language of this novel is, I think, a pretty accurate reflection of Woolf's world, which is limited to the middle classes.

Hybrid discourse can be used for undercutting the pretensions of characters or institutions in a fiction, and is a common source of irony (in Sperber and Wilson's terms, it is echoic: the element of dissociation, the co-presence of two 'voices' they stress is present). For example, at the beginning of *The Prime of Miss Jean Brodie* an opposition is set up between the attitude of Miss Brodie and her pupils and the mores of the school:

1. they had been immediately recognizable as Miss Brodie's pupils, being vastly informed on a lot of subjects irrelevant to the authorised curriculum, as the headmistress said, and useless to the school as a school. These girls were discovered to have heard of the Buchmanites and Mussolini, the Italian Renaissance painters, the advantages to the skin of cleansing cream and witch hazel over honest soap and water . . . (1961/1965: 5).
2. [they] were all famous in the school, which is to say they were held in suspicion and not much liking (1961/1965: 6).

In the first extract the narrator echoes the words of the headmistress. The passive (*were discovered*) in the second sentence is, as often happens, used to conceal agency. It cannot be attributed to any individual; it may reflect the views of an individual or group within the school world. It suggests the mutterings of those who come in contact with Miss Brodie's pupils. The reference to *honest* soap and water again echoes the views of others, without specific attribution. *Honest* is a non-restrictive modifier. Such epithets have an interpersonal function: they do not help us to identify the referent, but tell us something of the attitude of the speaker (Halliday 1985: 163; see also Epstein 1980). The clichéd phrase also reflects badly on the teachers whose attitude is conveyed, and contrasts with the exotic and original Miss Brodie. Her educational policies and her pupils are set in opposition to the more traditional mores of the school world. In the second extract the term *famous* is redefined in terms of its meaning in the school situation. (There is, of course, a further play, since so many children's stories contain the word 'famous' in the title or text. It hardly carries the strength of *fame* in other types of discourse.) These are clear instances of hybrid discourse, where a number of different voices are identifiable in the text, without the reader necessarily being able – or indeed needing – to decide precisely who they are. Common opinion, the views of parents, the views of teachers in the school . . . it hardly matters.

The narratorial voice in this novel, which so readily aligns itself with various characters, groups of characters, or a particular stance, as well as occasionally being neutral, is unstable; its ventriloquial character makes the reader's task more intriguing, in that no centre of authority is clear. The onus is on the reader to make complex judgements about the nature and value of Miss Brodie's influence upon her 'girls'. Bakhtin notes that narrators can align themselves more or less closely with the language of their characters, there can be an almost complete fusion of voices (1981: 315), just as throughout the novel as a genre there can be varying distances between aspects of the narrator's language and those of the characters. In this fiction, varieties of language are the means whereby the situation of the girls, the influences upon them, their sources of information and their interpretation of them as they develop are demonstrated. The novel's language reflects the cultural diversity of the city in matters of religion, attitudes to education (where Miss Brodie is pitted against her more traditional colleagues), the arts and sexuality. It is the potential to do this that makes novels such rich and complex literary forms.

Spark does not show the totality of the linguistic repertoire of the city: another side of Edinburgh is shown in the fiction of Welsh, which characteristically mingles a standard with the colloquial language of drug addicts and the young residents of Edinburgh's 'schemes'. This is characterised as code switching by sociolinguists: its effect is often to promote solidarity, though it can, of course, be a distancing device (see Fasold 1990: 40). The overall effect is mimetic of some Edinburgh speakers; in this short story the narrator is bi-dialectal. His language suggests he belongs to two different groups:

There were more than adequate toilet and shower facilities in the pavilion, which contained the footballers' changing-rooms as well as my bothy. So my outgoings were purely drink and drugs which, though substantial enough, with a bit of dealing, insurance and credit-card fraud, could be met fairly comfortably while allowing me to save. How good was that?

And yet it wisnae such a good life. There was the small problem of actually having to be on the job. (Irvine Welsh, 'Park Patrol', in *The Acid House*, 1994: 179)

I find myself surrounded by seventy-odd sweaty players and nippy, rid-faced officials. At that point, yes, I wished I'd got ma arse intae gear and turned the showers oan. My strategy on such occasions is tae come out fighting and act even more disgusted with the shower problem than they are. Steal those clothes of righteous indignation.

– Listen, mate, I said, shaking ma heid angrily, – ah fuckin telt the cunts the other week that the immersion was dodgy. (1994: 180)

The language here presents a rather confused picture. It makes sense for the narrator to address his interlocutors in the same dialect as they speak, so promoting solidarity. It approaches an anti-language in that its use is designed to set its speakers against authority. What is less clear is why he should mix the standard with dialect forms in the narrative proper. It seems to be more or less random. Normally one expects some motivation for choice of register and indeed for variation in pronunciation. The combination of sociolects found here is common in Welsh's writing; it is, of course, also typical of most speakers' language use, where there is substantial variation according to context, situation, interlocutors, and so on. To that extent, the heteroglossia displayed here is typical of most peoples' language use. What is lacking is a motive for the variation displayed here. It does not contribute organically to the narrative in the way that Spark's ranging over a series of sociolects does. On the other hand, the Scots have for many years been concerned that their language should be recognised (though many of them might not think that the variety Welsh uses is particularly worthy of attention). So there is a strong element of national pride involved in writing in the vernacular. That this attracted negative comment from English reviewers at the time perhaps proves the point. There is a further problem: many readers experience difficulty in reading texts that look so unfamiliar. Spelling is a matter of convention; there is no unanimity in the spelling of some of these words. However we pronounce a word, we are accustomed, on the whole, to a standard spelling, so this is likely to be a barrier even to speakers of the variety. Some give up the struggle. There is thus a problem of politeness here: readers face additional processing problems, and may feel that the spelling system adopted is in itself a face threatening act. However, familiarity breeds ease as well as contempt. If writers and readers conclude that it is worthwhile and desirable that a whole range of varieties should be available, it can be expected that an increasing number of works will appear in not only Scots, but other varieties, and in this way the heteroglossia characteristic of society will be more fully reflected in written texts. In a society which is so concerned with standardisation and the loss of individuality, this can be seen as a good thing: in Bakhtin's terms, it is the triumph of centrifugal over centripetal forces in language. But, as he argues, we need sufficient standardisation to make communication easy. There are no easy answers here: we seem to be in an era of transition, and the difficulties readers experience now may, in time, disappear.

7.15 CONCLUSION

Relevance theory is a most interesting contribution to understanding the pragmatics of discourse. As Pilkington shows (1991, 2000), it can offer a view of what constitutes literariness. Relevance theory is flawed to the extent that its definition of context is limited: it is telling that Sperber and Wilson rely on metaphors deriving from computers and economics to explain the workings of the human mind. It is clearly superior to the co-operative principle in its analysis of metaphor, and more generally in its explanation of how we access weak implicatures to arrive at an interpretation of an utterance. This at least in part explains how we can arrive at different interpretations. Perhaps its greatest contribution is its analysis of echoic language use. This encompasses not only irony, where it is of major significance, but also all forms of indirect discourse, where the duality of voices is marked.

Relevance theory is a cognitive theory, whereas Bakhtin is a literary scholar who is interested in identifying and categorising some of the effects of the multilayered discourse that characterises fictional discourse. The source of hybrid discourse is often to be found in free indirect discourse (whether reporting speech or thought). The combination of narratorial and character perspectives within a single syntactic unit is also a fruitful source of heteroglossia and irony. The other major source is the layering characteristic of fictional discourse, where we have narrator(s), characters and often reports of the perceptions of others outside the fiction, filtered through the language. This explains the sources of heteroglossia. Irony is considered more fully in the context of relevance theory, but it is worth reiterating here that the 'echoic' account of irony favoured by Sperber and Wilson fits excellently with the doubling of voices, and the consequent instability of the text that Bakhtin stresses. However, that is not putting it in the terms he would choose: for Bakhtin, it is not instability but rather the variety of experience that is conveyed in this way. But, from my perspective, what is most significant about these aspects of text is that the text becomes unstable: in the conflict of voices, where the narrator's voice is mingled with that of characters, the centre of authority is diminished, and the onus on the reader to construct the meaning of the text is greater than in fictions that do not exploit these resources. It is interesting to note that writers like Woolf, who display so much of the thoughts of their creatures, are finally less complex than those who maintain a strong narratorial voice, but allow free range to the disparate voices of the characters within the fiction. This lends great richness to the texts, which is less prominent in novels which do not exploit the range of idiolects and sociolects available, such as those of Austen and Woolf.

In the next chapter I shall consider the usefulness of echoic discourse in approaching parody and irony, and the contribution relevance theory makes to the explication of metaphor.

Chapter 8

Tropes and Parody

In this chapter I shall consider two tropes: metaphor and irony. I then move on to a discussion of parody, which shares with irony a large echoic element.

8.1 METAPHOR: INTRODUCTION

Metaphor is too wide an area to discuss fully in a context such as this: its bibliography extends from Aristotle. But despite all the attention, metaphor remains challengingly enigmatic. None of the theories proposed to explain metaphor is wholly satisfactory. This may be because it is rooted in the workings of the human mind (see Paprotté and Dirven 1985; Lakoff and Johnson 1980; Mey 1994; Pilkington 2000); we need more evidence from psycholinguists before any just assessment can be made. Metaphor was once defined as saying one thing and meaning another. This view has long since been dismissed, as linguists and philosophers have taken an increasing interest in it. Much remains to be discovered: the proliferation of metaphor in everyday language suggests that it is deeply rooted in the human mind (see Carter 2004). It is prevalent in all discourse types; there is a sheer ludic element here: we enjoy it. Metaphor is very common, yet also elusive. It sometimes requires a context to tell us whether an utterance is to be interpreted metaphorically or literally: *He is a hawk*, overheard at a bus stop, does not tell us whether it is a reference to a bellicose politician, and hence tritely metaphorical, or to a part taken in a play, in which case it is literal. One way of identifying some metaphors is the use of the word *literally*. An example from a catalogue description of a crystal bowl: *on its own it's magnificent, but when we added ice nuggets we were literally stunned. The whole effect is one of living light.*

Metaphor is a scalar phenomenon: there are dead metaphors in common use ('a dead duck'), which requires no special interpretive effort, through fairly conventional metaphors, to the original creations of speakers or writers. It is possible to revive dead metaphors through appropriate contextual buttressing. In *The Inheritors* Golding describes the thought processes of a group of Neanderthal people, who are on the verge of possessing language. They perceive nature as animate, and themselves as part of it. For them, *a puddle of water lay across the path* (1955/1961: 11) is literal (see Black 1993).

I will discuss some current pragmatic approaches to metaphor, and then look at how it works in texts. (I will not discuss traditional methods of analysing metaphor. Good accounts are found in Leech 1969 and Goatly 1997.) Metaphor poses the question: why don't we say what we mean when the language allows it? It does not always allow it, of course – Sterne had a lively awareness of the use of metaphor:

> my uncle Toby *fell in love:*
> – Not that the phrase is at all to my liking: for to say a man is *fallen* in love, – or that he is *deeply* in love, – or up to the ears in love, – and sometimes even *over head and ears in it,* – carries an idiomatical kind of implication, that love is a thing *below* a man . . . (*Tristram Shandy* VI, 37)

It is difficult to find another way of expressing coming into the state of loving in English; Chaucer uses a comparable metaphor, though predictably it is more elegant to suggest the encompassing nature of love: *ye loveres, that bathen in gladnesse* . . . (*Troilus and Criseyde* I, 22). (Deignan 1997 shows that these metaphors are still common in English.) The language does not seem to allow us to talk about falling in love without using a metaphor. Metaphor has always been one way of extending the lexicon.

8.2 FUNCTION OF METAPHOR

Cooper (1986, and see Mey 1994: 301) notes that we use language for purposes other than communicating beliefs. Therefore, given the prevalence of metaphor, we must assume that it is not a perverse use of language, as, he suggests, the use of archaism is (1986: 78). It is part of everyday conversation, and should be explained in those terms, not as aberrant language use. He is particularly concerned with the social function of metaphor. In addition to the kinds of speech acts that concern linguists, he notes that there are songs, poems and all kinds of literary discourse, whose function is understood by their audience: they are 'not received or judged as if they were information-giving devices, but rather as creations to be evaluated by such criteria as imaginative power, internal balance, and the capacity to evoke moods' (1986: 104). He calls these maverick utterances. He puts metaphor (and other creative uses of language, including in-group language such as army or prison slang) into this category. In his view, the principal power of metaphor is to open up new lines of thought, of original thinking. It is a case where the journey is more important than the destination. Another likely motivation for using metaphor is to induce a state of 'relative linguistic virginity' (150). Seeing the familiar in a new light – or making us see it clearly for the first time – is certainly one of the effects of metaphor (which perhaps helps to explain why poets use metaphor so commonly when discussing trite topics like love); as Waugh observes, 'metaphor creates an image of reality by connecting apparently quite disparate objects' (1984: 17).

Cooper concludes that a prime motivation for using metaphor (and irony) is the cultivation of intimacy. The producer of the metaphor, by doing so, credits his audience with the capacity to understand and appreciate it. This entails shared cultural experiences, the ability to reason analogically, familiarity with the tradition of meta-phorical expressions, and so on. By appreciating the metaphor, the audience shows that they are indeed members of this sub-set of the human race. In other words, metaphor is important socially, to foster and maintain bonds. Furthermore, if we are to understand metaphor (and irony) we have to recognise that part of the interpre-tive process is to identify the attitude of the speaker. Since 'attitude' is hardly some-thing that can enter into the paraphrase of a metaphor, it strongly suggests why metaphor resists paraphrase (1986: 161). In this he is interestingly close to Sperber and Wilson's analysis of poetic effects (1995: 217ff.), and to Blakemore's discussion (1993), which considers the importance of the speaker's judgement about the hearer's resources in formulating an utterance. The cognitive capacities of the audience and our judgement of their encyclopaedic knowledge will affect how we express ourselves. All of this strongly suggests that metaphor is to be included within the realm of politeness phenomena: it anoints our positive face, despite the fact that, initially, the effort required may seem to be a FTA. Thus it has a powerful interpersonal element: it pays us a compliment, stimulates thought, and gives pleasure.

8.3 CONCEPTUAL METAPHORS

Lakoff and Johnson (1980), Lakoff (1987) and Lakoff and Turner (1989) develop the view that metaphor is part of the human cognitive system: thus it is fundamen-tal to thought, as well as expression. Their argument is concerned particularly with those metaphors which suggest how the mind (or perhaps, a language or culture: much research is required before one can assume cross-linguistic validity for their examples, if not for the theory) perceives or shapes reality. Thus they focus particu-larly on structures where the metaphorical element is carried by, for example, a prep-osition. Examples of metaphors based on concepts – such as *down* is bad, while *up* is good or positive, time is money, death is departure – pervade the language (see Lakoff and Turner 1989: 221–3). These are all conceptual metaphors. They consider that poetic metaphors are often grounded in the common conceptual metaphors of a language (which helps to explain why they are often readily understood). Lakoff at least is a proponent of the Whorfian hypothesis, and has been to some extent respon-sible for reviving interest in it. Conceptual metaphor might be one example of a Whorfian influence on our thought. Lakoff (1987) argues that we use such meta-phors as part of our reasoning and thought on topics. Some of them are therefore dangerous: for example, lust is conceptualised as a war, madness, heat, hunger. Similarly, that an argument is conceptualised as a battle (*he won the fight, I beat him*) may have unfortunate repercussions.

The mind is the topic in a number of metaphors. This may be, in part at least, because we still do not understand much about its workings, so metaphor allows us to grapple with a rather elusive problem. In one conceptual metaphor the mind is conceived of as a container. Consider such common expressions as *in mind, out of your mind, at the back of my mind*. This metaphor has an interesting history: St Augustine (*Confessions* X, discussed in Carruthers 1990: 146) writes of memory:

those innumerable fields, and dens, and caves of my memory, innumerably full of innumerable kinds of things, . . . through all these do I run and flit about, on this side, and on that side, mining into them so far as ever I am able, but can find no bottom.

Carruthers traces a series of metaphors for the mind, from antiquity through the Middle Ages, which compare the mind to containers: dovecots, beehives, storage rooms, even Chaucer's *male*, the bag from which pilgrims take their stories: in other words, their memory. One point of these metaphors is that the contents of the mind are organised, making retrieval easier. It should be recollected, of course, that, until the advent of books, rolls were kept in rooms with partitions arranged in the manner of dovecots or beehives, with pigeonholes for documents (Carruthers 1990: 33–45).

An example of how concept metaphors can appear in developed form in literary texts would produce many examples. To take the metaphor of the mind as a container, St Augustine, in the passage cited above, calls it a *den* or *cave*. Locke (who disapproved of metaphor) comments on how the mind searches for hidden ideas: *they are roused and tumbled out of their dark cells into open daylight* . . . (*An Essay Concerning Human Understanding*, 1710/1975: II, 10). More recent writers have compared the mind to a junk room or attic: *Who wouldn't be astonished if his memory was brutally rifled – if from all the rags and clutter of twenty-five years a shining half-forgotten image was lifted into the light?* (Brown, 'The Two Fiddlers', 1974: 23). In this metaphor, a character meets a friend whom he has not seen for twenty-five years, and believes to be dead. The friend is unchanged by the passage of time, thus making the *shining half-forgotten image* apposite, in contrast to the time-ravaged observer.

In the next example, the basic concept of mind as a room is also used: this time it is apparently a well furnished but unkempt room:

Memories are like possessions: furniture, ornaments. Some are always in the room of your mind, some decayed, some lost; and some are there on the walls – of no further profit or use and never to be shared or revealed. (Ellis, *The Skeleton in the Cupboard*, 1988/1989: 50)

A slightly different use of the container metaphor from the same text shows that the metaphor is subject to variation:

There is fortunately a mechanism in us which works like the gates of a lock, interrupting and blocking the flow of memory, of immediate awareness. Once the gates are closed, although we know the water is there and it is still the same, we can disregard it . . . (Ellis, *The Skeleton in the Cupboard*, 1988/1989: 38)

In this extended metaphor memory is compared to water in a lock: 'forgetting' is closing the lock gates. But it appears that the memories the character seeks to obliterate remain, like detritus floating in water. It suggests how we can control memories, though not obliterate them: the water remains in the canal even if we ignore its contents. So the mind is the lock, with the water representing memories (*the flow of memory*). On the other hand, if one considers the normal function of a lock – to allow boats to move through hilly terrain – the metaphor becomes more difficult to interpret. Locks enable motion through control of water levels. The metaphor may therefore have to do with ways of controlling memory so that it can be useful, and not hamper other activities. No doubt further reflection would suggest more possibilities. The effect of all these passages is of course quite different: what they have in common is a source in the concept metaphor of the mind as a container. The Brown metaphor suggests the violent actions of a thief. All are attempts to capture aspects of memory, and its workings.

The next examples are concerned (as St Augustine is) with memory and its possible uses.

> The imagination doesn't crop annually like a reliable fruit tree. The writer has to gather whatever's there: sometimes too much, sometimes too little, sometimes nothing at all. And in the years of glut there is always a slatted wooden tray in some cool, dark attic, which the writer nervously visits from time to time . . . (Barnes, *Flaubert's Parrot*, 1984/1985: 115)

Closely similar is: *words still come welling up from that damp unvisited cellar where they were laid down* . . . (Bennett, *Telling Tales*, 2000: 87)

It is debatable whether the Barnes metaphor has to do with the imagination, as the text suggests, or with the mind (which *gathers* the fruits of imagination?). But it is clear that the third sentence must refer to memory, and the mind, this time as an attic. These examples suggest that, in one form or another, and with surprisingly little modification in most cases, mind and memory are encoded in very similar ways. A more violent example is: *He's astonished himself to think he's taken in so many words in the last few years, harpoons aimed straight at the brain, and that he actually remembers them* (Shields, *Larry's Party*, 1997/1998: 85). Here the brain remains a container (as vulnerable as a whale); the metaphor resides in the (implicitly copular) metaphor relating words to harpoons.

In another example, a character is meditating: *Images flitted through his mind* . . . *One by one the pictures chased each other, and he held open his mind's door, and let them pass through until the house was empty* . . . (Mantel, *Fludd*, 1989/1990: 78). Here, as in the following example, the character is controlling his thoughts, or at least attempting to empty his mind of unwanted ones. The punningly named Pensieve is used by the wizard Dumbledore when he feels his brain is too full, and when he wants to see connections between various thoughts and memories:

> 'One simply siphons the excess thoughts from one's mind, pours them into the basin, and examines them at one's leisure. It becomes easier to spot patterns and links, you understand, when they are in this form.' (J. K. Rowling, *Harry Potter and the Goblet of Fire*, 2000: 519)

In the same text the protagonist's inability to think is explained: *Harry's brain filled with a sort of blank buzzing, which didn't seem to allow room for concentration,* (296).

Given the origins of this metaphor in antiquity, it seems possible that it is indeed a conceptual metaphor which is available to a number of cultures and languages. The alternative explanation – that all derive from the classical and medieval models – is possible, but perhaps less likely. Clearly, the metaphor is ubiquitous.

8.4 THE CO-OPERATIVE PRINCIPLE AND METAPHOR

First, the co-operative principle reassures us that communication is intended: so a metaphor will be treated as a matter of implicature, or some kind of indirect speech act, in order to ensure that meaning is conveyed, since the literal meaning is usually impossible to sustain. In his very brief comments on metaphor, Grice (1975/1989: 34) notes only that the maxim of quality is exploited in metaphors such as: *You are the cream in my coffee.* (One of the flaws of the approach of Searle and Grice to metaphor, exemplified here, is a reliance on copular metaphors which seldom illuminate the teasing problems posed by more complex metaphors.) A Gricean approach to metaphor should take the following into account.

The maxim of **quality** is exploited, in that metaphor typically involves the misapplication of a term: for example, the violation of selection restrictions by treating inanimates as animate, or *vice versa*, or the common strategy of discussing abstract entities in concrete terms – it is probably easier to understand abstractions in terms of concrete items. An example is *tendrils of doubt* (Trevor, 'Reading Turgenev', 1991/1992: 34). A different kind of information is supplied than one might expect or require. The information may offer a different view of the topic of the metaphor than we previously held. In fact, the maxim of quality seems to function as a signal of metaphor, while other maxims may be more important in interpretation.

The maxim of **quantity** is often involved in metaphor: too much, or too little, information is offered. *You are the cream in my coffee* does not tell you whether I like cream, though it is conventionally interpreted as praise. On the other hand, in an example cited above, we are offered a view of memory, and how the mind works, which fulfils the maxim: *Who wouldn't be astonished if his memory was brutally rifled – if from all the rags and clutter of twenty-five years a shining half-forgotten image was lifted into the light?* (Brown, 'The Two Fiddlers', 1974: 23).

Metaphor always challenges the maxim of **manner**. Since this involves how something is expressed, it is within the competence of the speaker to vary it. It is therefore highly evaluative (see above, Chapter 3) in its effects. It always demands some effort to decode, to a greater or lesser degree. Trevor's metaphor, for instance, might be thought to be unnecessary, since he could have said something like *she became dubious.* But in his metaphor, doubt acquires some characteristics of living things, which grow, and the tendrils can potentially kill or damage their support. This may change our view of doubt: it becomes menacing and dangerous. (Note also that 'doubts' can grow metaphorically – a dead metaphor.)

The maxim of **relation** is perhaps the most significant for the analysis of metaphor (as it probably is for the processing of all kinds of discourse, as suggested by Sperber and Wilson's elevation of something like it into the only necessary condition for successful communication). What is clear is that some metaphors are more relevant than others (at least to some readers). Thus, in the metaphors for mind considered above, the Brown metaphor is thematically very important, and marks one – if not the – most important moment in the narrative. When we note that Trevor's *tendrils of doubt* is used of a bride contemplating her husband, we can scarcely be optimistic about her future: the rest of the fiction explores its relevance.

8.5   RELEVANCE THEORY

Like Cooper, Sperber and Wilson (1986/1995) consider that metaphor (and other figures of speech) should not be relegated to a special category, but form part of ordinary language use (see also Vicente 1996). Their approach to figurative language has been developed by Pilkington (2000) with considerable subtlety. Briefly, the relevance theory argument is that any utterance can be placed on a continuum of literal to looseness of expression: we use whichever is most economical in the circumstances. For example, when we set out shopping last weekend I said *I have no money*. The implicature I intended was that I needed to visit a cash machine before shopping. Nor did I mean the utterance literally, but it was more economical than saying that I had, say, £5.47 in my purse. If, on the other hand, I had been talking to my financial advisor, then precision about financial details would clearly have been necessary. On this cline, metaphor is at the looser end; it thus requires more interpretive effort. A successful metaphor will reward the reader with a complex array of very weak implicatures, which repay the extra processing effort expended. How far one goes in this process appears to be up to the individual. We continue to access implicatures until we are satisfied (see Pilkington 2000: 105). Thus different readers may come to different interpretations, through accessing more, fewer or different implicatures. As with Cooper's analysis of metaphor, this approach strongly suggests why paraphrase of metaphors is impossible – and that in turn explains why they are so prevalent. One use of metaphor is to convey concepts which are not lexicalised; another is to suggest attitude to a topic. It follows that these metaphors cannot readily be paraphrased. Consider the examples of metaphors for the mind cited above in 8.3: they are grappling to express concepts about the mind and how it works that have no adequate expression in English. Similarly, the metaphors for falling in love point to a gap in the lexicon. Metaphor is also a convenient way of conveying complex thoughts, not least because the onus is on the interpreter to work out the range of possible meaning(s) intended.

The more poetic the metaphor, the more complex are the effects. Context plays an important part in interpreting metaphor, as it does for any utterance. Recall that Sperber and Wilson's view of context is that it is largely the responsibility of the hearer, who accesses whatever information is needed to understand a particular utterance. This includes not only the preceding verbal interaction, but also – on the assumption that the utterance is relevant – items retrieved from the encyclopaedic memory to make sense of it. In the case of literary discourse, the context is buttressed by careful text creation. Indeed, this is a major feature of literary discourse. It explains why we are prepared to give it much attention, and why that attention is rewarded by deepening insights. It is also clear, of course, that literary discourse is organised in such a way as to suggest fruitful lines of thought, and so generate weak implicatures. Metaphor is prevalent in everyday language, but, generally speaking, it does not generate as many implicatures or contextual effects as in written texts, because spoken words are evanescent.

8.6 EXTEND THE EXAMPLE

The line of argument followed here is based on relevance theory: to explore weak implicatures generated by a metaphor. Looking at hints on pages 31 and 49–50, you are invited to develop the argument, bearing in mind that lexical chains buttress metaphors and create resonance in the text. I regret I am not allowed to quote from 'A Painful Case.'

8.7 METAPHOR: CONCLUSION

I have reviewed here a number of useful approaches to metaphor. Lakoff and his colleagues make a valuable contribution in suggesting why metaphor is so prevalent, as it often arises from conceptual metaphors, which structure thinking. In turn, these metaphors explain why it is that we are able to assimilate more poetic and complex metaphors. Grice's approach can be fruitful, provided it is developed; he seemed not to be very interested in figurative language. Relevance theory has been criticised for failing to take into account the social element of metaphor, stressed when Cooper and Goatly both refer to the interpersonal function of metaphor in the creation and maintenance of intimacy. This point applies equally to language which is frequently metaphoric, such as professional jargon and the language developed in closed communities like schools, prisons and the military. To some extent the failing of relevance theory is amended by Pilkington's attentive study of poetic effects. It may not be by chance that he largely avoids the metaphor that underlies Sperber and Wilson's work: that of the computer. People are not computers. We may do some things more slowly, but others we perform both more rapidly and certainly more subtly. Pilkington's work, combined with that of Cooper and Goatly, contributes to our understanding of how metaphor works on us, as well as in texts. In contrast to similes, in which a comparison is spelled out, and little interpretive freedom is given to the reader, metaphor allows much variety in the interpretation of a metaphor; however, it is a freedom affected by the context in which the metaphor occurs. Some metaphors are buttressed by surrounding text in a way which makes them resonant, and contribute a good deal to the interpretation; they become more than local elements in the structure of a text.

The value of metaphor is to encourage us to think anew on familiar topics, to grapple with the unknown or inexplicable (which may account for the proliferation of metaphors for the mind). Finally, we enjoy metaphor for its playful element: linguistic games are prevalent, from riddles in the playground onwards. That is why we are prepared to go on seeking for added meanings or, in relevance terms, weak implicatures. Pragmatically speaking, the usefulness (and hence prevalence) of metaphor may be accounted for by economy, speed and the fostering of interpersonal relations.

It is on these grounds that metaphor can claim a place in a book on pragmatics of literary discourse: it is an interpersonal, as well as a textual, device.

8.8 IRONY: INTRODUCTION

I will now consider approaches to irony, which shares at least some analytical problems with metaphor, and certainly encodes the ludic element in language use.

> There is no agreement among critics about what irony is, and many would hold to the romantic claim . . . that its very spirit and value are violated by the effort to be clear about it. (Booth 1974: ix)

Given this observation by a most competent reader, one can only embark on a discussion with great hesitation. I shall confine myself to pragmatic approaches to the topic. This is appropriate, since irony is conventionally defined in dictionaries as 'saying one thing and meaning another' and is dependent on the context, our judgement of the speaker and hearer, the relationship between them and the topic under discussion for its interpretation. Wales (1989) summarises various types of irony, and she notes that it can arise from a discrepancy between the views of character and narrator – this is particularly relevant here. Narrators know more than their characters, and this knowledge may be shared with the reader. There are often instances when the reader is privy to information not available to all the characters. So, in *Pride and Prejudice*, when Mr Bennet receives a letter from the egregious Mr Collins, warning him of the dangers of Elizabeth's marrying Darcy when she has realised that she loves him and has just been visited by his aunt, Mr Bennet says, *And pray, Lizzie, what said Lady Catherine about this report? Did she call to refuse her consent?* (1813/1972: 373). That is precisely the case, but Mr Bennet speaks in ignorance, and his daughter is in no position to confirm it. Narrator and readers can share the irony – Elizabeth is too involved to appreciate it.

A marked disparity between what is said and the situation is often indicative of irony. In the spoken language, intonation and even facial expression may suggest we are confronted with an ironic utterance. Lexis is sometimes a guide. Another possible hint of irony may be a departure from the textual norm (what Fowler 1981: 75 calls localisation). Contradiction of what has gone before may also suggest irony. For example, at the end of Spark's *Not to Disturb*, servants who stayed up all night while their employers commit murder and suicide (which they have predicted, if not quite plotted) the narrator says of them: *by noon they will be covered in the profound sleep of those who have kept faithful vigil all night* . . . (Spark 1971/1974: 96). In fact, they have connived at the deaths, from which they intend to profit mightily.

8.9 THE CO-OPERATIVE PRINCIPLE

Pragmatic approaches to irony include Grice's discussion in the light of the co-operative principle (1989). He considers that it results from a violation of the maxim of quality: if a speaker says something that is patently false, the hearer assumes he is implicating the opposite. In Lodge's *Therapy* a hospital porter wheeling a patient along a circuitous route to the theatre remarks: '*Got to take the scenic route today . . . Theatre lift's broken, ennit?*' (1995/1996: 9). This is a case of saying the opposite of what is meant; the phrase has entered at least contemporary British English to describe an indirect way of reaching an objective, doubtless a tribute to the sign-posting activities of various tourist authorities. Cope's 'Engineer's Corner' (1986) is an instance of an ironic poem which says the opposite of what it means:

We make more fuss of ballads than of blueprints –
That's why so many poets end up rich.
While engineers scrape by in cheerless garrets.
Who needs a bridge or dam? Who needs a ditch?

> . . .

No wonder small boys dream of writing couplets
And spurn the bike, the lorry and the train.
There's far too much encouragement for poets –
That's why this country's going down the drain.

The poem is a comment on an advertisement placed in *The Times* by the Engineering Council, suggesting that Westminster Abbey should have an Engineer's Corner. But one should note that ironies in this text are pointed not only by the advertisement, but because many of its assertions are contrafactual: it is common knowledge that poets do not ride around in Daimlers; the (romantic) image of the poet is of someone starving in a garret; little boys (probably) do not dream of writing couplets. Furthermore, the language is trite and cliché-ridden (poets always *scrape by* in garrets; they do not just live there); the last line contradicts much in the poem: if engineers are so hard done by, who has produced the drains for the country to go down? (This is a neat example of a metaphor in common use whose force is revived by the context.) Of course, the reader has to bear in mind the possibility that the Engineering Council might endorse the sentiments in the poem: the *locus* of the irony is rather slippery here. The poetic voice is saying 'the opposite of what she means', as in the conventional definition of irony, but it may echo sentiments attributable to the Engineering Council. Saying the opposite of what is meant is no doubt a common form of irony. In *Heart of Darkness* Marlow, the narrator, has just landed in the Congo. He sees a group of prisoners, and notes their shackles and misery, and the conspiratorial look of their black guard who: *seemed to take me into partnership in his exalted trust. After all, I also was a part of these high and just proceedings* (Conrad: 1902/1983: 43).

But Grice's account does not cover all ironies: Mr Bennet in *Pride and Prejudice* remarks: '*I admire all my three sons-in-law highly,*' said he. *Wickham, perhaps, is my favourite; but I think I shall like* your *husband quite as well as Jane's*' (1813/1972: 387). Since Wickham has brought disgrace on the family and been compelled to marry under duress, while the other two men are highly desirable (financially and in terms of social status), the implicature is clear. But Mr Bennet is not saying the opposite of what he means. Similarly, in Lodge's *How Far Can You Go?* the narrator is explaining the attitude of the Roman Catholic church to contraception. The official line is maintained, but a commission is investigating it. A Vatican spokesman is asked how it is possible for the Pope to maintain the current teaching, while asking for it to be reconsidered. He replies that: *the Church was in a state of certainty, but when the Pope had made his decision, whatever it was, the Church would pass from one state of certainty to another* (1980/1981: 105).

8.10 PRINCIPLE OF IRONY

Leech considers that there is a principle of irony, which builds upon his politeness principle (Leech adds a number of principles to Grice's conversational principle. The politeness principle, which has many maxims attached, simply urges us to be polite). Leech interprets irony in the light of the politeness principle:

> If you must cause offence, at least do so in a way which doesn't overtly conflict with the Politeness Principle, but allows the hearer to arrive at the offensive point of your remarks indirectly, by way of implicature. (1983: 82)

This suggests that his view of irony is apparently limited to ordinary conversation. But irony is not confined to encoding rude remarks about one's interlocutor. It is commonly used to express disapproval of things over which we may have no control. One might remark on the cleanliness of the streets, or the well-kept, pothole-free roads, intending an oblique comment on the local authority. The example of the hospital porter cited above cannot be explained as an attempt to avoid causing offence: he is only trying to keep the patient cheerful. There is no motivation of politeness in using irony in such circumstances. It is presumably used to bestow modest interest on a banal remark. (Leech's interest principle is in fact covered by relevance theory: in the perhaps marginal increase in contextual effects such an indirect way of expressing a thought conveys.)

8.11 RELEVANCE THEORY AND IRONY

Wilson and Sperber (1989: 101–3) consider that in irony, a speaker echoes words or a thought attributable to someone else, while dissociating herself from it. The thought echoed need never have been expressed, and may not be attributable to a specific individual. It may represent a cultural norm or aspiration, or refer to a type of person or attitude. An example is the first sentence of *Pride and Prejudice* (1813/1972), often cited in works on irony: *It is a truth universally acknowledged that a single man in possession of a good fortune must be in want of a wife.* It becomes clear that this is not endorsed by the narrator, and its hyperbolic quality in any case renders it unlikely to be entertained by the reader. Nevertheless, we do not believe that no rich bachelor wants to marry. It is not the opposite that is implicated, but something rather different. In context it is readily identified as echoing the thoughts of Mrs Bennet, mother of numerous daughters. As soon as she is introduced into the narrative, she announces the imminent arrival of a wealthy young bachelor in the neighbourhood, and remarks how beneficial that will be for her daughters. In the same novel Elizabeth is responding to the effusions of Mr Collins on the topic of his dire neighbour Lady Catherine: *Elizabeth tried to unite civility and truth in a few short sentences* (1813/1972: 244). The narrator is here echoing Elizabeth's thoughts – and the difficulty of combining the two qualities – with her own comment on the brevity of her remarks. The short passage exemplifies the difficulties in which the protagonist finds herself, confronted by two people who are so unlike anything she can consider admirable.

Wilson and Sperber note that there is no guarantee that the communication of irony will be successful. It is undoubtedly a risky kind of communication. Since relevance theory assumes that any utterance is maximally relevant, then if irony or other indirection is used it is presumably because the speaker considers that it is the most expeditious in the circumstances. The intention of the speaker must be inferred by the hearer: if the effort is adequately rewarded, then it is reasonable to assume that the utterance is intentional. The processing difficulties caused by an irony are rewarded by the extra cognitive effects it generates. It is a kind of utterance that works by implicature. Context will be very important in determining whether something is interpreted ironically or not. Mrs Bennet in *Pride and Prejudice* would miss the irony in the first sentence of the novel, since it is her opinion that is echoed. Sperber and Wilson consider that irony always expresses disapproval. Sometimes, however, it seems that it may be no more than detachment that is conveyed. This is perhaps the case when Mr Bennet tells his piano playing daughter *You have delighted us long enough* (*Pride and Prejudice*, 1813/1972: 142). Traditional accounts of irony are in difficulties with remarks of this kind, since in most accounts of irony it is assumed that the meaning is the opposite of that expressed. It is not necessarily the opposite of what is said that is conveyed, but a comment on the current situation. Sperber and Wilson's example of an ironic utterance from *Candide* – *When all was over and the rival kings were celebrating their victory with Te Deums in their respective camps* . . . (1995: 241) – is used to show that it cannot mean the opposite of what it says; as they suggest, it is a garden-path utterance which rewards readers by allowing them to reflect on the dishonesty of politicians. The reflections of readers are constrained by the utterance, but they are freer than if Voltaire had made his point by, for example, referring to the immediate political situation, the relevance of which might now be lost. We may recall the end of the first Gulf War, when both sides claimed victory. The 'echoic' element in this presumably refers to the statements of the two kings, echoed by Pangloss and endorsed by Voltaire. This shows the characteristically embedded nature of much irony in literary texts, where it is not always easy to decide on which level a particular irony is to be located.

One difficulty with Sperber and Wilson's account of irony is their requirement, which is crucial to relevance theory, that the first plausible interpretation of an utterance must be the one intended by the speaker. They accept that the overall effect may be quite complex, given the number of weak implicatures that may be accessed and used to enrich an interpretation, but:

(h)aving found an interpretation consistent with the principle of relevance – an interpretation (which may itself be very rich and very vague) which the writer might have thought of as an adequate repayment for the reader's effort – why not go on and look for ever richer interpretations and reverberations? If we are right, and considerations of relevance lie at the heart of verbal communication, such searches go beyond the domain of communication proper. Though the writer might have *wished* to communicate more than the first interpretation tested and found consistent with the principle of relevance, she cannot have rationally *intended* to. (Wilson and Sperber 1989: 116, their emphases)

I argue that literary writers do, at the very least, hope that their readers will go the extra mile, regardless of the principle of relevance. This, of course, is to suggest that relevance is not the only motivation underlying communication: we do it because we enjoy it. Pilkington (2000) allows for much reading and re-reading in order to access as many weak implicatures as the reader is capable of, or has the patience to pursue. There are so many games we play with language, from hyperbole to meiosis, needless use of metaphor, irony, puns and other less respectable activities, that it is hard to avoid the conclusion that we do it because we enjoy it. Otherwise what point is there in Sterne's constant language games?

– 'My sister, mayhap, quoth my uncle *Toby*, does not choose to let a man come so near her ****.' Make this a dash – 'tis an Aposiopesis. – Take the dash away, and write *Backside*, – 'tis Bawdy. – Scratch Backside out, and put *Cover'd way* in, – 'tis a Metaphor. (*Tristram Shandy*, 1760–7/1980: II, 6)

Wilson and Sperber's explanation of ironic utterances is more satisfactory than others because it accounts for cases where the speaker conveys the opposite of what she says; but also for instances where the criticism is muted. The assumption that an ironist intends the opposite of what is said misses the more teasing ironies. The ironist, in this view, always echoes an opinion while dissociating herself from it. The reasons for such dissociation are manifold. This view of irony fits the use of quotation for ironic purposes, and for understatement. They note that, in this view, irony is essentially similar to indirect discourse and other cases of echoic utterances which are all interpretations of thoughts or utterances attributable to someone else (1989: 107).

Wilson and Sperber argue (1989: 103) that the existence of echoic utterances, and the possibility of interpreting any utterance as echoic, strongly suggests that there is no maxim of quality, as Grice and his followers hold. It is certainly the case that we can defuse a difficult situation by saying *I was only being ironic*, but that is a rescue operation; most of the time we surely judge utterances on the basis of the maxims, certainly including quality.

However, Wilson and Sperber's echoic account of irony is not as great an innovation as they seem to suppose. A traditional critic, such as Booth, discusses metaphors used to describe irony, mentioning *eiron*, 'mask' and 'persona' (1974: 33). He points out that the value of such accounts (also implicitly present in the term 'echoic') is that they remind us that there are two voices, or perspectives, and that simple 'translation' from one to the other is impossible. In this respect, irony and metaphor are fundamentally similar. You cannot paraphrase them, because the whole communicative framework is involved, with our assessment of the two voices, their relationship, and ours with them. One of the problems with both Sperber and Wilson and the accounts of irony in the speech act tradition is that they tend to examine decontextualised utterances, and all too often the ironies are very simple. Irony is embedded in a communicative situation, whether spoken or written, and so involves the situation, relationships, and so on. In short, it is a discoursal phenomenon, and needs to be examined in that light. In a broader sense, this criticism can be levelled at relevance theory: it does not consider the sociocultural context in which all language use is negotiated.

It does seem clear that irony depends upon the ironist's ability to see something from two conflicting perspectives. It is less clear that one of the perspectives need be condemned outright, as most commentators seem to require. It is the detachment (perhaps even from both perspectives) that is the marker of irony. A single word or phrase can trigger an ironic interpretation. When Marlow, in *Heart of Darkness*, described the death of his predecessor in the Congo, in an argument over a couple of hens, he says *he had been a couple of years already out there engaged in the noble cause* (1902/1983: 34). Similarly, in *The Secret Agent*, Mrs Verloc is described as a *widow* immediately after she murders her husband (1907/1963: 215). We do not usually call murderesses *widows*. It is clearly a risky textual strategy whether in spoken or written discourse, partly perhaps because of the difficulty in identifying a linguistic element which would help to confirm its presence. It is thus that the onus for recognising ironic intent must lie with the hearer or reader. No amount of theorising has yet, apparently, found a way around this. In the end, it is sensitivity to context which allows us (fallibly) to think that we are dealing with irony. We have all surely experienced attempts at irony which have not been picked up by our interlocutor: the result is embarrassment on both sides. We recall that Cooper (1986) suggests that one of the effects of metaphor is the signal of membership of an 'in' group, competent to recognise the complexities encoded in metaphor. In this respect, irony is similar to metaphor: this has often been recognised as one of irony's effects. We are pleased when we identify an irony, and flattered that we are part of the select group that appreciates it (see Booth 1974; Stockwell 2002).

8.12 OTHER TYPES OF ECHOIC DISCOURSE

The concept of echoic utterances is a fruitful one, which is not limited to irony. It is essentially Bakhtin's hybrid discourse, the combination of two perspectives or voices within a single utterance. This mingling is perhaps clearest in various forms of indirect discourse, where voices of narrator and character are combined within a single syntactic utterance (see Wilson and Sperber 1989: 107, where they suggest that indirect speech and echoic utterances should be treated together as interpretations of an attributed thought or utterance). Indeed, it is not easy to mark a clear distinction between an echoic utterance and FID. In NRTA the effect may be particularly marked: it is often unclear to what extent it is the character's thoughts, and to what extent it is the narrator's obliquely expressed attitude toward them; that is why it is so frequently the *locus* of irony. In the following passage we begin with NRTA in the first sentence. The second and third sentences can be interpreted as either a continuation of the NRTA, or FIT, while the last sentence is clearly the narrator's ironic comment on his thoughts:

> He felt almost heartened, at this tender gesture from her. Possibly she did care about his feelings; possibly he was something more to her than a household object, at her disposal. Oh, the relentless optimism of the man! (Hilary Mantel, *Vacant Possession*, 1986/1987: 96)

No doubt this is why novels are often regarded as being fundamentally ironical. This interpretation of ironic utterances links it clearly to what Pascal (1977) calls the dual voice in his study of FID. It also helps to explain how difficult interpretation of irony can be, owing to the uncertainty of identifying the source of the dual voice, where it begins and where it leaves off.

8.13 IRONY IN FIRST-PERSON NARRATIVES

First-person narratives which are generally regarded as ironic pose interpretive challenges. It is not clear that any theory of irony will permit a reader to decide with any certainty that such a text is to be interpreted in a particular way. Eco (1984, in a discussion of symbolism) considers that it is up to the reader to decide to interpret a particular text symbolically. Arguably the same is true of irony. Wilson and Sperber (1989) note that their explanation of irony offers no clues as to its recognition. It remains a risky strategy, which is liable to misfire. There are, of course, clues as to the intention in most texts commonly regarded as ironic, but it can be particularly difficult to identify these in first-person narratives.

As we have seen, a common source of irony is the conflict between the voices of narrator and character. An obvious source of potential ironies in first-person narratives occurs because of the gap between the narrator and the implied author (see above, Chapter 1). The implied author communicates with the reader 'over the head', as it were, of the narrator, who may be unaware of the ironies generated by his discourse. (Many of these narrators are morally and/or intellectually limited.) I shall consider aspects of Twain's *Huckleberry Finn*, a novel set before the Civil War in a slave-owning state. The narrator/protagonist is a boy, the son of the town drunkard. The beginning offers a clear example of a gap between the narrator and his creator:

> You don't know about me, without you have read a book by the name of *The Adventures of Tom Sawyer*, but that ain't no matter. That book was made by Mr Mark Twain, and he told the truth, mainly. There was things which he stretched, but mainly he told the truth. (1884/1966: 49)

This is not saying the opposite of what is meant; indeed one may take it that Huck means what he says. On the surface level, he is presenting himself as an essentially honest narrator, and implicitly inviting the reader to trust him. The irony resides in the fictional character guaranteeing the veracity of his creator. Huck is, like Twain, mostly honest.

The major moral crisis of the novel revolves around Huck's agreeing to help a runaway slave, one of his few friends. Jim confesses to him that he has run away, because he believes he is about to be sold. Huck is shocked, but keeps his word: *'People would call me a low down Abolitionist and despise me for keeping mum . . .'* (1884/1966: 96). As they journey down the Mississippi toward freedom, Jim is increasingly excited but Huck suffers from a gnawing conscience (145):

> I begun to get it through my head that he *was* most free – and who was to blame for it? Why, *me*. I couldn't get that out of my conscience, no how nor no way . . . It hadn't ever come home to me before, what this thing was that I was doing. But now it did; and it staid with me, and scorched me more and more.

The disparity between Huck's actions and his self-criticism is marked. The voice of his conscience is the product of his society, which he echoes. Some time later Jim is seized and handed over for a reward. Huck is deeply disturbed. He reflects that it would be preferable for Jim to be a slave where he was known, than to be sold on, so he decides to write to his owner. But then he considers the opprobrium that will attach to him for helping a runaway. He realises that, as long as he can conceal his act, he would not suffer disgrace (282–3):

> The more I studied about this, the more my conscience went grinding me, and the more wicked and low-down and ornery I got to feeling. And at last, when it hit me all of a sudden that here was the plain hand of Providence slapping me in the face and letting me know my wickedness was being watched all the time from up there in heaven, whilst I was stealing a poor old woman's nigger that hadn't ever done me no harm, and now was showing me there's One that's always on the lookout, and ain't agoing to allow no such miserable doings to go only just so fur and no further, I most dropped in my tracks I was so scared . . . something inside me kept saying, 'There was the Sunday school, you could a gone to it; and if you'd a done it they'd a learnt you, there, that people that acts as I'd been acting about that nigger goes to everlasting fire.'

He tries to pray, but realises that he cannot because he is not in a state of repentance; he knows that he has no intention of writing to Miss Watson. *You can't pray a lie – I found that out* (283). Finally he writes the letter. *I felt good and all washed clean of sin for the first time I had ever felt so in my life, and I knowed I could pray now* (283). However, he reflects yet again on his adventures with Jim, the kindness Jim had shown him. He looks at the letter (283):

> It was a close place. I took it up, and held it in my hand. I was a trembling, because I'd got to decide, for ever, betwixt two things, and I knowed it. I studied a minute, sort of holding my breath, and then says to myself:
> 'All right then, I'll *go* to hell' – and tore it up.

Towards the end of the novel he is joined by his old friend Tom Sawyer, who insists on helping with the project of freeing Jim (305):

> That was the thing that was too many for me. Here was a boy that was respectable, and well brung up; and had a character to lose . . . and yet here he was without any more pride, or rightness, or feeling, than to stoop to this business, and make himself a shame, and his family a shame before everybody.

The final irony comes when it is revealed that Jim's owner has died, and freed him in her will. Huck is certainly aware of both the law and the teachings of the church – witness his references to providence, and his understanding of the nature of repentance. He has a pretty subtle understanding of that issue. The sad irony is that Huck lacks the self-confidence to reject the views of his society: he ignores them, but blames himself as evil for doing so. He feels he has nothing to lose, but cannot understand why Tom Sawyer is prepared to help Jim. And his innate goodness and sense is not sufficient to allow him to understand why Jim says that once he is free, he will try to buy his children. If the owner will not sell, he will find an abolitionist to rescue them from slavery. Set against Huck and his moral vision is the rest of society: the novel aligns God, Sunday school and *civilisation*, which is not at its best in a church service attended by two feuding families, all carrying guns: *It was pretty ornery preaching – all about brotherly love, and such-like tiresomeness . . .* (169). The sermon is duly praised by the congregation, but the feud breaks out again the same day, killing several.

Huck's acts are good, and his moral judgements are, on the whole, correct; they are juxtaposed to a thoroughly corrupt society, reflected in his 'conscience', whose promptings he rejects. Huck has the dual vision required of an ironist but he lacks the maturity to turn it into irony. Twain's attack on society is the more powerful for being delivered by a young, uneducated narrator: the ironies should not be lost on the reader. At the end of the novel another good-hearted woman tries to take him in hand: *But I reckon I got to light out for the Territory . . . because Aunt Sally she's going to adopt me and sivilise me and I can't stand it. I been there before* (369). In order to appreciate the ironies in this text we compare the value systems we hold, those of Huck, his society, and the implied author. It is the disparities between these that are the source of irony, together with the implicit attack on Southern society, and the devastating view of the church; it is Huck's difficulty in abandoning the teachings of church and society, though they run counter to his best instincts, that give rise to the major ironies in the novel.

Huck is unaware of the effect he has upon his readers. Many first-person narrators have this kind of innocence; an example is Spark's narrator in 'You Should Have Seen the Mess' (1958/1987). This short story is an autobiographical essay. There is nothing to suggest why the protagonist chose to write it, and she reveals her attitudes in an unself–conscious way. Her sole criterion for judging things or people is cleanliness (summed up in the title, so it is no guide to the implied author's views). The reader may well conclude that the implied author is being highly ironic at the expense of the social and educational system which produced this young woman. However, if the reader shared her prejudices and upbringing, the ironies might well remain undetected: the story would fit such a reader's preconceptions and judgements. The only direct hints in the text are reactions of other people to the young woman: for instance, an old woman living in a fourteenth-century cottage is amused at the suggestion that she should ask the council to rehouse her. (Again, this is a matter of cultural assumptions: Lorna cannot understand that this could be regarded as a desirable residence, even without indoor plumbing.) She tells us that she was good at English in school, though her language belies this. These are the few hints that suggest that the implied author does not endorse her views. A reader who shared her values would see no irony. Yet again, it reminds us that all the codes, standards, attitudes in society are implicated in irony. If we share the views of the implied author, we may find the text deliciously ironical. If not, we may not. It is one of the pleasures of irony.

Spark uses the short story to attack the values of the society that produced her protagonist, and the thoroughly immature young woman herself. Twain also uses Huck to attack the society of which he is a peripheral member, but supports Huck. In both cases, the force of the ironic attack is on the societies depicted. Twain likes Huck; Spark probably does not care for her character.

8.14 IRONY: CONCLUSION

There seems to be no single approach to the slippery phenomenon of irony that is always helpful to its elucidation or analysis. What does seem clear is that irony always involves the juxtaposition of two perspectives on a topic. To that extent Wilson and Sperber are right to emphasise the element of dissociation characteristic of irony, but it does not seem to me that it is also necessary that it express disapprobation. If it is true that such juxtaposition is essential to irony, then it is clear that almost any instance of FID is potentially ironic. That might be a most powerful motivation for using the device, and explain its prevalence.

Irony is a complex phenomenon, which engages us on various levels. If we appreciate it, we feel ourselves to be part of the 'in-group' addressed, and are therefore not only entertained, but flattered. It engages us more deeply in the text. If we miss the irony, it is a fairly significant face threatening act, to say nothing of the misreading and so misinterpretation of the text. Given how often irony does misfire (at least in spoken language), it is clear that irony is a thoroughly dangerous strategy. It is preeminently a face threatening act. Recognition of irony promotes solidarity; when it is missed, it promotes exclusion. Nevertheless, the sheer enjoyment that irony offers guarantees that we continue to risk much to use it. It can be a fruitful way of improving interpersonal relations by promoting feelings of intimacy, and flattering us as being competent to recognise it (see Booth 1974; Stockwell 2002).

8.15 ECHOIC DISCOURSE AND PARODY

Parody is a complex phenomenon, and depends much upon the reader's knowledge, memory and interpretive skills. It is pre-eminently echoic; and this suggests that it can fruitfully be considered in the light of relevance theory (see Wilson and Sperber 1989: 104). The essential difference between irony and parody is that parody relates to the linguistic form of an utterance, whereas most cases of irony relate to the context of the utterance: at the least, it is often extra- or non-linguistic. They consider that in both cases the speaker is dissociating herself, or is critical of the item parodied or ironised. It is not clear, particularly in the case of parody, that this is invariably the case. They perhaps overstate this way of looking at irony (and indeed parody.) It seems often to be the case that ironists and parodists in particular are simply playing games with language. Is the following irony, parody or both? *On the last day of summer Mrs Bohannon fell in love. The poplars, fallaciously pathetic, looked horrified, their branches rising on the wind like startled hair, and a pilgrim cloud wept a few chill tears* (Ellis, *The Other Side of the Fire*, 1983/1985: 7). It seems to me that it combines both, so anticipating the contents of the novel.

The echoic approach also illuminates what happens when intertextuality is important in a text. Intertextuality is sometimes close to parody. It might seem obvious that all intertextuality is inherently echoic: it need not necessarily be ironic. On a large scale, Ellis' *The Other Side of the Fire* is echoic, ironic and parodic. The parody works on the linguistic level as well as through the action. It is a modern retelling of the legend of Hippolytus (though the young man escapes with his life). The fervent pursuit by the woman who falls in love with her stepson is given an added twist by his homosexuality. Evvie, another character in this novel, is an undergraduate who divides her time between writing essays on Horace, and a Mills and Boon style romance intended to make her fortune. She is therefore an apprentice author in the fields of academic discourse and fiction writing. First, a sample of her novel:

> 'He strode feverishly the wide length of the Great Hall. On the vast table the tall candles guttered fitfully in the icy draught that blew through the ancient arras . . .' 'Cool it,' said Evvie, crossing out 'arras' and substituting 'broken panes in the mullioned windows.' . . . He glared wildly around until his eye fell on the regimental sword that hung above the massive fireplace . . .' 'Dashed uncomfortable,' muttered Evvie, but she left it there. (Ellis 1983/1985: 85)

The reader hardly needs to be told that he is the victim of frustrated love. Notable features of the style here include the heavy use of modifiers: adverbs and adjectives are prominent. *Blew* is the only verb without an adverb; *eye* the only noun without an adjective (see Nash 1990 for a study of this style.) The adjectives are predominantly interpersonal epithets in that they convey the speaker's attitude (see Halliday 1985: 163). (There is also the oddity of the phrase *the wide length*, since *wide* normally refers to the shorter dimension, and *length* to the longer one.) The syntax is straightforward, with a predominance of subjects in initial position in the sentences (except for the second, where an adjunct occupies the first position). There is a single relative clause: *that blew through the ancient arras*. The language is trite, but entirely appropriate to its purpose.

Next, a sample of Evvie in academic mode:

'The Victorians', began Evvie, 'steeped as they were in the Romantic and evangel-
ical movements, despised, because they did not understand, those arts of rhetoric
that the eighteenth century had found congenial. To the Victorians sincerity rather
than art was the hallmark of great poetry, just as belief, or at any rate agonising
doubt, was the hallmark of religion. Than Virgil or Lucretius no poets were more
sincere; and even such love-lorn elegists as Propertius and Catullus could be
admired without restraint, for their agonies and ecstasies, however sordid, were
clearly founded in experience and truth . . . These are the poets who appeal to a
modern taste, as they appealed to the mind of the eighteenth century; but to the
Victorians, who were betwixt and between, they did not seem quite to reach up
to that level of high seriousness at which art, religion and love were supposed to
join forces.' (1983/1985: 73)

The style of these two passages is highly contrastive. Evvie's academic prose is
complex, involving subordination, causal constructions and syntactical inversion.
The lexis is naturally also very different (though it is worth noting that both texts are
about emotions). The verbs predominantly refer to mental processes (*understand,
despise, admire, appeal*), in contrast to the novel, where the reader has to infer that
the laird is thinking from his physical activity. Similarly, references to the loves of the
Roman poets are mentioned in abstract terms: *agony and ecstasy, experience and truth*.
This text is also marked by trite metaphors: *steeped, hallmark* are both used in non-
literal senses, and in contexts that are highly predictable. Evvie is not insensitive to
dead metaphors in context: she notes, in her novel, the incongruous effect of his *eye
fell on the regimental sword*. The trite language, including the dead metaphors, of both
texts has a pragmatic function: it situates the reader in the appropriate context; it tells
us what kind of text we are reading, and therefore how we should approach it.

Thus we have stylistic contrasts which suggest the contrasting purposes and audiences for each text. Both texts reflect the different purposes they are designed to serve;
they contribute to the polyphonic effect of the novel in which they are embedded,
in Bakhtinian terms, and so illuminate the complex society that gives rise to such
texts. Both these styles contrast with the narrative style of the fiction in which these
texts are embedded. But, perhaps more interestingly, the novel in which they are
embedded itself deals with *agonies and ecstasies*, though of a type which would hardly
be likely to be acceptable to the editors of women's romances. Ellis' style in her own
fiction avoids the stylistic infelicities of her creature: the novel can be regarded as a
critique of the styles she parodies. In this way, the novel is echoic in the Bakhtinian
sense, reflecting the diversity of the society itself. It will be seen that this book parodies a number of genres including the 'young artist' type of novel. In this respect also,
it is a clear example of Bakhtin's heteroglossic discourse. As he points out (1981:
301), it is particularly characteristic of comic novels.

Parody is often ludic: witness the regular feature in *The Spectator*. It may exclude
some of its potential audience (just as irony does), often because the reader fails to
recognise the source. The same problem applies to intertextual references in general
(which I here understand to refer to the echo or quotation of other literary texts).

The echo or quotation of another literary work, because of the displacement of context, can have a parodic effect. For example: *Some men are born to country houses, some achieve country houses, others have country houses thrust upon them* (Wodehouse, *Company for Henry*, 1967/1980: 28). Sometimes, of course, the source is made clear in the text (which might suggest a lack of confidence in the reader). Wodehouse has no such qualms.

Another use of parody can be rather cruel in revealing the mind of a character. In *Ulysses* (1922/1968: 346) Joyce parodies the style of women's magazines. A group of young women are looking after some small children. One of them, Gerty, is gradually focalised. The narrator is displaced by character focalisation, in the same parodic style, interspersed with her spoken language. The implicature is that Gerty thinks in the style of the magazines she reads, though she has the sense not to speak in that manner. Essentially a passage of NRTA with touches of FIT shows the mind of a character: she is wholly without independent personality, thinking in the terms suggested by her reading. A possible implicature is that this highly derivative language reflects accurately her reading, her limited intelligence, and how she thinks. In that sense, the language of the magazines has become her language, part of her idiolect. The combination of her thoughts (FIT) and the narrator's parodic language are an example of Bakhtin's *double oriented speech*. That is, the words can be attributed to both narrator and character. At the same time it parodies the language of women's magazines. Individual readers will no doubt differ in their interpretation of these effects: does Gerty think in the same terms as the magazines she reads, or is the narrator only showing the kinds of influence on her thinking (which is clear in her thoughts on iron jelloids, female pills and so on)? The focalisation here is marked by the deictic *those, that*. Parts are clearly in FIT: the question is whether most of the passage is. In contrast, when she considers the arguments with her friends, the (highly contrastive) lexis and syntax suggest her normal speaking voice. The implicatures of this style are interesting. They suggest a character whose derivative thoughts come from her reading: her personality is shaped by her favourite magazines. (I am not allowed to quote from Joyce, so borrow the book from a library!)

8.16   PARODY: CONCLUSION

Parody, a pre-eminent case of echoic discourse, is not only entertaining, but often serves as a critique of the society depicted.

8.17   CONCLUSION

Metaphor, irony and parody all have a strongly interpersonal function. All are potentially FTAs, with the reward – if we appreciate the effect – of being counted amongst the elect (if not, of course, we are excluded, which probably means we will not return to that fiction). All are challenging to the reader, making demands on our encyclopaedic knowledge, and our capacity to assimilate the local effects they create into our overall interpretation of the text. Irony and parody encode two perspectives, inviting us to disentangle them. All contribute to creating the 'tone' of the fictions in which they occur; most of them have a playful element – the sheer joy in their creation and appreciation. In the next chapter I will consider symbolism, which, like the topics discussed here, places much responsibility for interpretation on the reader, thus promoting engagement with the text.

Chapter 9

Symbolism

9.1 INTRODUCTION

I shall here consider first a pragmatic approach to symbolism. Then, I shall discuss
some possible symbolic readings of fictional texts, in order to exemplify the theory,
and then illustrate some of its limitations. These limitations are perhaps inherent to
any consideration of a textual feature whose interpretation depends on rather more
than the immediate context of utterance.

9.2 THEORY

An interesting pragmatic approach to symbolism is offered by Eco (1984). His suggestions about the creation and reception of symbol place it firmly in the interpersonal context which characterises pragmatic approaches to interpretation. We have
noted the ubiquity of the Gricean maxims. Indeed, if Grice is correct and, in broad
terms, it is difficult to imagine that something like the co-operative principle does
not guide our normal interpretation of discourse, it is perhaps not surprising that
Eco approaches symbolism via the maxims. The use of the Gricean maxims for the
interpretation of symbolism 'naturalises' it, showing that it forms part of the normal
communicative resources we use in interaction. What Eco offers is his view of how
symbolism 'works' and a possible explanation of why it is used. This approach does
not place major constraints on interpretation; what it does is to suggest how and why
we arrive at symbolic readings, and even why we decide that it is an appropriate
reading strategy to adopt. Indeed, it is an essential part of Eco's view that readers will
vary in their interpretations according to their encyclopaedic knowledge and, generally, what they are able to bring to the text, in the way of deriving appropriate implicatures via the Gricean maxims. It is therefore an approach that will not appeal to
those who, like Sperber and Wilson, think that one of the main deficiencies of the
Gricean maxims is that insufficient constraints are placed upon the implicatures
which may be derived from them. This they consider to be irrational and contrary
to how language works (Sperber and Wilson 1995: 200). The point, however, is that
symbol is allusive and elusive; it is not easy to pin down, and, as Eco stresses, it suggests, rather than making an explicit statement. In that respect, it works in a way

close to what Sperber and Wilson describe as 'poetic effects' (1995: 236–7; see Chapter 7 of this book).

Eco's definition of symbol is narrow. In his analysis, a symbol is idiolectal, that is, it has value only in its context: anything else is only an emblem, or the quotation of a previously existing symbol. Thus many items that are commonly described as symbols are, for him, emblems, or quotations of a symbol. Many such emblems are visual rather than verbal; they are particularly common in the visual arts, as well as in daily life – from crosses on churches to road markings, Remembrance Day poppies, and mourning colours are not symbols, but signs with a single clear meaning, though the meanings are culturally conditioned. Unlike metonymic emblems, such as a skull on a grave, they are accessible only to members of a particular cultural community. Eco's definition of symbol also excludes using the term in relation to items such as fire, which is often interpreted to signify domestic comfort, warmth and hospitality. It can equally represent destruction, according to the context in which it is found. These meanings are conventionalised, and therefore not symbolic. In Golding's *Lord of the Flies* (1954/1958) the children light a signal fire in the hope of being rescued from their island. Ironically, help comes when the island has been set alight with murderous intent. At least two of the conventionalised values of 'fire' are thus encoded here: neither, as it stands, is symbolic in Eco's terms.

In contrast to the emblem, a true symbol for Eco offers a range of indeterminate meanings, which neither the author nor the receiver is able to pin down fully. He argues that the potential for a symbolic interpretation is triggered by an apparent violation of one or more of the maxims – particularly those of quantity, manner or relation. An excessive attention to some textual detail, which appears to be insufficiently motivated by the surrounding co-text and the stylistic norms of the text, invites symbolic interpretation on the grounds that it is otherwise unjustifiable. Symbolism is thus seen as an example of textual implicature, which invites the reader to explore possible meanings (and the motivation for encoding them allusively) in the usual way. He stresses that a symbolic interpretation is an optional extension of meaning. A symbolic passage is always interpretable on a literal level: it is up to the reader, on the basis of experience of the text, the genre, and encyclopaedic knowledge, to go further. The violation of one or more of the maxims results in an 'over-encoding' of meanings. A further feature of symbols, as suggested by their optionality, is that the text does not require a symbolic interpretation to be understood: like allegory, to which Eco compares it, the text remains interpretable on a literal level. Allegory is, of course, much more clear-cut: the Slough of Despond and Mr Christian do not invite interpretative freedom. One feature shared by allegory and symbol is that both usually require some cultural knowledge to interpret them. Symbolism, on the other hand, is the result of interaction between text and reader; it is an optional interpretative strategy which the reader may choose to adopt. In this respect it contrasts with, for example, metaphor, which is constructed by the author and requires a non-literal interpretation to be understood at all.

9.3 EXEMPLIFICATION

The above account of this approach to symbolism shows that it is essentially dependent upon the reader's sensitivity to the maxims. One problem, of course, is that readers are individuals, and decisions about whether or not a maxim has been exploited will vary from one reader to another, as – to some extent at least – will their encyclopaedic knowledge, including their experience of other texts and cultural factors which may be relevant to interpretation. Consider this passage from Hemingway's 'The Snows of Kilimanjaro'. This novella has two layers of narrative. On the outer level, Harry, the protagonist, is dying. He recollects various episodes of his past, which he had intended to turn into stories, but had avoided writing. Thus, on the outer level of narrative, Harry is a character-focaliser almost throughout, and on the inner level he is narrator. Thus mentally, if not physically, he dies re-established as a writer, at least in his own mind. One of these passages represents what is apparently his earliest memory:

> There was a log house, chinked white with mortar, on a hill above the lake. There was a bell on a pole by the door to call the people in to meals. Behind the house were fields, and behind the fields was the timber. A line of lombardy poplars ran from the house to the dock. Other poplars ran along the point. A road went up to the hills above the edge of the timber and along that road he picked blackberries. Then that log house was burned down and all the guns that had been on the deer foot racks above the open fireplace were burned and afterwards their barrels, with the lead melted in the magazines, and the stocks burned away, lay out on the heap of ashes that were used to make lye for the big iron soap kettles, and you asked Grandfather if you could have them to play with, and he said, no. You see they were his guns still and he never bought any others. Nor did he hunt any more. The house was rebuilt out of lumber now and painted white and from its porch you saw the poplars and the lake beyond; but there were never any more guns. The barrels of the guns that had hung on the deer feet on the wall of the log house lay out there on the heap of ashes and no one ever touched them. (Hemingway, 'The Snows of Kilimanjaro', 1939/1964: 456)

What is most striking about this passage is the emphasis placed upon the guns, which occupy a large proportion of the text. Syntactically, the repeated description of the guns is marked off from the rest of the passage by heavy use of recursive structures in a post-nominal position, where the rest of the paragraph is marked by simple syntax and short sentences. These descriptions violate the maxim of quantity (too much) and manner (repetition, and deviation from the textual norm, as recursion is not common elsewhere in this text); relation is more questionable: relevant to whom? It is notable too that the guns form part of the domestic interior; nothing is said of their function. Harry's youth is suggested not only by the fact that he wants the gun barrels to play with, but that they are identified only by their location – not by name as an adult might do. The memory is focalised in the child, and the adult narrator cannot, or will not, interpret it, for himself or the reader. The fragment of (presumably) free direct discourse (*you see they were his guns still*) points also to childhood memories, with a puzzled question to an adult, and a reply which would not impose on a rabbit. For the child, the guns are clearly numinous, but it is not easy to say what they might represent: adulthood? masculinity? the world of which he is not yet part, but expects to join? The memory might represent the innocence of lost childhood, in which guns are part of the interior of a house, and are 'played with', not used for killing. The guns might also suggest the social role of the grandfather in protecting and providing for the family. It seems that Harry as protagonist does not understand why he is not allowed to play with the guns; as narrator no doubt he does understand. In this respect, the guns seem to be symbolic in Eco's sense: the narrator cannot, or will not, spell out what they mean; the reader can guess something of their significance from the juxtaposition of this memory with the next paragraph, which details the suicide of a hotel proprietor who is unable to continue his business when inflation wipes out the money he had saved to open in the new season. The implicature of the juxtaposition suggests an interpretation on the lines that for grandfather the loss of his guns was an equivalent disaster. One might then interpret grandfather's survival as a kind of death in life (possibly analogous to the gangrene that is killing Harry). The reader may draw analogies between Harry's fate and that of the grandfather; she may possibly think of destroyed lives, and infer that the grandfather feels that he has outlived his usefulness with the end of the pioneering life in the American West, or simply the destruction wrought by the passage of time. But none of these possible values is stated explicitly in the text.

Following Eco, one can propose that the reader is free to assign whatever meanings seem relevant to the guns in interpreting this passage. He writes of a 'nebula' of possible interpretations (1984: 161), and argues that in symbolism the writer has no intention of spelling out what he means. The child protagonist, to judge by the embedded dialogue, is puzzled and uncomprehending. But it is clear that the amount of space devoted to the guns, and the fact that they are described only as part of the contents of the house, does satisfy Eco's requirement of being pragmatically 'uneconomic'. One should note that the maxims do no more than provide an explanation of the mechanism whereby we recognise the possibility of symbolic reading of a text: the reading itself will depend upon the reader's encyclopaedic knowledge, and judgements as to whether or not the maxims of manner and relation in particular have been exploited here. Why, unless to draw special attention to the guns, should the syntax change, and so much space be devoted to them? The motivation for using a symbolic mode in a context such as this may be twofold. On the one hand, Harry may find it unnecessary, and even painful, to analyse his emotions and memories in detail. From a narratorial perspective, in a text such as this, which is characteristic of Hemingway's style in avoiding explicit commentary and emotive comments (it corresponds to Simpson's B (N) neutral style), it gives the reader free rein to consider the emotional impact the memory holds for Harry.

In his account of symbol, Eco insists upon a distinction between genuine symbols and other signs, which are not unique to a particular textual environment. Thus what are commonly accounted as symbols (such as the attributes of saints in Christian iconography, or mourning colours) are not, in his terms, symbolic. In the short story considered here, there are numerous examples of such signs. Vultures surround the dying man; and when he realises the imminence of his death it was as *a sudden evil-smelling emptiness and the odd thing was that the hyena slipped lightly along the edge of it* (1939/1964: 453) As he recedes into unconsciousness, death comes *and rested its head on the foot of the cot and he could smell its breath . . .* (461). The association between hyenas and death is clear – like vultures, they are scavengers.

The man then imagines that the plane which was to have taken him to hospital comes, and he is flown to the summit of Kilimanjaro. Helen, his partner, is awakened by the cry of the hyena to find him dead in his cot. In the epigraph to the story, we are told that Kilimanjaro is the Masai House of God, and that there is the dried and frozen carcass of a leopard near the summit. *No one has explained what the leopard was seeking at that altitude* (443). The reader might establish a range of analogies between Harry and the leopard: both die outside their normal situations; both are *seeking* something (though only the reader is aware of this). One might therefore make symbolic associations between Harry and the leopard, and conclude that Harry, having 'written' in the last hours of his life, has redeemed himself, and so is worthy of the 'House of God'; (leopards are viewed as types of Christ in medieval bestiaries). On the other hand, one might stress the hyena, whose cry awakens Helen when he dies. When, earlier in the day, he engages in a period of self-examination and repentance he thinks: *What was his talent anyway? It was a talent all right but instead of using it he had traded on it* (450). He echoes the Parable of the Talents in St Matthew's Gospel, where the servant who does not double his lord's money is cast into outer darkness; the hyena in this story is *just outside the range of the fire* (461). This suggests another possible range of symbolic interpretations of the text: the one that Harry gives to his experience of death, in which he dies justified and goes to the House of God, versus the alternative, in which, like the hyena and unprofitable servant, he is cast into outer darkness (Matt. 25: 30).

It is interesting that Eco should use Grice to suggest ways in which symbolism may operate in texts. Because of the nature of implicature, and the heavy reliance any such use of the maxims must place on the reader's encyclopaedic knowledge, it is not difficult to see why symbolism remains a slippery and intractable area. One might conclude that the grandfather's guns are susceptible to an interpretation along the lines of the maxims, without coming to a conclusion either as to their precise significance to the reader, Harry, or indeed the grandfather. On the other hand, the explication of possible values attaching to the hyena and leopard in the interpretation may seem too clear and explicit to warrant the use of the term symbol as Eco defines it.

9.4 CHARACTER AS SOURCE OF SYMBOLISM

Eco's account of symbolism seems to imply that it is most commonly found in the narrator's voice in a narrative, but this is not always the case, though it is perhaps the commonest. I shall now consider examples of symbolism where focalisation is rooted in a character. An example of a character 'reading' symbolically may be found in 'The

Snows of Kilimanjaro' when Harry says: '*Never believe any of that about a scythe and a skull,*' he told her. '*It can be two bicycle policemen as easily, or be a bird. Or it can have a wide snout like a hyena*' (1939/1964: 461). The remark, made shortly before he slips into unconsciousness, is perhaps not said aloud, since his companion does not respond. It would in any case have been opaque to her; the reader understands the references to bicycle policemen, who occur in his memories of Paris, though they are not obviously linked to death; they may therefore be symbolic here. The vultures around the camp have been mentioned, as has the hyena, which, finally dislimns, is one of the forms in which death appears to Harry (461). As scavengers, vultures and hyenas are metonymically associated with death, and they are emblematic rather than symbolic. As with any implicature, much depends on the reader's ability to pick up and interpret. There is no guarantee of correct interpretation. This is equally the case with many conversational implicatures in ordinary discourse, which interlocutors may fail to pick up.

Another case of a character creating symbols is found in Woolf's *To the Lighthouse*, which is dense with metonyms, metaphors and other tropes. The narrator guides the reader through the thoughts of the characters, offering comment and interpretation. This 'narrated monologue', as Cohn (1979) labels it, guides the reader through the intricacies of the thoughts and memories of the characters. At the beginning of the novel the narrator associates Mr Ramsay with sharp, cutting instruments, and makes clear that James, in particular, wishes that he could attack his father with a knife or axe. Towards the end of the novel, James, now an adolescent, recalls allusively the moment when his father so annoyed him:

> in what garden did all this happen . . . Something, he remembered, stayed and darkened over him, would not move; something flourished up in the air, something arid and sharp descended even there, like a blade, a scimitar, smiting through the leaves and flowers even of that happy world and making them shrivel and fall. 'It will rain,' he remembered his father saying. 'You won't be able to go to the Lighthouse.' (1927/1964: 210)

It is questionable whether one can apply the co-operative principle to one's inner thoughts. To the thinker, clearly, the maxim of relation is fulfilled, and apparently excessive dwelling on one thing or another may violate the maxim of quantity for the reader – but surely not for the thinker. The pact, if such it be, that the CP be observed, exists at the higher level, in the relationship between narrator and reader. In novels of the type of *To the Lighthouse*, the narrator is presumed to be obeying the CP, and certainly exercises, as all narrators do, powers to reveal or conceal what a character is thinking. Therefore the reader can reasonably assume that the thoughts of the character are, finally, relevant and can be used in interpretation.

Grice's maxims are conversational: it is neither easy nor always rewarding to attempt to apply them to the thoughts of characters, even when, as in this case, they are relatively focused. But some observations can be made, in the light of the maxims, on the grounds that, if they condition the way we talk to each other, they may not be wholly irrelevant to the way we develop our thoughts. One must always bear in mind that the obsessions that Woolf charts for many of her characters are interpretable in context, and they have the function of showing the reader what a character is like. What does emerge here is the relevance to James of his early memories: not only that, but his recollections of the emotion he felt are encoded both in the language the narrator has used at the beginning of the novel to describe them – the new element is the wheel crushing the foot – and in the recognition of its innocence. Arguably, this is at least quasi-symbolic: James is grappling with his developing feelings of sympathy for his father, and a growing understanding of Mr Ramsay's emotional immaturity which lessens his responsibility for his callous behaviour.

9.5 SYMBOL ON THE NARRATORIAL LEVEL

A nudge towards symbolic interpretation in Golding's *Lord of the Flies* is found in the table of contents, where generic noun phrases occur: 'Fire on the Mountain', 'Huts on the Beach', 'Painted Faces and Long Hair', 'Beast From Water', 'Beast from Air', 'Shadows and Tall Trees', 'Gift for the Darkness', 'Cry of the Hunters'. This contrasts with the other chapter headings. The degree of deviation from the norms varies, but 'Gift for the Darkness' and 'Cry of the Hunters' both seem to expect the indefinite and definite article respectively, while 'Huts on the Beach' and 'Painted Faces and Long Hair' are not deviant at all. 'Fire on the Mountain', 'Beast from Water' and 'Beast from Air' seem to point to more than their literal meanings – we would normally expect not a generic here, but an article preceding the noun.

Golding's *Lord of the Flies* shows how naturalistic elements are open to an optional symbolic interpretation. The boys who have crashed onto a desert island find a conch; when it is blown, the boys assemble. It is natural that they should elect Ralph, who has the conch, their leader. The conch immediately assumes the function of the mace in regulating their meetings: the child holding the conch has the right to the floor. This is symbolic in a conventional sense (but not in Eco's), and one which culture has conditioned readers to accept without particular thought. The conch is a natural item, which assumes cultural significance by its use and analogy with the mace. Piggy's glasses come closer to assuming a symbolic meaning. For him, they are simply essential to his life. They are, of course, the product of civilisation (like the mace); they are, generally speaking, of practical rather than symbolic value, though in appropriate contexts they may carry a nebula of associations (scholarship, and so on). They denote the attention of parents or the state to the health and comfort of a small boy. The children use them to light the fire. When Jack steals them, the boys initially assume he had come for the conch (thus incidentally suggesting their understanding of its value), but, for Jack, the glasses have taken its place, and represent his dominion: *The chief led them, trotting steadily, exulting in his achievement. He was a chief now in truth; and he made stabbing motions with his spear. From his left hand dangled Piggy's broken glasses* (1954/1958: 160). It is not a complex symbol, and perhaps Eco would reject it as being symbolic at all, but the reader can attribute multiple meanings to the spectacles, particularly if they are considered in connection with the conch. From Jack's perspective, they are, at the very least, emblematic of his power. He rejects the value of the conch.

Just before Piggy is murdered, he goes to the Tribe to demand the return of his glasses, carrying the conch, whose authority they no longer recognise: *Piggy lifted the white, magic shell* (171). Then, as the boys confront each other, Ralph and Piggy stand together, Piggy holding out *the talisman, the fragile, shining beauty of the shell . . .* Another boy dislodges a stone. *The rock struck Piggy a glancing blow from chin to knee: the conch exploded into a thousand white fragments and ceased to exist* (172). As is the case with many descriptions, these could be held to violate the maxim of quantity: the reader probably knows what a conch looks like; the *magic* aspect has been suggested already in the narrative. More significant perhaps is the deflection of attention from the death of Piggy to the destruction of the conch. This strongly suggests its importance; the fragility of the conch links it metaphorically to the rule of law and the parliamentary procedures with which it is already associated via the mace. Since this interpretation depends on cultural knowledge, it seems to fall clearly into what Eco regards as emblem, rather than symbol. The reader reaches the interpretation, as with true symbolism, through the Gricean maxims: particularly, in this case, the maxim of quantity (it seems extraordinary that more attention should focus on the destruction of the conch than on the death of Piggy) and manner – the description is very full. The maxim of relation must be invoked also, to understand why the narrator considers that this emphasis is the most appropriate. It is only at the very end of the novel that Piggy's death is truly acknowledged, in the NRTA of Ralph's thoughts, when he is able to weep *for the end of innocence, the darkness of man's heart, and the fall through the air of the true, wise friend called Piggy* (192).

For Jack, the glasses clearly represent his dominion. The essential difference between the conch and Piggy's spectacles lies in the fact that the conch has, through its similarity to the mace, associations for the reader which are a generally acknowledged part of the culture; the glasses are much more open to various interpretations, the richness of which will vary from one reader to another. There are interesting features to the history of the glasses. They are essential to Piggy; they are used to start the fire. Once stolen, they embody Jack's chieftainship. Not only that: Piggy refuses to acknowledge the fact of Simon's murder until his glasses are stolen. It is only then that Piggy is able to confront the truth about his death (162). This emphasises the extreme of violence in both cases, and enhances our sense of the brutality of the theft.

The connection between power and Piggy's spectacles is suggested most explicitly at the very end of the novel, when the officer sees Jack, who decides not to claim leadership of the boys: *A little boy who wore the remains of an extraordinary black cap on his red hair and who carried the remains of a pair of spectacles at his waist, started forward, then changed his mind and stood still* (191). What is interesting about the glasses is precisely that, to an outsider, they have no meaning. The naval officer merely notices them, without understanding the value they have acquired, just as he fails to recognise that the *extraordinary black cap* Jack is wearing was part of his uniform as a chorister. Symbols, then, are very much in the eye of the beholder. They remain, to some, entirely without special value.

The description of Jack is balanced by that of the officer: *It was a white-topped cap, and above the green shade of the peak was a crown, an anchor, gold foliage. [Ralph] saw white drill, epaulettes, a revolver, a row of gilt buttons down the front of a uniform* (190). The revolver is a mark of authority, just as the glasses are when worn at Jack's waist. The revolver is at least useful, whereas Piggy's glasses, for Jack and his tribe, have only a symbolic value. The theft of the glasses has changed their meaning. The maxim of manner can be invoked here: the description of the boy and the officer are sufficiently similar (caps, item at waist) to allow the reader to move beyond the text to consider the comparable roles played by the two in their respective situations. This makes the end of the novel particularly dark; the *deus ex machina* who arrives to rescue the boys can only return them to the world which, at the beginning of the novel, we are told had been destroyed, apparently by atomic weapons. The boys have systematically destroyed their island refuge; Jack is as dictatorial as any adult.

Lord of the Flies begins with the striking appearance of Jack's choristers, still dressed as though in the cloister, in their cloaks and caps. This is, at least, emblematic of their role in society at home; it has a more immediate effect in that Jack is able to maintain discipline over the choir, and this is one of the sources of the destruction of their idyllic time on the island. This description is balanced by the appearance of the officer at the end. The fiction suggests that the world the boys knew has been destroyed by an atomic war (78). Yet the naval officer – who is on duty – is wearing dress whites, with gold epaulettes. He is seen by Ralph (whose father is a naval officer), and may suggest an inversion of the choristers at the beginning of the novel. The officer brings salvation from the burning island. Yet no reading of the text can be favourable to military might. The descriptions of clothes – perhaps particularly in a fiction where most of the characters are more or less naked for much of the time – seems a clear case of over-encoding in Eco's terms. Gricean maxims, particularly those of quantity and relation, are also invoked in this interpretation. (Clothing is regularly used by authors as a means of characterisation, and to indicate social situations and relationships, so this goes only a little further than a reader might expect.) The impetus to interpret the clothing symbolically in this context is, as Eco stresses, always an optional reading. It makes sense of the text because, in both cases, the narrator seems to adopt a perspective aligned with Ralph, and the sighting of the choristers and the naval officer are, for him, significant moments. It seems that the children's rescue is formulated in terms which are very much part of the schema of rescue from desert islands (at least, at the time this novel was written). What it lacks in verisimilitude, it gains in thematic importance.

The ends of novels often achieve closure by integrating and adumbrating reinterpretations of earlier parts of the fiction. This activity may in itself lead to varying interpretations of the end of the novel. The end of this fiction initially seems up-beat. The boys are rescued. If Europe has been destroyed by war, it is, on the one hand, improbable that the Navy would be cruising peacefully around desert islands; on the other hand, the whole course of the novel suggests that we should look hard at admired traditions and aspects of British culture. The naval officer, echoing the unreflective attitudes of *The Coral Island*, expected that British boys would have coped better with the situation. Indeed, the boys themselves have this attitude at the beginning: *'After all, we're not savages. We're English, and the English are best at everything'* (42). The Navy is presented as the instrument of rescue, but its primary function is warlike; it is war that has brought them to the island in the first place. Similarly, the choir when it appears on the beach, still dressed in its cloaks and caps as though in the cathedral precincts, not only suggests a characteristic element of English culture, but is also an obvious reminder of religious values. The discipline, which is, no doubt, essential to a cathedral choir, is rapidly turned to evil by Jack, who is accustomed to the unwavering obedience of the other choristers, and turns it to his own ends. Jack also, perhaps predictably, abandons his leadership role when adult authority reasserts itself. Navy and choir may represent, metonymically, their society. But their role in the novel also invites the possibility of exploring the possible values – the alternative, quasi-symbolic values – attributed to them, as well as reading the end naturalistically.

As we integrate elements of a fiction, we are also able to reinterpret them, particularly towards the end of the novel. A sense of closure is achieved, the ends are tied together, things are explained, order reigns. It is partly the reader's responsibility to achieve this, by knitting together elements scattered through the text, and bringing them to bear on interpretation. The boys have learned that some of the schemata they accepted have no validity – such as the officer's naïve expectation that British boys would have behaved better. It is at this point that Ralph, weeping for the death of Piggy, shows himself more mature than the adult.

As Eco points out, symbolic interpretation is always an option, open to the reader, but by no means compulsory. It can, however, help us to achieve integration of a text, and may suggest motivation for certain of its features. The descriptions at the end of this novel are a case in point: particularly when linked to earlier descriptions, the contrast between the choristers and the naval officer is very pointed. Both are seen first from Ralph's perspective. The function of the officer's gun and Piggy's broken glasses are comparable, powerful markers of authority.

The Gricean maxims suggest that interpretation should be sought via the maxims of manner and relation. From the reader's perspective, the description of Jack is a reminder of his nature. But it is focalised through the officer, who does not recognise the remnants of his chorister's cap, or the values attributable to the glasses. This is, then, not relevant to the officer, who is scanning the scene, but very relevant to the reader. The apparent violation of the maxim of quantity at this point – we hardly need reminding of Jack's uniform – perhaps has another function. At the highest level of processing the text, we integrate these elements. The choice of interpretation available is quite wide. Uniforms generally denote membership of an organisation, discipline, position in society. As the Navy and cathedral choristers are particularly linked to Englishness, the scope is further widened. When we consider that the officer – nescient though he is – does rescue the boys, the contrast between religion and warfare (whether aggressive or defensive) does not seem particularly apposite. But if the society that produced these children no longer exists, their rescue seems at best limited, and a far from happy ending. They are to return to a world which they have successfully mimicked on their island. The facile equation of the two elements I have been considering here as representing religion and the state respectively does not seem helpful. The values that individual readers will bring to their assessment of these two entities will doubtless vary widely. But the various schemata that we bring to our consideration of choirs and navies will most likely have been altered, if not overturned, by the experience of reading the novel.

Ultimately, a reader is guided by a search for maximal sense, or relevance. Like nature, we abhor a vacuum. Grice's maxims are really no more than the statement of a compact which is assumed to exist between interlocutors: communication makes little sense unless we assume the *bona fides* of those we talk too, and certainly of the texts we read. Recall that Thorne (1988) argued that, in processing literary discourse we look for maximal significance, and go as far as necessary to integrate all textual elements into the interpretation. We look beyond the literal meaning, in our interpretive search. That is why, I think, we have descriptions of the appearance of both Jack and the naval officer just as we are approaching the end of the text (and so eagerly awaiting closure), which might seem to violate the maxim of quantity in providing more information than we require. (As a delaying tactic, it is also an evaluative device.) The maxim of manner is also relevant: the children are seen by the officer, and the reader is reminded that Jack is a little boy, whereas the reader has made the distinction of the boys themselves: Jack is a *big 'un*. There is, in Eco's terms, over-encoding here, and that serves as a trigger to interpretation. The change in perspective urges a re-examination of the text. We may wonder whether or not the children are truly 'rescued'. We may see that the society which produced them, and has apparently destroyed itself, is not very different from the society they created on the island, which they also destroyed. The novel challenges some of the assumptions we tend to carry with us: about, for instance, the value of discipline. The officer is who, where and what he is in obedience to higher authority, and he saves the children. Jack's choristers are also trained in obedience, and allow his thuggishness full sway.

9.6 CONCLUSION

Symbolism, like irony and some other pragmatic strategies, presents difficult interpretative problems. Irony may, quite simply, fail to be recognised: it does not announce itself in the way that, say, metaphor does. In this it is like symbolism. Despite the confidence with which Eco approaches symbol via the Gricean maxims, the fact that symbol relies to such a large extent on the encyclopaedic knowledge of readers, is embedded in a cultural matrix which readers may share to a greater or lesser extent, and the sheer idiosyncrasy of readers approaching texts – even the same text at different times may attract a different reading – we cannot hope to secure total agreement on this kind of textual interpretation. The same applies to the need for the reader to decide that something in the text has been 'over-encoded' and so draws attention to itself in such a way as to trigger a possible symbolic interpretation.

There are a number of weak links in any chain of argument about symbolic readings: the maxim of manner, for example, is not only under the control of the writer, but also involves the judgement of the reader. So Eco's idea that over-encoding triggers symbolic interpretations lies very much in the reader's perceptions of possible contrasts in style between the passage in question and the rest of the text. Thus, for example, the description of Piggy's death in *Lord of the Flies* seems sufficient to me to trigger a symbolic interpretation, but another reader might argue that its cold accuracy reflects simply a child's unemotional view of the event.

The combination of features that make up symbols means that there is perhaps no certain way of interpreting them, as Eco argues. The reasons for this are basically that their optionality always leaves it open to the reader to accept the invitation to read a text symbolically or not. Symbols are rooted in the pragmatics of situation and use. Their interpretation depends crucially on encyclopaedic knowledge, and our interpretation of the maxims. Therefore it is partly a matter of recognising culturally accepted associations similar to those that Lakoff argues underlie the metaphors that structure our thought. Similarly, the crucial role of the maxim of manner in Eco's approach to symbol serves to underline its significance in interpreting all discourse. One has only to consider the way in which novelists use reporting clauses (*he asked anxiously/ thoughtfully/irritably*, and so on) to be aware of how essential manner is to interpretation. But, in the case of literary discourse and particularly when it comes to symbols, as we have seen, decisions as to whether the maxim is being exploited are, as in everyday life, very much up to the individual. This is perhaps why Eco is so insistent that symbol, that most elusive of figures, can only suggest, never be definitively pinned down. It is also perhaps part of the reason why Eco considers that it is up to the reader to decide to interpret a text symbolically: we can all think of times when we have misinterpreted a glance, an intonation pattern.

All of this suggests that symbolism is a complex phenomenon, which is not readily amenable to explanation, or to the kind of clarity that Sperber and Wilson demand when they say that the problem with a Gricean approach is that it allows for uncontrolled implicatures. In fact, many symbols seem to be rooted in a metonymic principle. This applies not only to the obvious emblems such as scythes and skulls in graveyards; it can also be seen in the value attributed to the conch in *Lord of the Flies*, and even to Piggy's spectacles: once they are stolen they represent power, like the revolver at the officer's belt, or the scalps ornamenting the waistband of an Indian brave. There are interesting similarities between symbols and metaphor: both require thinking in terms of analogy, both allow great interpretative freedom, they depend upon the talents of the receiver to decode and tease out the possible implicatures, and adopt those that seem to enrich the interpretation most. Both also make demands upon the encyclopaedic knowledge of the decoder; both are, to varying degrees, outwith the control of the author of the text (see Cooper (1986: 117) who argues that the interpretation of an utterance is outside the control of the speaker).

As we saw above, Lakoff and his collaborators offer a persuasive explanation not only for how metaphor works, but why it is important because of the way in which it assists, even models, thought. Arguably, symbolism operates in a similar way: like metaphor it invites an open-ended exploration of possible meanings, assessed in the context of the work. We use symbols to arrive at a richer meaning than we could attain without them. In considering *Lord of the Flies*, we can perhaps see how these apparently disparate theories are in fact quite similar in the way they offer ideas about how our interpretative processes work.

In the next chapter I shift direction for the last time, in considering how the thoughts of characters are depicted. This can involve any of the topics considered already.

Chapter 10

Psychonarration

10.1 INTRODUCTION

In this chapter I shall consider the various ways in which the mental activity of fictional characters is shown. The term psychonarration was coined by Cohn (1979) to cover this area. Authors have always been interested in depicting the thoughts of their characters. Homer offers insights into the thoughts of heroes at critical moments in their lives, in the form of NRTA, soliloquies and dialogue with gods or goddesses which are presumably not overheard by anyone else. Shakespeare uses soliloquy; this can be somewhat unnatural, but is accepted as a normal convention of the genre. In both cases the mind disclosed is expressing itself in syntactically well-formed utterances. It is usually concerned with matters of great significance. The focus of interest began to change when Locke in the eighteenth century developed his ideas about how the mind works, based upon introspection in *An Essay Concerning Human Understanding* (1690/1975). Sterne plays with Locke's concept of free association as one of the principal structural elements of *Tristram Shandy*, though in his case it is really not-so-free association: each of his characters has idiosyncrasies and illogicalities of thought which are exploited to witty effect (see Locke 1690/1975: 11, xxxiii). Sterne marks a departure from the depiction of logical, coherent thought as somehow representing the norm for mental activity. With the further development of psychological theories and insights in the nineteenth and twentieth centuries, novelists attempt to mirror what they think goes on in the mind. The great change in the use of psychonarration in the twentieth century is not so much a matter of the techniques employed – these were already in use – but in the subject matter to which they were applied. Interest now focuses not on the significant/critical moments in life, but much more on a concern with the texture of ordinary existence: there are attempts to reflect the unique experiences of individuals.

William James in *Principle of Psychology* (1890) argues that reality is not an objective, given entity 'out there', but is perceived subjectively and is actively interpreted by the consciousness of each individual. He suggested the terms 'stream' or 'river' as the metaphors by which it might best be described; the metaphor *stream* has been adopted by many literary critics. A wide range of techniques is available to show the inner workings of the minds of fictional characters.

The reproduction of speech and thought is a relatively simple matter. Where it becomes more complex is when it is used in combination with narratorial comments (as it always is when there is more than a bare reporting clause) and in those instances when it becomes difficult to distinguish between the voices of narrator and character. The depiction of thought is the prime source of the so-called 'interior monologue' and 'stream of consciousness' techniques in fiction that can render the texture of a work very complex. There is no agreed definition of these terms, which are essentially literary rather than stylistic. They are avoided here. The term psychonarration will be used to cover this area of fictional discourse. These techniques are now well integrated into the range of stylistic devices available to writers. I will now look at the range of possibilities, and exemplify them.

10.2 THE MEANS TO DEPICT CONSCIOUSNESS OF CHARACTERS

These include:

  narrator's comments, description and observation
  narrator's report of thought acts (NRTA)
  indirect thought (IT)
  free indirect thought (FIT)
  direct discourse (DD)
  free direct thought (FDT)

These are arranged in a cline of decreasing narratorial involvement, with FDT being the 'freest' of intrusions or marks of authorial presence. It should be remembered, however, that even in a text which has no signs of narratorial presence other than indications of whose mind we are examining (such as Faulkner's *As I Lay Dying* where the chapter headings identify the character), there must be a narrator who has decided whose mind to reveal and when, and who controls the juxtaposition with the thoughts of others. Thus there is something slightly spurious in the freedom granted the fictional characters: they remain very much the creatures of their creator. In most cases, and certainly the more interesting ones, these grammatical options are used in combination, making for a very flexible text, though it may present more difficulties to the reader.

10.3 NARRATOR'S COMMENTS

Sometimes a narrator will analyse the mental disposition of a character, in terms which might well not occur to the character and, as in this case, combine it with comments on the character's attitude:

  Nina had a much longer-term project in mind, which she kept to herself, for she
  was convinced that sooner or later she would separate from Rowland, marry again,
  have children, study. But in the meantime, shrewd woman that she was, she knew

there was a life to be lived as comfortably and pleasantly as possible. (Spark, *The Finishing School*, 2004: 69)

10.4 NARRATOR'S REPORT OF THOUGHT ACTS (NRTA)

It is often thought that NRTA (like NRSA) has limited uses; it does not involve the reader in a particularly empathetic way. NRSA is often used for less significant elements in the narrative: for example, for a speech which is not worth reproducing fully, but where the content must be communicated for the development of the story. In fact, NRTA is more complex than that, and has various uses. It can embody the judgement of the narrator. It is more distancing than other forms of reporting thought (and we note that it is only in fiction that we are privileged to know the thoughts of others). Because of the narratorial presence, we often have the co-presence of two consciousnesses, with the potential for irony that affords. It is often combined with other forms of thought presentation.

A simple case of NRTA is: *Rowland regretted his early efforts to persuade Chris not to write the book* (Spark, *The Finishing School*, 2004: 64). NRTA can be combined with any other method of thought presentation. NRTA is a particularly useful device for it allows the narrator to express the thoughts of people and even animals which are not normally accessible. Here Focus, a Persian cat, is going for a walk (his perspective is suggested by the word *sinister*):

> He was perfectly sensible of the dangers inherent in being so attractive, and was taking no risks. Aunt Irene had a very sinister sepia-tinted photograph of one of her relations wearing a hat which looked to Focus as though it might well be related to him. (Ellis, *The 27th Kingdom*, 1982: 123)

It can also be used to report the thoughts of a dying man: *In the split second before he died Peter remembered these words, and remembered that, unlike Bridget, Frances had not disputed the likelihood of his death* (Vickers, *Instances of the Number 3*, 2001/2002: 44). And Conrad uses NRTA in *The Secret Agent* to show the thought processes of an idiot:

> He could say nothing; for the tenderness to all pain and all misery, the desire to make the horse happy and the cabman happy, had reached the point of a bizarre longing to take them to bed with him. And that, he knew, was impossible. For Stevie was not mad. It was, as it were, a symbolic longing . . . (1907/1963: 139)

The narrator comments ironically on Stevie's thoughts (*bizarre longing*), which suggests certain limits to his sympathy for the character. It also shows sharply that two consciousnesses are at work here: hence the irony, the distancing from the character (which is not seen in the passage above about Focus), so we have Bakhtin's hybrid discourse. It diminishes our sympathy for the unfortunate Stevie . . . and perhaps for the narrator too.

An extreme form of NRTA is found in Golding's *The Inheritors*, a novel which describes the activities of a group of Neanderthals who are on the verge of acquiring language. Golding uses a number of devices to show how they think. Most obviously, he uses a normal reporting clause: *He remembered the hyenas* . . . (1955/1961: 40). The narratorial voice in *The Inheritors* tries to reproduce the mind-set of the characters through modifications to the patterns of standard English (see Adriaens 1970; Halliday 1971; Black 1993). The Neanderthals believe they exist on the same level as all other beings; they do not distinguish clearly between animate and inanimate. In this passage Lok, the focaliser, has a sighting of *homo sapiens*:

> As he watched, one of the farther rocks began to change shape. At one side a small bump elongated then disappeared quickly. The top of the rock swelled, the hump fined off at the base and elongated again then halved its height. Then it was gone. Lok stood and let the pictures come and go in his head. One was a picture of a cave bear that he had once seen rear itself out of the rock and heard roar like the sea. Lok did not know much more about the bear than that because after the bear had roared the people had run for most of a day. This thing, this black changing shape, had something of the bear's slow movement in it. He screwed up his eyes and peered at the rock to see if it would change shape again. There was a single birch tree that overtopped the other trees on the island, and was now picked out against the moon-drenched sky. It was very thick at the base, unduly thick, and as Lok watched, impossibly thick. The blob of darkness seemed to coagulate round the stem like a drop of blood on a stick. It lengthened, thickened again, lengthened. (1955/1961: 79)

The character's thought processes are shown; it is up to the reader to infer that a man is first hiding behind rocks, then climbing a tree. For Lok, that the rock should change shape is a reasonable hypothesis, since in principle he believes that everything is more or less animate. The word *picture* (which variously means thought, memory and communication in the text) here refers to memories. They are apparently random: the point is perhaps that the *picture* of the bear is highly relevant. It is unknown and dangerous. Lok seems to see the connection primarily in terms of the movement of the rock. The text suggests a mind which makes connections, but is not analytical or reflective. Lok's attention then shifts to the tree: the narrator shows the sharpness of his observation, using a simile which is not inappropriate to the character's experience: *a drop of blood on a stick*. Lok notes the oddity of the movement. This passage consists primarily of the narrator's description of Lok's thoughts; it manages to convey his very limited language. When he (implicitly) compares his new experience with memories of a bear, the onus is on the reader to make explicit why he does so, just as we have to infer that a man is climbing the tree.

In *To the Lighthouse* Woolf uses a comparable technique to show the mind of James, who is a small child at the beginning of the novel, so it is reasonable to depict his thoughts in terms of visual images. He always associates thoughts of his father with sharp objects, a knife, a scimitar and beaks. At the end of the novel he is a teenager, whose rage at his father goes back to childhood:

James kept dreading the moment when he would look up and speak sharply to him about something or other. Why were they lagging about here? he would demand, or something quite unreasonable like that. And if he does, James thought, then I shall take a knife and strike him to the heart.

He had always kept this old symbol of taking a knife and striking his father to the heart. (1927/1964: 208)

Here we find Woolf's characteristic blending of NRTA with a character's thought – in this case the imaginary FDT he attributes to his father, moving into DT in the last sentence (Cohn 1979 calls this style narrated monologue).

In the final example of NRTA, from *Tristram Shandy*, we have an impossible narrative situation – a first-person narrator who nevertheless reports as though he were endowed with all the privileges of omniscience. Furthermore, he is an infant when this scene takes place:

– – My young master in *London* is dead! said *Obadiah*. – –

– – A green sattin night-gown of my mother's, which had been twice scoured, was the first idea which *Obadiah's* exclamation brought into *Susannah's* head. – – Well might *Locke* write a chapter upon the imperfection of words. – – Then, quoth *Susannah*, we must all go into mourning. – – But note a second time: the word *mourning*, notwithstanding *Susannah* made use of it herself – – failed also of doing its office; it excited not one single idea, tinged with either grey or black, – – all was green. – – The green sattin night-gown hung there still.

– – O! 'twill be the death of my poor mistress, cried *Susannah*.

My mother's whole wardrobe followed. – – What a procession! her red damask, – – her orange-tawny, – – her white and yellow lutestrings, – – her brown taffata, – – her bone-laced caps, her bed-gowns and comfortable under-petticoats. – – Not a rag was left behind. – – 'No, – – *she will never look up again,*' said *Susannah*. (Sterne 1760–7/1980: V, 7)

Susannah's words are wholly appropriate to the situation, while her mind dwells on the possibility that she will inherit her mistress's wardrobe when she goes into mourning, or dies of grief. What is most interesting is the striking disparity between what Susannah says and what she is thinking: in this Sterne is quite similar to a passage in *To the Lighthouse* where the thoughts of various characters are examined during a dinner party. Unlike Woolf, the narrator stresses the incongruity between thoughts and words, without noting that such subterfuge is essential to civilised life. Sterne is here having a dig at Locke: in the chapter following the one cited from *An Essay Concerning Human Understanding*, Locke suggests that words referring to concrete things should be identified in dictionaries by pictures, rather than words (III, xi). The narrator's ironic presence allows the juxtaposition of words and thoughts, one of the principal merits of the less direct ways of showing thought.

These examples show the wide range of effects that can be achieved by using NRTA. It is a very flexible device which allows the juxtaposition of the character's thoughts with narratorial comment.

10.5 INDIRECT THOUGHT (IT)

Sternberg (1991) points out the inherent ambiguities and uncertainty present in all forms of indirect discourse, since the original is spoken by one person, in a particular context, and is repeated (more or less inaccurately) by someone else, in another context. This observation applies generally to all forms of psychonarration as well as to all varieties of reported speech. Indirect thought, being common, requires little exemplification: *she did not think that he was the conscience-ridden type who would make a habit of it* (Ellis, *Pillars of Gold*, 1992/1993: 169). The emotive lexis here conveys the character's unorthodox view of conscience and establishes it clearly as the character's thought, rather than NRTA. IT can, of course, be neutral in conveying an attitude: *Bridget remembered the nun whom she had seen only once since that first leave-taking* (Vickers, *Instances of the Number 3*, 2001/2002: 126).

10.6 FREE INDIRECT THOUGHT (FIT)

Pragmatically speaking, this category is the most interesting and challenging of the various methods of thought presentation. A degree of uncertainty as to the extent to which it reflects the perspectives of character or narrator complicates the reader's task. It is characterised by the co-presence of two 'voices': the character's is essentially echoic, as it is embedded in the narrative, while the narrator's voice may encode a quite different perspective, or set of attitudes. One of the merits of using FIT is that it fits seamlessly into normal past-tense narratives; it is therefore a rather unobtrusive device:

> He watched the anxious parent ravens and their brood, three puffed-up, sooty young thugs, almost ready to fly.
> One of the adult ravens arrived and tried to stuff a morsel of live stuff into the bill of one of the young. But the young raven turned its head, the wriggling meal was not to its liking. Was it full? Anorexic? Or plain rebellious? Apparently, not even ravens were immune to concerns about their offspring. This notion that a creator had influence over the objects of its creation – where on earth did that idea come from? A parent, even a raven parent could tell you it was nonsense . . . (Vickers, *Mr Golightly's Holiday*, 2003: 216)

Free indirect discourse is commonly the locus of ironic comment, when the narrator distances himself from his character, whether by means of lexical choice, direct or oblique comment. (In this particular instance, part of the irony resides in the fact that Mr Golightly is God.) It is often in indirect discourse that some of the subtlest of fictional effects are achieved. Varieties of free indirect discourse also contribute to the 'polyphonic' nature of fictional discourse, most obviously in the blending of the voices of narrator and character.

10.7 DIRECT THOUGHT (DT) AND FREE DIRECT THOUGHT (FDT)

The distinction between DT and FDT is, of course, the presence or absence of a reporting clause. The element of echoic discourse is absent in these types (together with the potential for distortion implicit in the metaphor 'echoic'). This passage is FDT: *She's jealous of me, wants him to pay her some attention. No nun she, ought to be ashamed. Goes after men. Priests. Tried it with Angwin. Chased her out of the presbytery* (Mantel, *Fludd,* 1989/1990: 111). The FDT passage exhibits the truncated syntax which is regularly used by novelists to suggest speed of thought, and intimacy. It has become a conventional marker of this type of thought presentation. The references are clear in context: a young nun is being beaten by her Mother Superior. Angwin is the local priest.

While it might seem obvious that FDT offers the clearest view of the mind of another, this is not always the case. Since the character is not intent on communicating, the text may be obscure, presenting interpretive difficulties to the reader. Faulkner's *As I Lay Dying* (1930) consists of a series of chapters, each labelled with the name of a character, whose thoughts and sometimes words are reproduced without any narratorial intervention. The reader has to piece together the narrative, rather in the way of assembling a mosaic. The situation in this passage is that Vardaman, a small child, is watching his brother Cash make a coffin for his mother, who is dead or dying.

> When they get it finished they are going to put her in it and then for a long time I couldn't say it. I saw the dark stand up and go whirling away and I said 'Are you going to nail her up in it, Cash? Cash? Cash?' I got shut up in the crib and the new door it was too heavy for me it went shut I couldn't breathe because the rat was breathing up all the air. I said 'Are you going to nail it shut, Cash? Nail it? *Nail it?*' (1930/1963: 54)

This text is hardly reader-friendly, nor should one expect it to be, since, except in the DD passages, Vardaman is not attempting to communicate with anyone. The prevalence of pro-forms (*it, her*) indicates that he is thinking of matters familiar to him. The first *it* clearly refers to the coffin, just as *her* is presumably his mother. The child's distress becomes clearer with his memory of being shut in the crib, unable to breathe. The peculiar sequence of tenses and temporal adverbials in the first sentence is opaque, as is the second sentence: what is the *dark* that *stands up* and *whirls away*? This kind of difficulty is predictable in a text of this type. Probably he remembers the incident of the crib because he associates it with the coffin. This style is realistic in the sense that we do not have to spell out to ourselves what we are thinking; however, when we talk to others, that is just what we must do if we want to be understood. It is challenging to the reader, and could therefore be described as fundamentally impolite. Individuals will vary in whether they think the effort is adequately rewarded, or indeed feel flattered that they belong to a community which appreciates the style.

The interpretive problems posed by FDT are quite similar to problems we encounter when eavesdropping, or listening to conversations we lack the information to understand. Carter (2004: 262) quotes a conversation between a couple who know each other well: it is opaque to an outsider. The difficulties, which are also common to FDT, arise from the over-hearer's difficulties in assigning value to pro-forms, and in sudden switches from singular to plural (which occurs quite regularly in conversation, for example when we speak of one person, but implicitly refer to their family by switching to the plural).

The flexibility of FDT is amply demonstrated in Joyce's *Ulysses*. Molly Bloom's soliloquy at its end comes as she is apparently falling asleep, and her thoughts range widely over the recent and distant past. The style is characterised by reduced syntax, absence of logical connectors, and apparently random associations of ideas. The tense varies, according to whether she is recollecting or looking to the future. Characteristic is the absence of punctuation marks, the (overt) absence of the narrator, while the sporadic use of capitals suggests Molly's emphases. Words may be run together. It is an effective way of suggesting the speed of thought. This style can accommodate quotation of other speakers, and indirect speech. While Molly's soliloquy takes place as she is drifting off to sleep, other instances of the technique are found when a character is interacting with others, and so is firmly placed within a narrative context. For example, when Bloom and his friend Goulding are discussing the opera, Bloom's thoughts wander to the relationship between music and mathematics, as both are based on numbers. He also engages in word-play, less obviously relevant to the subject under discussion, but characteristic of how his mind works. This is typical of Bloom's style of thinking, and so contributes to his characterisation, and the texture of the novel (*Ulysses*: 1922/1968: 277).

This is naturalistic in the sense that it reflects the way in which our words do not always reflect our thoughts. Here Bloom is playing with words, his thoughts arising from the word *number*, it finishes with the near-identical pronunciation of *symmetry/cemetery*. In this and the next example juxtaposition of thoughts and words is an effective device in showing the disparity between them:

> What Frances thought was: Why does she have to be so *different*? Aloud, she said, 'I don't know that I want so terribly to "talk" either – though there are things I could probably only say to you.' (Vickers, *Instances of the Number 3*, 2001/2002: 12)

10.8 MIXED STYLES: NARRATED MONOLOGUE

Cohn (1979) coined the term narrated monologue to describe Woolf's style. The term neatly captures the co-presence of two 'voices' in the fiction. The narratorial voice guides the reader, offering interpretation and contextualisation of the character's thoughts. The combination of all the resources to show a character's mind is a notable characteristic of her technique. The whole range is deployed, from DD through the varieties of indirect discourse and narrator's description of the character's thoughts. A notable example of this style is found in *To the Lighthouse* (1927). All of the techniques discussed in this chapter are used, except for the extreme of FDT found in Molly's thoughts in *Ulysses*. An interesting feature, though rather uncomfortable, is the juxtaposition of the thoughts of various characters. At a dinner table scene in *To the Lighthouse* the guests all hope that their thoughts will not be revealed to their companions (1927/1964: 108). It is unnatural, and impossible outside fiction, that we should be privy to the thoughts of others; there is something voyeuristic about it. But somehow it seems more natural if we have the thoughts of only one character at a time. No doubt we have all feared that others might discover our thoughts. A feature of Woolf's approach is that she is interested in the ordinary thoughts of ordinary people. She does not usually distinguish her characters by idiolectal traits, so we are often confronted with genuine difficulties in attributing sentences or even parts of them to the voice of character or narrator. We have two consciousnesses which are closely aligned, so no great contrast between them is found. Consider this:

> Jasper offered her an opal necklace; Rose a gold necklace.[1] Which looked best against her black dress?[2] Which did indeed? said Mrs Ramsay absentmindedly, looking at her neck and shoulders (but avoiding her face), in the glass.[3] And then, while the children rummaged among her things, she looked out of the window at a sight which always amused her – the rooks trying to decide which tree to settle on.[4] Every time, they seemed to change their minds and rose up again into the air again, because, she thought, the old rook, the father rook, old Joseph was her name for him, was a bird of a very trying and difficult disposition.[5] He was a disreputable old bird, with half his wing feathers missing.[6] He was like some seedy old gentleman in a top hat she had seen playing the horn in front of a public house.[7]
> 'Look!' she said, laughing.[8] They were actually fighting.[9] Joseph and Mary were fighting.[10] Anyhow they all went up again, and the air was shoved aside by their black wings and cut into exquisite scimitar shapes.[11] The movement of the wing beating out, out, out – she could never describe it accurately enough to please herself – was one of the loveliest of all to her.[12] Look at that she said to Rose, hoping that Rose would see it more clearly than she could.[13] For one's children so often gave one's own perceptions a little thrust forward.[14]

We are confronted here with genuine difficulties in attributing sentences or even parts of them to the voice of character or narrator. The contrast would be sharper if there were idiolectal or indeed attitudinal differences between them.

Sentence 1 is narratorial description; the next sentence is clearly FID, though it is not clear which of the children speaks. Then sentence 3 begins with Mrs Ramsay's FIT, then changes to narrator's description, which continues as Mrs Ramsay switches her attention to the rooks outside and the passage moves into NRTA (sentence 5 marked by *she thought*). Sentences 6 and 7 are plausibly FIT. Sentence 8 begins with DD, with a reporting clause. Sentence 9 and 10 are FID (*actually* suggests spoken language; the repetition is more likely to be attributable to Mrs Ramsay, trying to interest her children, than to the narrator). Sentence 11 is plausibly Mrs Ramsay's

FIT, as is the beginning of the next sentence, except for the parenthetic clause between the dashes (probably narratorial). Sentence 13 begins with FDD, but finishes with NRTA. The final sentence is FIT. Sentences 8 and 13 may refer to the same utterance: the first time with quotation marks to indicate DD, in 13 we have FDD with a reporting clause. Yet both refer to the same incident, perhaps even to the same utterance.

Austen shows some similarities to Woolf in showing the minds of (some) of her characters. The technique is used sparingly, usually at moments of crisis. The thoughts are reasonably well ordered, both logically and syntactically. In *Pride and Prejudice* Elizabeth is visiting the house of Mr Darcy, whom she thinks she dislikes; an unexpected meeting leads her to change her mind. The passage is crucial in the development of the novel (as is true of most examples of psychonarration until recent times). The procedure is largely to use varieties of (free) direct and indirect discourse. Austen's narrators and the character whose views are portrayed are usually closely aligned, both linguistically and socially. Austen is not particularly concerned to create idiolects for her characters, but they are differentiated according to how close their language is to that of the narrator: thus one problem in this passage is that it is not always possible to be certain whether some parts should be attributed to the narrator or character.

> There was certainly at this moment, in Elizabeth's mind, a more gentle sensation towards the original, than she had ever felt in the height of their acquaintance.[1] The commendation bestowed on him by Mrs Reynolds was of no trifling nature.[2] What praise is more valuable than the praise of an intelligent servant?[3] As a brother, a landlord, a master, she considered how many people's happiness were in his guardianship! –[4] How much of pleasure or pain it was in his power to bestow! –[5]How much of good or evil must be done by him![6] Every idea that had been brought forward by the housekeeper was favourable to his character, and as she fixed his eye upon herself, she thought of his regard with a deeper sentiment of gratitude than it had ever raised before; she remembered its warmth, and softened its impropriety of expression.[7] (Austen 1813/1972: 272)

Sentences 1 and 2 are narratorial, though the second sentence may also reflect Elizabeth's judgement. The third sentence is more problematic. It is easiest to interpret as an example of gnomic generalisation, in which case it is most easily attributable to the narrator. However, given the closeness of views of character and narrator, one might interpret it as Elizabeth's; in that case, the second sentence can be interpreted as FIT, unmarked by an attribution. It does not matter, of course, in our overall interpretation of the novel which view we adopt, but it is a teasing example of how slippery the voices of character and narrator can be, and how difficult it can be to attribute clauses to one or another with certainty. Sentences 4 and 5 represent Elizabeth's thoughts in FIT; the first sentence has a reporting clause, while the punctuation, with its liberal use of exclamation marks, also shows that this is the character's thought. Sentence 6 is perhaps FDT. Sentence 7 rounds off the passage with NRTA (and is not without irony, as Elizabeth fixes the painting's eye upon herself).

Narrated monologue has been used by many writers since Woolf. An example follows:

> Not for the first time Eric tried to imagine how he'd feel if he murdered her.[1] Not how he'd feel while he was doing it – the act, no doubt, would give him a momentary satisfaction – but how he would react afterwards.[2] His principal emotion, he thought, would be embarrassment.[3] Murder was neither respectable nor sophisticated; for the rest of his life he would feel miserable and shy if anyone so much as glanced at him.[4] The whispers – *'He murdered his wife, you know.'*[5] He had no real fear of the immediate consequences since he thought he would only spend a few years in jail with remission for good conduct.[6] He could give a course on engineering to the other inmates.[7] A number of wife-killers had got off very lightly recently.[8] He had once asked a customer, a solicitor from Edinburgh, about the complexities of divorce.[9] The man had advised against it these days.[10] It was a lengthy, expensive and disruptive business, fraught with recrimination and ill-feeling.[11] It was quicker and neater, he said, to murder your spouse, plead intolerable provocation or insanity, or what you would, pay your debt to society and emerge from open prison to resume life with your property intact and no maintenance payments to worry about.[12] (Ellis, *The Inn at the Edge of the World*, 1990/1991: 1)

This passage comes from the beginning of the novel; there is therefore no evidence that allows the reader to identify possible idiolectal traits, and so distinguish narrator from character. This factor tends to make analysis more difficult. Sentence 1 is NRTA, as indicated by the reporting verb *tried to imagine*, and *not for the first time* is a comment which is unlikely to come from the character. The second seems to be a combination: the first clause, with its contracted verb, suggests character rather than narrator and would thus be FIT; the second and third clauses are most likely NRTA, though one could argue that they are also FIT. The reporting verb of sentence 3 suggests it is also NRTA, sentence 4 is perhaps NRTA also. In sentence 5 the syntax is truncated; it includes DD (from imaginary people), which suggests we are moving into FIT. Sentence 6 is NRTA. Sentence 7 is interpretable as FIT, with *inmates* rather than *prisoners* suggesting a sympathetic attitude to criminals, from one who already imagines himself inside. Sentence 8 seems to be FIT: *recently* (together with *these* in sentence 10) suggests character focalisation because of the proximal deictics. Sentence 9 is narratorial. The final sentences are the lawyer's ID, embedded within the character's thoughts. Cohn's term 'narrated monologue' neatly captures the oscillating movement between narrator and character. One difference is that Ellis is ironic in a way that Woolf is not.

10.9 CONCLUSION

Subtle effects are achieved by the deployment of the full range of techniques available to authors: this is a very flexible area. Almost paradoxically, the narrator's description of the character's thoughts and NRTA may offer the most complex views, precisely because the presence of a narrator permits an analytical approach and can show the perspective of several characters as well as the narrator. And as has been noted already, the varieties of indirect discourse lend themselves readily to echoic language features; thus passages depicting the consciousness of characters often combine the perceptions of both narrator and character, creating a Bakhtinian polyphonic discourse. That is one of the reasons that such passages may often seem ironic.

While it might seem obvious that FDT offers the clearest view of the mind of another (for example, in Molly Bloom's thoughts at the end of *Ulysses*), this seems not always to be the case. Partly, no doubt, this may be because the character is not intent upon communication with another: the text may therefore be relatively obscure, presenting interpretive difficulties to the reader, who may not necessarily be rewarded by particularly valuable insights.

In some respects, the development of the extremes of psychonarration, as exemplified by Joyce and Faulkner, seem to represent a dead end in the development of fictional discourse. There are doubtless many reasons for this. One may be that these extremes are not, in fact, particularly naturalistic. Readers will vary in their reactions and the extent to which they think they represent with any verisimilitude the way people think. In passages such as Molly Bloom's soliloquy, there is little of the polyphonic discourse that characterises much fiction, though she does occasionally quote others' words. Without a narrator, the dominance of a single voice is almost inevitable, though other characters may supply some elements of dialogism. The loss here is the dimension of ironic comment on the character, the juxtaposition of more than one point of view which, arguably, is one of the most interesting and characteristic features of the novel. It is notable that many novels and short stories which are presented from the single perspective of an 'I' narrator nevertheless manage to encode other perspectives on their matter. Another advantage of a narrator is the speed with which focalisation can shift from one character to another – for example, in the dinner party scene in *To the Lighthouse*; it also means that anyone (or almost any thing) can, briefly, be a focaliser, including the cat Focus, cited earlier in this chapter.

Psychonarration contributes to characterisation, though perhaps in odd ways. It may give readers the 'feel' of what it is like to be a particular person; this is limited if there is little or no interaction with other characters. One particularly interesting example of characterisation occurs at the end of *The Inheritors*, an extract of which is cited above, from the perspective of the Neanderthal protagonist. In the last part of the novel, when the Neanderthals are dead, one of the new people is the focaliser: *I am like a pool, he thought, some tide has filled me, the sand is swirling, the waters are obscured and strange things are creeping out of the cracks and crannies in my mind* (Golding 1955/1961: 227). Here FDT is deployed to show the mind of a modern man. It is particularly effective in context because of the contrast with the presentation of the only partly verbally formulated thoughts of the people. Metaphor is present here too: *cracks and crannies in my mind*. (The mind as a container again!) Elsewhere in the novel the narrator suggests that simile is a powerful tool for thought: it is easily employed here. Thus the shift in focalisation, with the use of FDT, is a striking way of contrasting the mental worlds of the two sets of characters in the novel.

The narrated monologue type of psychonarration, exploiting most or all of the available techniques, has proved influential, and is in regular (though often sparing) use by contemporary novelists, including Ellis, Vickers and Rankin. It is remarkable, and an indication of its value, that it should have been assimilated into the detective story.

Chapter 11

Conclusion

11.1 THE LITERARY-CRITICAL APPROACH

Literary language is almost endlessly protean. I therefore consider it appropriate to include in a book on the pragmatics of literary discourse in fiction accounts of how literary scholars approach these texts. Scholars like Culler (1975) have shown how what linguists call schemata mediate our understanding of texts. Our culturally acquired knowledge of genre, which begins with the rhymes and fairy tales read or told to small children, carries over into our adult reading. It predisposes us to certain reactions, and is part of the creation of the context in which we read.

The formalist approach to fiction, as developed by Genette, is helpful to interpretation. The proportions of text suggest the interest of the narrator and direct us to attend to the features the novelist is most concerned with. The same applies to the temporal organisation of a text – that is, the order in which the story is told. These are essentially matters covered by the maxim of manner. They all generate massive implicatures about what is most significant in a text, and therefore control how we read, as well as having more immediate local effects.

In Chapter 1 I referred to Thorne's argument that we read literary texts with a different kind of attention than we give to other types of written text. We do this because we expect to be adequately rewarded for our attention (with what Sperber and Wilson call weak implicatures). Thorne seems to be prepared to go farther than the relevance theoreticians in searching for his rewards: this may well be true of many readers. Pilkington (2000) believes that poetic effects can be used to explain 'literariness'. If that idea were developed sufficiently, relevance theory might be able to offer a theory of literature. It is not at all clear to me that Sperber and Wilson would endorse as intensive and lengthy a search for implicatures as Pilkington does, though he might well argue that he is within the theory: it is just that, like any successful reader, he is not satisfied until a very long search for weak implicatures has taken place.

11.2 CONTEXT

Moving to more linguistic approaches, context is crucial to all utterance interpretation. As a preliminary to interpreting any discourse, it is helpful to know who produced it and the circumstances surrounding its production. What is required is a definition of context that seems to possess psychological verisimilitude – that is, it may reflect how real people react to discourse. It needs to be sensitive to the whole range of experience and knowledge we bring to any discourse. In that respect Werth, and Sperber and Wilson, are superior to the discourse analytical tradition (exemplified in Brown and Yule 1983) who see it as a combination of the preceding discourse and the physical situation of the participants. Sperber and Wilson's definition includes anything in our encyclopaedic knowledge that may help us to access explicatures and implicatures. Werth (1999) goes well beyond this, in that he believes that an adequate definition of context will include encyclopaedic knowledge, and our relations with other participants in the discourse. His view of context is that it is text driven: that is, the discourse recipient activates all those elements required for its interpretation: their retrieval from our encyclopaedic memory, and memory of the preceding discourse, and any other factors we consider relevant to interpretation. He also takes into account our view of the speaker/writer in social and sociolinguistic terms. That would include, in a literary text, our assessment of the reliability or otherwise of the narrator, our memory of other texts by the same author (to the extent that we can recall these), and their social situation. That is, at its most extreme, we may adopt a different view of the narrator of a Virginia Woolf novel to one by, say, Irvine Welsh. We are, of course, perfectly aware that novelists can create a *persona* for themselves as readily as they create characters. The narrator of *Tom Jones* is, generally speaking, a friendly, almost avuncular voice, guiding his readers into the intricacies of novel reading. He can, however, as we have seen, verge on the abusive (see Chapter 4). One of the great merits of Werth's study of context is that he allows all of these elements to enter into interpretation. It seems, to me at least, that this is how we proceed in the real world, which presumably carries over to our reading of fiction.

11.3 SPEECH ACT THEORY

This approach, while clearly of great interest to the analysis of ordinary language, seems to me to have less to contribute to our understanding of literary discourse than other theories considered here. The classification of all the speech acts in a novel is usually a rather arid exercise. Most of the narrator's language usually consists of representative speech acts; characters' discourse is predictably more varied, with plenty of expressives and directives. Sterne and Fielding use directives (in Sterne's case often ill-formed: Tristram cannot appropriately invite us into his study!) while Fielding has an educational project in mind: teaching us how to read a novel. However, in one crucial respect speech act theory is extremely helpful in drawing attention to the significance of malformed speech acts: these can be a most useful way of pinning down the nature of unreliable narrators in particular. The use of representative speech acts by a first-person narrator commenting on the motivation, opinions or thoughts of another character is an obvious example.

11.4 GRICE'S CO-OPERATIVE PRINCIPLE

Grice's co-operative principle and the associated maxims are very useful, despite their primary association with spoken language, for the interpretation of written texts. Grice has identified the likely way in which we approach any discourse: with the assumption (strengthened in relevance theory) that we are intending successful communication, that we are being essentially co-operative on some level. We therefore assume *bona fides* in our interlocutors. As we have seen, some of the maxims are of less obvious usefulness in reading fictional discourse. When I am reading a newspaper, I can decide fairly readily whether or not I am satisfied with the quantity of information offered (the quality is more difficult to judge). It is not at all clear how the maxim of quantity applies to other kinds of writing. We must either trust the author, or decide that she is unnecessarily prolix. The case of withholding information is different: this can serve a useful purpose, most easily observed in detective fiction, or in texts which depend on maintaining an air of uncertainty about outcomes. This applies to short stories like Joyce's 'A Painful Case,' where we never discover the truth about Mrs Sinico's death, and to teasing fictions such as James' *The Turn of the Screw*. It is notable in the latter case that the opera version is, at least in one respect, much less effective than the novel: the ghosts are on stage, singing vigorously. However much the music may contribute, the opera traduces the novel, whose point depends on the uncertainty generated by a discourse mediated through several hands, and coming ultimately from a young governess who says she has seen ghosts, though apparently no one else has.

The maxim of quality is not obviously significant when it comes to fiction. It is, after all, fiction. It is of course applicable in character-to-character interactions. It is also relevant to our interpretation of first-person narrators: is the governess in *The Turn of the Screw* self-deluded, lying or telling the truth? The maxim of manner is also problematic. Almost anything could be expressed in another way; this maxim has nothing to do with the veracity of the utterance, and everything to do with its expression, which is entirely under the control of the speaker or writer. This maxim is therefore very useful in assessing literary texts. *How* something is expressed can indicate the attitude of the speaker or writer; Labov's evaluative devices all involve the maxim of manner. It is also useful to consider the manner maxim in relation to Genette's study of the temporal organisation of texts. As I have tried to show, the order in which information is released affects how we read, just as the proportion of text devoted to different aspects of the narrative opens fruitful lines of interpretation.

The maxim of relevance is also very problematic: relevant to what or whom? In a literary text, or indeed any written text, we assume that all textual elements are relevant – otherwise an editor would have queried them. However, our assessment of the relevance of individual textual items to the whole is a matter that deeply involves the reader's judgement, and contributes to our engagement with the text. Because a novel has only words to create a world, items will be used with implied significance which might not bear much weight in the real world. An economical way of creating a character, suggesting age, background and social position might be to describe their

clothing. Distressed jeans, with tears already in place when purchased, are an identifying feature of some young people today, whereas to say that someone was wearing
well-pressed jeans will instantly add about thirty years to her age. So a description of
clothes can be relevant, and economically suggest a range of implicatures we might
derive.

11.5 RELEVANCE THEORY

Sperber and Wilson argue that the weakness of Grice's co-operative principle lies in
the uncontrolled way in which it permits us to access possible implicatures, with no
limits placed on our efforts. They consider that only relevance guides interpretation:
no other maxim is required. We proceed on the assumption that any communicative
act is relevant, and access implicatures until we are satisfied. Relevance theory is not
particularly interested in literary discourse, though it has been developed by followers of Sperber and Wilson to accommodate it more readily. However, their analysis
of weak implicatures, and poetic effects in particular, does not seem to be under great
control either: we proceed until we are satisfied and, as we have seen, this will certainly be at different points for each reader. Relevance theory does offer some elegant
explanations of common features of language use which are often treated as special
cases, particularly metaphor and irony. The demystification of these, and the demonstration that they can be accounted for as part of ordinary language use, is a valuable contribution. The relevance approach to metaphor suggests that it can be
accounted for in terms of ordinary language use: we use more or less precise ways of
expressing ourselves on different occasions, and for different purposes. Thus metaphor is at the looser end of the spectrum between precise and looser ways of conveying our meaning. This explanation also suggests why metaphor engages us so deeply,
as it demands a great deal of interpretive effort by the hearer. The freedom to access
different implicatures (arising in part because the encyclopaedic knowledge of individuals varies), to say nothing of the varying amounts of effort we are prepared to
put in, explains why interpretations will not be identical for all readers, or even the
same reader at different times. The relevance explanation of metaphor, treating it as
an interpretation of the speaker's thought is persuasive. It fits well with Lakoff's view
that many metaphors derive from concept metaphors – this view explains how it is
that we begin to work out what a metaphor in a particular context 'means'. Sperber
and Wilson's account (developed by Pilkington) encourages freedom to work out the
implicatures, without imposing a grid to constrain interpretation.

11.6 ECHOIC DISCOURSE

The relevance account of echoic discourse makes a major contribution by offering a
model for the interpretation of irony and other forms of echoic language, including
the whole range of varieties of indirect discourse. Not only is this an elegant analytical tool, it explains how it is that we can interpret something ironically – or not. It
explains how it is that we can miss ironies, particularly if the ironist is echoing a

thought we may sympathise with. (In this respect it is similar to Eco's account of symbol, which, as we saw, he regards as an option open to the reader when interpreting a text.) And, by showing that it is part of everyday language use, it de-mystifies it. The echoic account of irony seems to cover all the manifestations of the phenomenon, holding on to the crucial element of distancing, with varying degrees of disapprobation. The relevance view is not committed to the view of irony found in, for example, Leech, which holds that irony must be totally condemnatory.

Bakhtin demonstrates the wide range of effects achieved in the novel essentially through the use of echoic discourse (his hybrid discourse): with a profound understanding of how literary language works, and attention to its details. He is highly sensitive to the essentially sociolinguistic and historical elements of all language use. In this he is a powerful counterweight to Sperber and Wilson, who ignore this huge and important aspect: language is spoken and written by people, who are all embedded in a series of social relations which strongly affect the ways they speak and write. Our previous experience – of reading, of each other – conditions what we say, and how we say it. Though Bakhtin and Sperber and Wilson have similar insights into echoic language, its uses and effects, Bakhtin is deeply concerned with the social contexts in which language is used, whether in spoken or written discourse; by bringing these together we gain great insights into how language works. Relevance theory proposes a cognitive theory of how we approach and interpret language; Bakhtin adds an essential dimension by situating all discourse in the historical and social context in which it is created and read, thus remedying one of the deficiencies of relevance theoreticians. He perceives that language is inherently dialogic: anticipating reactions and ready to respond to them again situates language in a social context.

11.7 LABOV AND NATURAL NARRATIVE

Labov's study of natural narratives, produced by (often gifted) people telling of their personal experiences, identifies crucial elements in fictions, whether written or spoken. The large-scale organisation of narratives he develops is not particularly original. But it can be helpful if we are baffled by a novel to remind ourselves that it may just be because there is, for example, no clear resolution. Contemporary novelists commonly avoid the coda: the *and they lived happily ever after* ending. Some modern novels do have explicit resolutions and codas: one such is Ellis' *The 27th Kingdom*, where all the threads and characters are brought together in a most unexpected way, and a prediction as to the future of one of the main characters is also adumbrated. The presence or absence of resolutions and codas is essentially a matter of fashion. It is perhaps more teasing to the reader to leave room for speculation about the future of the ink blots we call characters. Similarly, the orientation section of novels is often dispensed with, or sharply abbreviated, though it was a more or less compulsory element in nineteenth-century fiction. Novelists may offer no abstract (why should they?) An abstract perhaps makes more sense in oral narratives, when it can be part of the attempt to claim the floor for a sustained turn (for turn-taking, see Schiffrin 1994). In a sense, it is a politeness strategy, designed to invite consent from the audience. It may seem less obviously relevant for a novel, which we can choose to read or not, though it is quite common for something like an abstract or similar enticement to appear on the back cover of a book. Even the complicating action can be dispensed with: Woolf's *To the Lighthouse* does not have a causally linked chain of events; instead, it is an account of the thoughts and interactions of a group of people over a ten-year period. Elements which in another fiction would count as major events – childbirth, and a number of deaths, including that of Mrs Ramsay, the main character – are mentioned only in passing. Yet the novel does have a resolution, in a moment of unity for all. Thus Labov contributes to our understanding of literary texts, through his analysis of textual organisation.

Our reactions are manipulated through the exploitation of the resources of evaluative devices (in effect, these are weak implicatures in relevance theoretic terms), guiding us in the directions desired by the narrator. Internal evaluative devices can be deployed much more densely in written narratives: in the case of figures of speech such as metaphor, as Pilkington (2000) points out, major interpretive effort may be invited to explore densely constructed text. Even if this were possible in spoken language, hearers do not have time to process the implicatures 'on-line'.

11.8 PSYCHONARRATION

The most intricate effects in fiction arise through the depiction of the thought processes of characters. We are soon embroiled in attempts to distinguish between the voices of the narrator and fictional characters. This is not always easy, and even if we are fairly confident of our analysis, the question remains: where does authority reside? The moment focalisation shifts into a character, we have a duality of voice that complicates interpretation. Even in NRTA the distance between the thinking character and narrator is variable. NRTA can be a summarising device, but it can equally echo words attributable to the character and encode the narrator's views. In this way it can convey attitude. In ID, as with any embedded discourse we experience difficulties in deciding where one voice begins and the other leaves off. This is most obvious when attempting to disentangle what goes on in FID. It is for this reason that some of the most intricate effects are found here, in the combination of voices. This is, of course, impossible in the real world: we cannot know what others are thinking. FIT is thus most unnatural. It is, nevertheless, one of the most powerful resources available to a novelist. It permits a flexible and nuanced combination of voices, with great potential for ironic effects. It can give us a very close view of a character, or imply criticisms and distance from the character. Because it is so difficult to disentangle, in a principled way, the voices involved in embedded discourse of this type, the reader is confronted not only with an interesting task, but is left with teasing uncertainty. There is something indecent about this prying into another's mind, whereas DT, without narratorial intervention, somehow seems more acceptable – more acceptable, but of course equally lacking in verisimilitude. There is additional pleasure to be derived from showing thoughts equally inaccessible: the first *he* in the following passage is a cat:

There was no one in the street, so he went for a little walk towards the church waving his tail, and there, sitting on a garden wall was that rat. Major Mason saw it too, only he didn't believe it. He was out for a constitutional, because he was determined to become very healthy now that he had given up drinking, and this rat vision struck him as most unfair. He knew it must be a hallucination because that dopey-looking cat was taking no notice of it at all. (Ellis, *The 27th Kingdom*, 1982: 123–4)

The first sentence is NRTA of the cat Focus. *So* suggests that it is because Focus sees no one that he decides to proceed with his walk. The reference in the second sentence to *that* rat shows that Focus recognises it as an old acquaintance; for those two words the focalisation switches to the cat. When Major Mason is introduced, the narrator begins with a description of his state of mind, but the proximal *this rat vision* suggests that we move briefly into his consciousness, though the rest returns to NRTA, until in the final sentence *that dopey looking cat* suggests we have moved back into his mind: a typical use of a fragment of FDT embedded in the narrator's discourse. NRTA is, of course, flexible: it can shadow the thoughts of a character more or less closely. Here, for instance, *very healthy* is probably a close echo of the Major's thoughts – the *very* gives the game away.

Perhaps the most interesting – pragmatically speaking at any rate – element I have considered here is the whole range of indirect language in fiction. It is here that the interplay between narrator and characters is at its most complex and enigmatic. We are in an area of uncertainty, which makes interpretation difficult or dubious. We are not always certain to which voice textual elements should be attributed and are therefore uncertain how much to rely on them. The language is refracted through different perspectives, with various degrees of embedding, so that precise attribution is impossible. It is this very problematic area of fictional discourse which is, perhaps, the most interesting and the most challenging to readers.

11.9 SUMMARY

Pragmatic theories are just that – hypotheses about how we process language. They are not specific to any particular language use. The assumption is that these are the ground rules we use in interpreting all discourse. Speaking would be pointless unless we assumed that our interlocutor was being co-operative; Grice's maxims suggest some of the ways in which that co-operation is carried out. Nevertheless, some fictions may seem to be inherently unco-operative. For me, at least, *Finnegans Wake* falls into that category. Whether in the longer term scholars will conclude that Sperber and Wilson are right to argue that only relevance is taken into account in processing discourse is uncertain. In purely practical terms, the Gricean maxims are very useful in reminding us of what we are doing when we process language – or creating a text ourselves. All these theories can assist our interpretive efforts, and guide our reading. They may even offer an explanation of why we react in particular ways to texts. If we feel that our confidence is misplaced, perhaps because of a seemingly irrelevant statement or description or apparently wilful violation of a maxim, the theories explain why we have this reaction.

I have tried to show the range of things we look for when reading novels: we probably begin with higher-order elements of the organisation of the text, then we move on to more 'micro' organisational features. While I have argued against the proliferation of maxims and principles, such as those suggested by Leech, in his interest principle he has surely put his finger on the one crucial aspect of literary discourse. Literature exists to interest us; if it fails in that, we have no motivation to read. I hope that the theories (and sometimes cumbrous terminology) presented here have not obscured the basic fact that we do – at least, should – read for pleasure.

I have sought to demonstrate the usefulness of a pragmatically-oriented approach to the language of fictional texts. An applied linguistic perspective adds a dimension to the reading of literature; it reminds us that it is rooted in ordinary discourse and situations. It also shows how it differs from them. The co-operative principle shows us how we relate to each other, and suggests the ground rules we use in interpreting discourse; these are clearly relevant to conversation (as first intended by Grice), and also help to illuminate literary texts. It is very hard to think that maxims we use in ordinary interactions would be suspended when we begin to read.

I argue that relevance theory makes its greatest contribution to the pragmatics of literary discourse with its approach to echoic language, which covers not only the variety of indirect discourse (both speech and thought) found in literary texts, but in illuminating how and even why we use irony. It explains why it is fallibly understood, or missed. Bakhtin, though using different terminology, shares with Sperber and Wilson an awareness of the echoic nature of much discourse, and situates this in a social and historical context, thus enriching the analysis.

There are communicative acts which can be regarded as intrusive, for example in inviting us to consider topics we may not wish to dwell on, in their language (offensive lexis, little known dialects, irony, intertextual references, and so on). Pragmatic theories offer a motivation for the use of metaphor and irony. Politeness theory offers an explanation of why parody and other tropes can cause irritation in an audience – or give much pleasure. It depends on whether we perceive them as face threatening acts, or as paying us the compliment of assuming we can understand them.

The theories of Genette are relevant to a pragmatic approach, because they cover aspects of the pragmatics of literary discourse which, in the real world, we would pick up from our interlocutors. The proportions of a text, for instance, are relevant to interpretation, but we also use such methods when we listen to someone's account of his day. Similarly, the voice of the narrator is of crucial significance in assessing a narrative. Both these approaches involve interpersonal elements.

It is the principled way in which pragmatic theories can deal with puzzling aspects of literary texts that, finally, makes it appealing as an interpretive and pedagogical tool.

Bibliography

Adriaens, M. (1970), 'Style in W. Golding's *The Inheritors*', *English Studies* 5: 16–30.

Bakhtin, M. (1981), *The Dialogic Imagination*, trans. C. Emerson and M. Holquist, Austin: University of Texas Press.

Bakhtin, M. (1984), *Problems of Dostoevsky's Poetics*, ed. and trans. Caryl Emerson, Manchester: University of Minnesota and Manchester University Press.

Bal, M. (1997), *Narratology*, Toronto: University of Toronto Press.

Black, E. (1993), 'Metaphor, simile and cognition in Golding's *The Inheritors*', *Language and Literature* 2: 1, 37–48.

Blakemore, D. (1992), *Understanding Utterances*, Oxford: Blackwell.

Blakemore, D. (1993), 'The Relevance of Reformulations', *Language and Literature* 2: 2, 101–20.

Booth, W. (1961), *The Rhetoric of Fiction*, Chicago: Chicago University Press.

Booth, W. (1974), *A Rhetoric of Irony*, Chicago: Chicago University Press.

Brooke-Rose, C. (1981), *A Rhetoric of the Unreal*, Cambridge: Cambridge University Press.

Brown, G. and G. Yule (1983), *Discourse Analysis*, Cambridge: Cambridge University Press.

Brown, P. and S. Levinson (1987), *Politeness: Some Universals in Language Usage*, 2nd edn, Cambridge: Cambridge University Press.

Carruthers, M. (1990), *The Book of Memory*, Cambridge: Cambridge University Press.

Carter, R. (2004), *Language and Creativity*, London: Routledge.

Chafe, W. (1994), *Discourse, Consciousness and Time*, Chicago: Chicago University Press.

Chambers, J. (1995), *Sociolinguistic Theory*, Oxford: Blackwell.

Clark, K. and M. Holquist (1984), *Mikhail Bakhtin*, Cambridge, MA and London: The Belknap Press of Harvard University Press.

Coates, J. (1988), 'Gossip revisited: language in all female groups', in J. Coates and D. Cameron, *Women in their Speech Communities*, Harlow: Longman, pp. 94–122.

Cohn, D. (1979), *Transparent Minds*, Princeton: Princeton University Press.

Cook, G. (1994), *Discourse and Literature*, Oxford: Oxford University Press.

Cooper, D. (1986), *Metaphor*, Oxford: Blackwell.

Culler, J. (1975), *Structuralist Poetics*, London: Routledge and Kegan Paul.

Culpeper, J., D. Bousfeld and A. Wichmann (2003), 'Impoliteness revisited with special reference to dynamic and prosodic aspects', *Journal of Pragmatics* 35, 1545–79.

Dahl, Ö. (1985), *Tense and Aspect Systems*, Oxford: Blackwell.

Deignan, A. (1997), 'Metaphors of desire', in K. Harvey and C. Shalom (eds), *Language and Desire*, London: Routledge.

Eco, U. (1984), *Semiotics and the Philosophy of Language*, Basingstoke: Macmillan.

Epstein, E. (1980) 'Non-restrictive modifiers: poetic features of language', in S. Greenbaum, G. Leech and J. Svartvik, *Studies in English Linguistics for Randolph Quirk*, Harlow: Longman.

Fasold, R. (1987), *Sociolinguistics of Society*, Oxford: Blackwell.

Fasold R. (1990), *Sociolinguistics of Language*, Oxford: Blackwell.

Fish, S. (1980), *Is there a Text in this Class?*, Cambridge, MA: Harvard University Press.

Forster, E. M. (1927/1962), *Aspects of the Novel*, Harmondsworth: Penguin.

Fowler, R. (1981), *Literature as Social Discourse*, London: Batsford.

Genette, G. (1980), *Narrative Discourse*, trans. J. Lewin, Oxford: Blackwell, from *Figures III* (1972), Paris: Ed du Seuil.

Genette, G. (1982), *Figures of Literary Discourse*, trans. Alan Sheridan, Oxford: Blackwell, from *Figures I* (1966), *Figures II* (1969), *Figures III* (1972), all Paris: Ed. du Seuil.

Genette, G. (1988), *Narrative Discourse Revisited*, trans. J. Lewin, Ithaca: Cornell University Press, from *Nouveau discours du récit*, Paris: Ed. du Seuil.

Georgakopoulou, A. (1993), *Binding, Unfolding and Evaluating Modern Greek Personal Storytelling: a Discourse-Analytic Study*, unpublished Ph.D. thesis, University of Edinburgh.

Georgakopoulou, A. and D. Goutsos (1997), *Discourse Analysis*, Edinburgh: Edinburgh University Press.

Goatly, A. (1997), *The Language of Metaphors*, London: Routledge.

Goffman, E. (1967), *Interaction Ritual*, New York: Doubleday Anchor.

Grice, H. (1989), 'Logic and conversation' in *Studies in the Way of Words*, Cambridge MA: Harvard University Press, originally published in P. Cole and J. Morgan (eds) (1975) *Syntax and Semantics*, vol. 3, New York: Academic Press.

Grundy, P. (1995), *Doing Pragmatics*, London: Edward Arnold.

Halliday, M. (1971), 'Linguistic function and literary style: an enquiry into the language of William Golding's *The Inheritors*', in S. Chatman (ed.), *Literary Style: A Symposium*, Oxford: Oxford University Press.

Halliday, M. (1978), *Language as Social Semiotic*, London: Edward Arnold.

Halliday, M. (1985), *An Introduction to Functional Grammar*, London: Edward Arnold.

Holquist, M. (1990), *Dialogism: Bakhtin and his World*, London: Routledge.

Huddleston, R. and G. Pullum (2002), *The Cambridge Grammar of the English Language*, Cambridge: Cambridge University Press.

Hurford, J. and B. Heasley (1983), *Semantics: A Coursebook*, Cambridge: Cambridge University Press.

Joseph, J., N. Love and T. Taylor (2001), *Landmarks in Linguistic Thought II*, London: Routledge.

Labov, W. (1972), *Language in the Inner City*, Philadelphia: University of Pennsylvania Press.

Lakoff, G. (1987), *Women, Fire and Dangerous Things*, Chicago: Chicago University Press.

Lakoff, G. and M. Johnson (1980), *Metaphors We Live By*, Chicago: Chicago University Press.

Lakoff, G. and M. Turner (1989), *More than Cool Reason*, Chicago: Chicago University Press.

Leech, G. (1969), *A Linguistic Guide to English Poetry*, Harlow: Longman.

Leech, G. (1971), *Meaning and the English Verb*, Harlow: Longman.

Leech, G. (1983), *Principles of Pragmatics*, Harlow: Longman.

Leech, G. and M. Short (1981), *Style in Fiction*, Harlow: Longman.

Levinson, S. (1983), *Pragmatics*, Cambridge: Cambridge University Press.

Locke, J. (1690/1975), *An Essay Concerning Human Understanding*, Oxford: Clarendon Press.

Lucy, J. (1993), 'General Introduction', in J. Lucy (ed.), *Reflexive Language: Reported Speech and Metapragmatics*, Cambridge: Cambridge University Press.

Lyons, J. (1969), *An Introduction to Theoretical Linguistics*, Cambridge: Cambridge University Press.

Lyons, J. (1977), *Semantics*, 2 vols, Cambridge: Cambridge University Press.

Mey, J. (1993/1994), (repr. with corrections) *Pragmatics*, Oxford: Blackwell.

Nash, W. (1990), *Language in Popular Fiction*, London: Routledge.

O'Donnell, K. (1990), 'Difference and dominance: how labor and management talk conflict', in A. Grimshaw (ed.), *Conflict Talk*, Cambridge: Cambridge University Press.

Paprotté, W. and R. Dirven (eds) (1995), *The Ubiquity of Metaphor*, Amsterdam: John Benjamins.

Pascal, R. (1977), *The Dual Voice: Free Indirect Speech and its Functioning in the Nineteenth Century European Novel*, Manchester: Manchester University Press.

Petrey, S. (1990), *Speech Acts and Literary Theory*, London: Routledge.

Pilkington, A. (1991), 'Poetic Effects: A Relevance Theory Perspective', in R. Sell (ed.), *Literary Pragmatics*, London: Routledge.

Pilkington, A. (1996), 'Introduction: relevance theory and literary style', in *Language and Literature* 5.3, pp. 157–62.

Pilkington, A. (2000), *Poetic Effects*, Amsterdam: John Benjamins.

Pratt, M. (1977), *Toward a Speech Act Theory of Literary Discourse*, Bloomington: Indiana University Press.

Rimmon-Kenan, S. (1983), *Narrative Fiction: Contemporary Poetics*, London: Methuen.

Schiffrin, D. (1994), *Approaches to Discourse*, Oxford: Blackwell.

Scholes, R. and R. Kellog (1966), *The Nature of Narrative*, New York: Oxford University Press.

Searle, J. (1969), *Speech Acts. An Essay in the Philosophy of Language*, Cambridge: Cambridge University Press.

Segal, E. (1995), 'Narrative comprehension and the role of deictic shift theory', in J. Duchan, G. Bruder and L. Hewitt (eds), *Deixis in Narrative: A Cognitive Science Perspective*, Hillsdale, NJ: Lawrence Erlbaum Associates, pp. 3–17.

Sell, R. (1991), 'The politeness of literary texts', in R. Sell (ed.), *Literary Pragmatics*, London: Routledge, pp. 208–24.

Semino, E. (1995), 'Schema theory and the analysis of text worlds in poetry', *Language and Literature* 4.2, 79–108.

Semino, E. (1997), *Language and World Creation in Poems and Other Texts*, Harlow: Addison Wesley Longman.

Short, M. (1986), 'Literature and language teaching and the nature of language', in T. D'Haen (ed.) *Linguistics and the Study of Literature*, Amsterdam: Rodopi.

Short, M. (1988), 'Speech presentation, the novel and the press', in W. Van Peer (ed.) *The Taming of the Text*, London: Routledge.

Short, M. (1996), *Exploring the Language of Poems, Plays and Prose*, London: Longman.

Simpson, P. (1993), *Language, Ideology and Point of View*, London: Routledge.

Sperber, D. and D. Wilson (1986/1995) (rev. edn), *Relevance: Communication and Cognition*, Oxford: Blackwell.

Stanzel, F. (1984), *A Theory of Narrative*, trans. C. Goedsche, Cambridge: Cambridge University Press, originally published in *Theorie des Erzählens* (1979), Göttingen: Vandenhoeck and Ruprecht.

Sternberg, M. (1991), 'How indirect discourse means: syntax, semantics, poetics, pragmatics', in R. Sell (ed.), *Literary Pragmatics*, London: Routledge.

Stockwell, P. (2002), *Cognitive Poetics, an Introduction*, London: Routledge.

Tannen, D. (ed.) (1993), *Framing in Discourse*, New York: Oxford University Press.

Thomas, J. (1995), *Meaning in Interaction*, Harlow: Longman.

Thorne, J. (1988), 'What is a poem?', in W. Van Peer (ed.) *The Taming of the Text*, London: Routledge, pp. 280–91.

Toolan M. (1992) 'The significations of representing dialect in writing', in *Language and Literature* 1.1, 29–46.

Toolan, M. (1998), *Language in Literature: an Introduction to Stylistics*, London: Arnold.

Toolan, M. (2001), *Narrative: a Critical Linguistic Introduction*, London: Routledge.

Uspensky, B. (1973), *A Poetics of Composition*, trans. V. Zavarin and S. Wittig, Berkeley: University of California Press.

Vicente, B. (1996), 'On the semantics and pragmatics of metaphor', in *Language and Literature* 5: 3, 195–208.

Vuchinich, S. (1990), 'The sequential organisation of closing in verbal family conflict', in A. Grimshaw (ed.), *Conflict Talk*, Cambridge: Cambridge University Press.

Wales, K. (1989), *A Dictionary of Stylistics*, Harlow: Longman.

Waugh, P. (1984), *Metafiction*, London: Methuen.

Weber, J. (1996), 'Towards contextualized stylistics: an overview', in J. Weber (ed.), *The Stylistics Reader*, London: Arnold.

Werth, P. (1999), *Text Worlds: Representing Conceptual Space in Discourse*, Harlow: Pearson Education.

Whittaker, R. (1982), *The Faith and Fiction of Muriel Spark*, London: Macmillan.

Widdowson, H. (1975), *Linguistics and the Study of Literature*, Harlow: Longman.

Wilkins, D. (1995), 'Expanding the traditional category of deictic elements: interjections as deictics', in J. Duchan, G. Bruder, L. Hewitt (eds), *Deictics in Narrative: A Cognitive Science Perspective*, Hillsdale: Lawrence Erlbaum Associates.

Wilson, D. and D. Sperber (1989), 'On verbal irony', in *UCL Working Papers in Linguistics*, vol. 1, London: University College Department of Phonetics and Linguistics: Linguistics Section.

Yule, G. (1996), *Pragmatics*, Oxford: Oxford University Press.

AUTHORS DISCUSSED

Austen, Jane (1811/1961), *Sense and Sensibility*, Harmondsworth: Penguin.

Austen, Jane (1813/1972), *Pride and Prejudice*, Harmondsworth: Penguin.

Barnes, Julian (1984/1985), *Flaubert's Parrot*, London: Picador.

Bennett, Alan (2000), *Telling Tales*, London: BBC Worldwide.

Bierce, Ambrose (1988), *The Collected Writings of Ambrose Bierce*, London: Picador.

Brown, George Mackay (1974), 'The two fiddlers', in *The Two Fiddlers: Tales from Orkney*, London: Chatto & Windus.

Calvino, Italo (1982), *If on a Winter's Night a Traveller*, trans. W. Weaver, London: Picador, originally published as *Se una notte d'inverno un viaggiatore* (1979), Turin: Einaudi.

Conrad, Joseph (1902/1983), *Heart of Darkness*, Harmondsworth: Penguin.

Conrad, Joseph, (1907/1963), *The Secret Agent*, Harmondsworth: Penguin.

Cope, Wendy (1986), 'Engineer's Corner' and 'Reading Scheme', in *Making Coffee for Kingsley Amis*, London: Faber.

Defoe, Daniel (1722/1978), *Moll Flanders*, Harmondsworth: Penguin.

Dickens, Charles (1864–5/1971), *Our Mutual Friend*, Harmondsworth: Penguin.

Ellis, Alice Thomas (1982), *The 27th Kingdom*, Harmondsworth: Penguin.

Ellis, Alice Thomas (1983/1985), *The Other Side of the Fire*, Harmondsworth: Penguin.

Ellis, Alice Thomas (1987/1989), *The Clothes in the Wardrobe*, Harmondsworth: Penguin.

Ellis, Alice Thomas (1988/1989), *The Skeleton in the Cupboard*, Harmondsworth: Penguin.

Ellis, Alice Thomas (1989/1990), *The Fly in the Ointment*, Harmondsworth: Penguin.

Ellis, Alice Thomas (1990/1991), *The Inn at the Edge of the World*, Harmondsworth: Penguin.

Ellis, Alice Thomas (1992/1993), *Pillars of Gold*, Harmondsworth: Penguin.

Ellis, Alice Thomas (1996/1997), *Fairy Tale*, Harmondsworth: Penguin.

Faulkner, William (1930/1963), *As I Lay Dying*, Harmondsworth: Penguin.

Fielding, Henry (1749/1973), *Tom Jones*, ed. S. Baker, New York: Norton.

Financial Times (27 October 1997), 'Observer', London.

Fitzgerald, F. Scott (1920/1962), 'May Day', in *The Diamond as Big as the Ritz and Other Stories*, Harmondsworth: Penguin.

Fitzgerald, F. Scott (1926/1962), *The Great Gatsby*, Harmondsworth: Penguin.

Golding, William (1954/1958), *Lord of the Flies*, London: Faber.

Golding, William (1955/1961), *The Inheritors*, London: Faber.

Hemingway, Ernest (1939/1964), '*The Short Happy Life of Francis Macomber*', in *The Essential Hemingway*, Harmondsworth: Penguin.

Hemingway, Ernest (1939/1964), 'The Snows of Kilimanjaro', in *The Essential Hemingway*, Harmondsworth: Penguin.

Hemingway, Ernest (1947/1964), 'In Our Time', in *The Essential Hemingway*, Harmondsworth: Penguin.

Ishiguro, Kazuo (2000/2001), *When We Were Orphans*, New York: Vintage.

James, Henry (1898/1969), *The Turn of the Screw*, Harmondsworth: Penguin.

Joyce, James (1914 /1977), 'A Painful Case', in *Dubliners*, London: Paladin.

Joyce, James (1916/1964), *A Portrait of the Artist as a Young Man*, London: Heinemann Educational.

Joyce, James (1922/1968) *Ulysses*, Harmondsworth: Penguin.

Lawrence, D. H. (1913/1948), Sons *and Lovers*, Harmondsworth: Penguin.

Lawrence, D. H. (1922/1995), 'Monkey Nuts' and 'Tickets, Please', in *England, My England and Other Stories*, Harmondsworth: Penguin.

Lodge, David (1975/1978), *Changing Places*, Harmondsworth: Penguin.

Lodge, David (1980/1981), *How Far Can You Go?*, Harmondsworth: Penguin.

Lodge, David (1984/1985), *Small World*, Harmondsworth: Penguin.

Lodge, David (1991/1992), *Paradise News*, Harmondsworth: Penguin.

Lodge, David (1995/1996), *Therapy*, Harmondsworth: Penguin.

Mantel, Hilary (1986/1987), *Vacant Possession*, Harmondsworth: Penguin.

Mantel, Hilary (1989/1990), *Fludd*, Harmondsworth: Penguin.

Mantel, Hilary (2003), *Learning to Talk*, London: Fourth Estate.

Munro, Alice (1996/1997), 'Fits', in *Selected Stories*, London: Vintage.

Private Eye (20 November 1992), London: Pressdram.

Rankin, Ian (1992/1998), 'A Good Hanging', in *A Good Hanging*, London: Orion.

Rowling, J. K. (2000), *Harry Potter and the Goblet of Fire*, London: Bloomsbury.

Shields, Carol (1997/1998), *Larry's Party*, London: Fourth Estate.

Spark, Muriel (1958/1987), 'You Should Have Seen the Mess', in *The Go-Away Bird and Other Stories*, Harmondsworth: Penguin.

Spark, Muriel (1959/1961), *Memento Mori*, Harmondsworth: Penguin.

Spark, Muriel (1961/1965), *The Prime of Miss Jean Brodie*, Harmondsworth: Penguin.

Spark, Muriel (1970/1974), *The Driver's Seat*, Harmondsworth: Penguin.

Spark, Muriel (1971/1974), *Not to Disturb*, Harmondsworth: Penguin.

Spark, Muriel (1987), 'Bang Bang You're Dead', in *The Stories of Muriel Spark*, London: The Bodley Head.

Spark, Muriel (1988/1989), A *Far Cry from Kensington*, Harmondsworth: Penguin.

Spark, Muriel (2004), *The Finishing School*, London: Penguin Viking.

Sterne, Laurence (1760–7/1980), *The Life and Opinions of Tristram Shandy, Gent*, New York: W.W. Norton & Co.

Thubron, Colin (1996/1998), *Distance*, Harmondsworth: Penguin.

Trevor, William (1991/1992), 'Reading Turgenev', in *Two Lives*, Harmondsworth: Penguin.

Twain, Mark (1884/1985), *The Adventures of Huckleberry Finn*, Harmondsworth: Penguin.

Vickers, Salley (2001/2002), *Instances of the Number 3*, London: Fourth Estate.

Vickers, Salley (2003), *Mr Golightly's Holiday*, London: Fourth Estate.

Walker, Alice (1992/1993), *Possessing the Secret of Joy*, London: Vintage Books.

Welsh, Irvine (1994), 'The Granton Star Cause' and 'Disnae Matter', in *The Acid House*, London: Jonathan Cape.

Wodehouse, P. G. (1919/1961), *A Damsel in Distress*, Harmondsworth: Penguin.

Wodehouse, P. G. (1937/1966), *Lord Emsworth and Others*, Harmondsworth: Penguin.

Wodehouse, P. G. (1967/1980), *Company for Henry*, Harmondsworth: Penguin.

Woolf, Virginia (1925/1964), *Mrs Dalloway*, Harmondsworth: Penguin.

Woolf, Virginia (1927/1964), *To The Lighthouse*, Harmondsworth: Penguin.

General Index

Anti-language, 95, 100, 103

Bakhtin, 92–102, 121; *see also* heteroglossia, hybrid discourse

Code-switching, 64, 88–91, 99
Competent reader, 37–8
Context, 3–4, 84–6, 91–2, 101, 108, 113–15, 150–1
Co-operative Principle, 23–35, 107–8, 110–11, 124–5, 129, 131, 133–4, 152
   Failure to observe a maxim, 24–5, 28–30
   Implicature, 28, 47, 51, 128–9
   Maxim of manner, 24, 26, 30, 56, 107, 125–6, 152
   Maxim of quality, 23, 30, 32, 56–7, 107, 110, 114, 126, 152
   Maxim of quantity, 23, 29–30, 107, 125–7, 131–3, 152
   Maxim of relation, 23, 31–2, 107, 125, 127, 131–2, 152

Deictic expressions, 4
   Article, 5
   Pronoun, 4, 13–15
Discourse
   Direct discourse, 65, 66–7, 70, 76, 138, 141, 143, 145, 147, 155
   Free direct discourse, 65, 68–70, 127, 138, 141–4, 146–8, 155–6
   Free indirect discourse, 67–70, 76, 95–8, 101, 115–16, 119, 122, 138, 142, 145, 146–7, 155
   Indirect discourse, 67–8, 142, 147, 155

Echoic language, 86–7, 92, 96, 112–16, 119, 153–4, 157

Face *see* Politeness

Genre, 37–9, 52
Gnomic utterance, 11, 14
Grice, H.P. *see* co-operative principle

Heteroglossia, 93–5, 97
Hybrid discourse, 95–8, 101, 122

Idiolect, 63, 95
Implied author, 54
Implied reader, 54
Interest principle, 34
Intertextuality, 49–50, 75, 92, 120–2
Irony, 75–6, 110–19, 134, 153
   And C.P., 110–12
   And relevance, 112–15

Labov, W.
   Evaluative devices, 40–3, 48, 74, 155
   Narrative theory, 39–43,154

Metaphor, 102–10, 121, 135, 153
   And C.P., 107–8
   Conceptual, 104–7
   Function, 103–4

Narratee, 54, 59–60
Narrative
   Duration, 44–6, 157
   Frequency, 46–8
   Instance, 57–61
   Temporal ordering, 43–4
   Voices, 53–4
Narrator, 11, 27, 30, 33–4, 42, 53–62, 138–9
   First person, 55–61, 116–19
   Third person, 61–2, 95–9
Narrator's report of speech/thought act, 64, 66, 70, 76, 97–8, 115–16, 122, 137–41, 145–8, 155–6

Index to Literary Authors and Works Cited

Undergraduate Lending Library